THE SECOND TIME AS FARCE

The Second Time as Farce:

Reflections on the Drama of Mean Times

DAVID EDGAR

LAWRENCE AND WISHART
LONDON

Lawrence and Wishart Limited
39 Museum Street
London WC1A 1LQ

This edition first published 1988

© David Edgar, 1988

Photoset in North Wales by
Derek Doyle & Associates, Mold, Clwyd
Printed and bound in Great Britain by
Billing and Sons, Worcester

To Neil

Contents

Preface

It's always dangerous to begin a collection of occasional pieces by remarking that it's always dangerous to produce such a volume, particularly when at least one of the pieces in question begins with the same line. But although I'm fully aware of the risks of the project, I'm pleased to be given the opportunity to undertake it. Playwrights are not really expected to write about their own business (Brecht has suffered particularly on this score); certainly, they are not encouraged to stray from aesthetics into the fields of public comment and political controversy, and, if they do so, they find their pretensions mocked rather than their arguments contested.

The fact that I have now amassed a fairly substantial scrapbook of theatrical and political pieces – the very cream of which have been selected for publication here – is due to a number of acts of faith, by the most heroic elements of the literary and journalistic establishment, who have chosen to take my thoughts on the theatre and other matters seriously. I should mention a clutch of literary editors (particularly Gillian Wilce and Harriett Gilbert of the *New Statesman*) who allowed me loose on political material; periodicals like the *Guardian* and *New Socialist* which allowed me to pontificate on non-dramatic subjects at greater length; and journals like the *Listener*, the *Dickensian* and *New Formations* which reprinted my talks and lectures on theatrical topics.

But pride of place must go to two considerable and doughty institutions: the journal *Race & Class* and its officers A. Sivanandan, Jenny Bourne, Hazel Waters and Danny Reilly; and *Marxism Today*, a periodical whose politics – under Martin Jacques's rigorous but impish editorship – are probably closest to my own, though as it happens I am not now (and have never been) a member of the organisation which publishes it.

One of the most famous aphorisms of that party's founding spirit comes, as is well known, at the start of *The Eighteenth Brumaire of Louis Bonaparte*, in which Marx asserts (via Hegel) that the events and even personages of history occur not once but twice, 'the first time as tragedy, the second as farce'. This statement might seem to trivialise history, but in fact does nothing of the kind.

For (as Marx goes on to hint) farce is all about unexpected nakedness and hasty disguise, about sudden slight and impulsive acts of retaliation; a more than suitable form for a period in which contemporary crises are answered by Victorian Values, and past humiliations are absolved by the resurrection of imperial prerogative. In the last decade, mass poverty has been dressed up as profligacy, and social indigence recast as individual iniquity. We have seen Suez avenged on the beachheads of the South Atlantic, and Saltley Gate metaphorically recaptured on the fields of Orgreave.

The second time as farce, indeed: but only if it is accepted – as any playwright knows and Marx well understood – that farce is a highly serious business.

Introduction:
Thoughts for the Third Term

In 1976, the Royal Shakespeare Company presented my anti-fascist play *Destiny* in its small Stratford theatre, The Other Place. By rights the play should have transferred to the company's London studio, but for various reasons it was resolved to try it out on the main stage (then the Aldwych), in repertoire with *King Lear*.

The show hit town at a propitious time. The spring of 1977 saw the limping Callaghan government in pact with the Liberals, the National Front reaching its (local) electoral zenith, and violence flaring on the Grunwick picket line. Perhaps it was no surprise that the only theatre not to lose business during the week of the Queen's Silver Jubilee was the Aldwych; appropriately bedecked with patriotic bunting, the theatre was showing a play in which a mad king provokes a murderous civil war between himself and the rest of the royal family; and another which suggested that the country was about to be taken over by the Nazis.

But history was to have its revenge. The television version of *Destiny* was broadcast on 31 January 1978, precisely 24 hours after Mrs Thatcher made her then notorious statement on *World In Action* to the effect that the indigenous population was frightened of being 'rather swamped' by people of an alien culture, a statement widely (and rightly) regarded as signalling that the Thatcher Conservative Party was fully prepared to articulate the kind of militant and exclusive nationalist resentment that had hitherto been the preserve of the fascist fringe. There were a number of things *Destiny* got right (I like to think), but it was massively wrong in its assumption that the Tory Party was terminally infected with the ethos of weakness and decline. It had spotted motive, victim and weapon (the sharpened Union Jack in the heart of the body politic), but it had missed the identity of the murderer.

Destiny was important to me because it gave me a political life above and beyond political theatre. In the early 1970s, the two were indistinguishable: my theatre work (largely in touring agitprop) *was* my political activity. In the late 1970s, it was liberating to discover that politics and theatre could operate not simultaneously but in parallel; that I could treat of British neo-fascism in one way in the theatre, and in quite another way in articles and speeches for the anti-racist and anti-fascist movement. And as it became clearer and clearer that my gently paternalistic Tory candidate in *Destiny* was a charming anachronism, I began to pursue a programme of thinking, reading and writing about Thatcherism which, although useful for my 1983 play *Maydays*, nonetheless had a quite independent life.

Like many others, I was struck by – and have written quite a lot about – the distinction between the free-market, entrepreneurial, individualist side of the New Conservatism, and the contradictory (or perhaps complementary) impulse towards traditionalism, nationalism and authority (an inconsistency – if inconsistency it is – well exemplified by the Thatcho/Powellite commitment to a free market in things, but fear of the free movement of people). And this discrepancy has become more significant the more it has been recognised as such, not just on the left, but on the right: as the economic liberals (including the heroin-legalisers and indeed the free-borderers) cross swords as well as making parleys with the social authoritarians.

One of the difficulties for those of us who think there is a dispute, and the authoritarians are winning it, is the fact that most of the government's actual legislative agenda has addressed its economic programme; that although quite full, the social legislative basket has been packed piecemeal, by way of moral panic (video nasties), knee-jerk statutory additions (hippy convoys), private members' legislation (kerb-crawling), or amendments to main bills ('free speech' in universities, sex education, and, of course

Section 28). In this respect – particularly if you remember the failures on hanging, abortion, and television sex'n'-violence (thus far) – the social programme can appear distinctly patchy, and one could be forgiven for regarding it as no more than political cosmetic, a sop to the wilder reaches of the Tory conference, a matter of mere rhetoric.

But in fact, of course, there is nothing mere about it. Indeed, the genius of Thatcherism has been precisely in the shaping of the political perspective, a project of re-education which has been enabled partly by the dextrous plasticity of its discourse. I am not alone in noticing how the welfare system, once the dampener of individuality and stunter of the nation's economic creativity, has been magically transformed into the promoter of irresponsibility, indiscipline and disorder; how the trade unions, once the brute force of corporate monopoly power (virtually, indeed, an arm of state) have mysteriously mutated into harbingers of anarchy. And this deft sleight of hand is reflected in the actual processes of change: the brilliance of Thatcherism is not (heaven knows) in its economics but rather in its politics, or, even ratherer, in its capacity to pursue political ends by fiscal means, to express essentially social objectives in political language, to achieve economic goals by way of a transformation of the culture.

And if that is so, then surely those capacities were developed in the aftermath of the events of July 1981, itself a time oddly comparable with the summer of 1977, as the bunting went up once again (for the Royal Wedding), but this time to flap against hastily erected boards and shutters guarding the shopfronts of Liverpool, Manchester and South London from the riotous young. For if 1977 had seen social democracy's chickens coming home to roost, then the 1981 riots marked the darkening of the sky above monetarism, as unemployment inexorably clambered towards three million, and the youth of the cities confirmed the darkest warnings about imminent civil strife.

The dramatic transformation of the government's fortunes in the subsequent twelve months is usually ascribed solely to the Falklands War, and the stiffening of all that bunting with the starch of real British blood. But the Falklands was not all that went on in the early months of 1982 (when, it may be recalled, the government's Gallup rating stood at 31 per cent). Indeed, at the same time, strategies were being developed that were to alter the government's fortunes in a much more profound way.

Thus, in the second Employment Act, (second-read in February), a clear economic objective (the reduction of wage pressure) was achieved by essentially political means (the offer of government funds for election of union leaders, predictably spurned by those leaderships, and thus cunningly casting the government as the democrats and the union bosses as the authoritarians). Similarly, in March and April, the ticklish economic and political questions raised by the 1981 riots began to be confronted by means of an increasingly sophisticated cultural critique of inner city life. Confronted by the self-evident connection between economic retrenchment and the political fact of the uprisings, a succession of government ministers (from Rhodes Boyson and Timothy Raison to Thatcher herself) set about constructing an essentially cultural explanation for youth alienation, which embraced inadequate schooling, single parenthood, 'sour media mores' and, crucially, the residual influence of 1960s permissiveness.

While, third, and even as our boys were liberating our kith and kin in the hills above Port Stanley, the so-called Ministerial Steering Group on Government Strategy was giving thought to the implementation of certain then unthinkable economic measures – the privatisation of education and national insurance, limiting the state's role to means tested benefits – in conscious pursuit of the political objective of isolating and ghettoising the underclass.[1] While the intended cultural consequences of such proposals were spelt out in the stated objectives of the Cabinet's Family Policy group, which met in September 'to identify, and to seek, ways of counteracting those factors which tend to undermine, or even prohibit, the exercise of personal responsibility and a sense of individual self-respect'.[2]

Meanwhile, of course, the government was heading

steadily towards its most spectacular first-term achievement: the sale of half a million council houses and flats.
Economically, this represented a considerable shift of
expenditure and savings from the public to the private
sector (in 1979, there had been 104,000 housing
completions; in 1982, the number dropped below 50,000
for the first time since the 1920s). Politically, the sale of
council houses occasioned a dramatic reduction in the
scope of local authority patronage and power (not least as
landlord). And culturally, of course, the privatisation of
municipal housing relocated people's arena of interest,
self-consciousness and belonging, from community and
class to individual and family.

Surely, it is the policy of council house sales which
demonstrates most clearly the innovatory character of
Thatcherism, as a new kind of ruling-class strategy,
pursued on a wide band of fronts, against a broad variety
of enemies, using an impressive array of weaponry. In the
first term, Thatcherism saw off what it regarded as the
primary economic enemy of inflation, largely by way of
reducing the monopoly industrial power of the trade
unions, via the economic mechanism of unemployment
and the political tactic of union reform. In the second
term, the government addressed the essentially political
task of disarming the left opposition in the municipalities
and elsewhere (including CND and politicised unions like
the Mineworkers), an objective realised by fiscal restraint
(rate-capping) and direct political gerrymandering (the
abolition of the metropolitan counties and the GLC).

While in the third term, faced with mounting evidence
that despite everything the nation appears to remain
stubbornly resistant to the *values* of untrammelled
enterprise and increasing inequity – that having lost the
economic and political argument the left still retains
positions on the *moral* highground – she is taking on the
culture.

And there are of course precedents for this progression.
In essence, the basic economic restructuring – from a still
predominantly Fordist to a fundamentally post-Fordist
economy – was completed in the first term: a hundred

IBM compatibles had been allowed to bloom, a hundred fast food franchises encouraged to contend. Politically, too, the Great Leap Centrewards (and the complementary anti-leftist campaigns in the town halls and the coalfields) has routed the socialist-roaders. But all kinds of ancient, atavistic loyalties and presumptions remain: stubbornly, backward elements cling to feudal notions of economic fairness and social justice. The time for the unleashing of the Great Bourgeois Cultural Revolution had and has clearly arrived.

I want to consider how this revolution may transform one sector – the performing arts – but before doing so it is hard to resist the temptation to point out that the economic and political victories were if not enabled then at least made a great deal easier by the abstention – and subsequently the defection – of large sections of the very British cultural establishment that is now under particular attack. When she came for the unions, such people were not in all respects displeased. When she came for municipal housing, they applauded. By the time she came for the Labour councils, they were already nuzzled up to David Owen. Now she has come for them – in the Universities, the Arts, the BBC, the Church – it surely requires superhuman restraint not to remind the Vice-Chancellors, the Artistic Directors, the Director-Generals and the Bishops that we did tell them so.

The Arts were a predictable battleground because – unlike, say, Fleet Street, or substantial parts of higher education – they have proved a site of considerable resistance to the New Right. Both television drama and the live theatre managed to retain a muscular commitment to the left-liberal consensus. In so far as that may now be changing, it represents a chilling paradigm for the culture as a whole.

The story of Thatcherism and the Arts can be told via three documents, two clustered around the Seizure of Power, the third much more recent. In 1978, the right-wing Selsdon Group produced a pamphlet whose simple message was contained in its title: *A Policy for the Arts: Just Cut Taxes*.[3] Its message was that if more money was left in the pockets of the people, then consumers could pay the market price for arts products, and private patrons enabled to make up any shortfall in production.

As with much late-1970s New Writing, the Selsdon pamphlet was keen to flavour its arguments with libertarian rhetoric, and implied that by releasing the Arts from the dead stranglehold of state control it would usher in a new age of radicalism and innovation. This was clearly not the position taken by the novelist Kingsley Amis, whose pamphlet *An Arts Policy?* was published a year later.[4] After a somewhat desultory rehearsal of the anti-statist argument, Amis moved quickly on to his real target: 'plays without plots, a canvas entirely covered with black paint offered as a picture, poems that are meaningless patterns of letters – I needn't go on'. He does, though: to blame subsidy not for stifling innovation but for encouraging the aesthetic self-indulgence of an avant-garde which does not need to appeal to its public through the market.

Elsewhere, Amis tossed in a cursory attack on political theatre – 'I cannot say I fancy paying the bills of some supposedly promising young person while he writes his political (equals left wing) or experimental (equals nonsensical) play, these apparently being the only two categories tolerated'.[5] Not surprisingly, the early, muscle-flexing period of Thatcherism saw the odd attack – by the Federation of the Conservative Students, Norman Tebbit, Teddy Taylor and the like – on subsidy for 'politically-inspired theatre companies', the presentation of plays like Howard Brenton and Tony Howard's *A Short Sharp Shock*, and, famously, the National Theatre's production of Brenton's *The Romans in Britain*. While more recently, of course, there have been intermittent attacks on the supposed tendentiousness of drama-documentaries or factually-based plays like Alan Bleasdale's *The Monocled Mutineer*.

But it strikes me that it was not until well into the Third Term that the cultural critique developed coherent form. On 10 January 1988, Professor Norman Stone wrote an article in the *Sunday Times* in which he singled out six contemporary British films as evidence for the view that 'semi-educated ambitious mediocrities' were presenting a 'childish caricature' of contemporary Britain in 'tawdry, ragged, rancidly provincial films' that 'might have come straight from the agitprop department of the late GLC'. Professor Stone clearly put his argument together at speed (he describes the central character of *My Beautiful Laundrette* as an Asian immigrant, and he thinks that women are a minority). But despite the solecisms (can a 'process' really 'shift intellectual goalposts'?) the argument is clear enough: that an alienated cultural establishment has set out to present a distorted, inaccurate and negative picture of a Britain in a state of apocalyptic decline. On the same day, the thesis was upheld in the *Sunday Telegraph*, in a piece titled 'Why Britain's eggheads look down on Mrs Thatcher'; of the seven luminaries pictured at the head of Graham Turner's article, four work in the theatre. And the issue was taken up again in the *Sunday Times* of 24 January, whose main leader argued that 'a small band of disillusioned intellectuals' was presenting a 'one-sided and inaccurate' picture of a Britain in the grip of terminal decay.

Would, in one sense, that it were so. In reality, however, the Thatcherite attack on the negativism of the 'metropolitan cultural classes' is considerably more questionable than its previous assault on the trade union militants and the local left (though, as in the latter case, it fits neatly into fashionable theory of a 'New Class' conspiracy between intellectual renegades and lumpen-proletarian shocktroops). For the truth is that, despite the heroic efforts of a few highly successful (nay, entre-preneurial) low-budget film makers, the economics, politics and now very ethos of Thatcherism has indeed begun to invade the bloodstream of the cultural industries, and by recognisably roundabout routes.

Thus there has been no direct censorship (up until Section 28 at least), the Arts Council has not been abolished, and the arm's length principle more or less preserved (the distance depending on one's view of the extent of Sir William Rees Mogg's reach). Despite the crises of the mid-1980s, the Royal Court has not been closed, and some (though by no means all) of the overtly political theatre troupes of the 1970s have been allowed to totter on. No, what has happened is the application of altogether more subtle – and yet typical – constraints on arts organisations; as steady but undramatic economic shrinkage, in combination with gentle but consistent political pressure, has prised open the cracks sufficiently to let the sap of Thatcherism seep through.

Rightly regarded as one of Britain and the world's great theatre troupes, the Royal Shakespeare Company believes that the works of Shakespeare need to be recaptured and made new for every generation. In the late 1970s, it put that belief into spectacular effect with Trevor Nunn's triumphant musical version of *The Comedy of Errors*, which led the same director (in collaboration with John Caird and, as it happens, me) to seek to revitalise another minor work of a great writer, and adapt Dickens's early comic novel *Nicholas Nickleby* for stage performance. Fired by that success, the same two directors set about to reclaim another dusty and ill-used classic, by stripping the pantomimic varnish off J.M. Barrie's *Peter Pan*, and exposing the original, with all its complexity and ambivalence, to the light of day.

What all of these projects had in common was that they devoted the same degree of rigour, commitment, innovatory zeal and, crucially, sense of purpose to the production of consciously popular theatre as the RSC dedicates to Shakespeare. But ten years on, things had changed. In the late 1980s, the company presented three perhaps unintentionally equivalent productions: another Shakespearian offshoot (*Kiss Me Kate*), a second children's classic (*The Wizard of Oz*) and a further adaptation (of the Stephen King horror-yarn *Carrie*). The difference between the second trio and the first was not merely that the latter had all been major films. Nor was it entirely that their best friends could not describe them as innovatory (though that was not unimportant). It was that between the first trio and the second the RSC had presented its hit musical version of Hugo's *Les Miserables* and as a consequence of that success had come to rely – financially and, in a real way, psychologically – on similar achievement in the commercial sector. The very genuine zeal to reclaim and to reinvent, the sense of crusading purpose that informed *Comedy*, *Nickleby* and *Peter Pan* had within two or three years of *Les Miserables'* undoubted trumph mutated into the equally compulsive but creatively damaging urge to prove work in the 'real world' of the market place. The RSC has coped with economic retrenchment before, and it is more than adept at the politics of subsidy. What it has not been able to resist is a cultural climate in which the only yardstick of personal success is lines round the block.

What is happening to the Royal Shakespeare Company is a microcosm of what has happened or might happen to a swathe of cultural institutions. The television companies already face a familiar barrage of pressures – from the fact of satellites, via the political question of the future of the specialist channels, to the prospect of direct censorial control.

But amid the gloom there are rays of hope. The government's belated discovery of personal morality, its sudden vulnerability on the issue of the sort of people it has made us (or more accurately, the sort of people it has rewarded), the ever-more credible association that is being made between greed and selfishness in the market place and in personal and social life gives the forces of progress an opportunity – if only they can seize it – to construct and promote a new, collective morality appropriate to our times.

And there is another characteristic of Cultural as opposed to Economic or Political Thatcherism, which opens a window of opportunity. One of the most striking differences between RSC popular theatre in the 1970s and RSC populism now is that the projects have become progressively less inventive, less innovatory, more and more bound by given notions of what in particular musical theatre is, which means of course what it has thus far been. In order to succeed in the subsidised sector, the RSC rightly felt itself obliged to innovate; to win in the market place, it seems constrained to be conservative. Indeed, now, if you want to find the formally radical in the theatre, you don't look to the major metropolitan institutions, stuffed with creative iconoclasts; you look to community theatre in small towns and suburbs, where local amateurs demand and provide new theatrical sites into which the professionals seem fearful to tread.

And what is true of the theatre applies writ large. Mrs Thatcher and her ideologues could and did present her economic policy as emancipatory (releasing the nation from the bonds of statism) and her political attack on the left as libertarian (freeing the people from the bully-boys and commissars). Her *cultural* policies admit of no such interpretation. They are essentially, inherently and inescapably reactionary, restrictive and indeed censorious. Far from opening up options and choices, she is seeking to close them down.[6] Having seen off the nanny state in the economy, she is now emerging as the Platonic Guardian of the culture, with her satraps sifting through the school books for anything that might be said to 'promote' homosexuality, and the Broadcasting Standards Authority seeing to it that we're all in bed by nine.

It's for this reason – among many others – that the left has got to embrace genuine political pluralism, not out of lip-service, nor out of a vague, residual anti-Stalinism, but as part of the very warp and weft of its politics. The obstacles to a revitalised political and cultural pluralism that will genuinely accommodate and embrace the new social movements that have emerged since the late 1960s are awesome. They encompass members of those very movements who seek to substitute a new totalitarianism for the old; they include a Labour leadership – and a hard left – which resolutely refuse to acknowledge that anything has changed.

But if those obstacles can be overcome, then the opportunities are great. Because while the left may not have had much economic or political success in the period since the end of the long boom, it has chalked up a number of achievements that have arisen out of movements which have had culture (in the broadest sense) at their very core. Unlike the traditional forms of left organisation, the women's, peace, green and anti-racist movements (including anti-apartheid) have been about not only what was thought and done, but what was worn, and eaten, and sung along to, and, yes, even enjoyed.

And surely there will be no chance (as well as no point) in a socialist victory in the early 1990s unless by then the left has managed to integrate the priorities of the new emancipatory movements into its central political platform; a project which will involve, among other things, the greening of its theory and the feminising of its practice. In such an endeavour, consciously socialist artists have a significant and challenging role to play (and more so, arguably, than when they felt obliged to do no more than agitate and propagandise). What is certain is that the effort to bring about a synthesis of the new cultural movements with a viable economic agenda is the left's most urgent political task.

Notes

1. See Peter Riddell, *The Thatcher Government*, Oxford 1983, p.162.
2. Ibid, p.137.
3. One of the offshoots of the outwardly-collapsing Monday Club, the Selsdon Group, was set up in the mid-1970s to defend the economic-liberal, laissez-faire policies associated with the pre-U-turn phase of the 1970-74 Heath government, policies initially formulated at a conference held in the Selsdon Hotel.
4. Kingsley Amis, *An Arts Policy?*, Centre for Policy Studies, London 1979.
5. Kingsley Amis, 'Speaking up for Excellence', in Patrick Cormack (ed.), *Right Turn*, London, 1978, p.56.
6. George Gale, Peterhouse graduate and scourge of the mindless 1960s, wrote an article in the *Times* (23 May 1987) titled 'Do we really need opera?'.

Theatre of Fact

The year 1968 saw a reawakening of radical theatre as it saw a resurgence of radical much-else. Ten years later, the time seemed right for reassessment. My contribution was a pair of articles written for the Socialist Workers Party's *Socialist Review* (April and May 1978), which were reprinted as one in *Theatre Quarterly* (Winter 1979).

Having managed (I think to my surprise) to write something both polemical and reasonably coherent about the content of what I do, I welcomed the invitation from radio producer Richard Ellis to address a question adjacent if not directly applicable to its form. In the early 1980s – as now – the issue of drama-documentary on television was a live one. The debate tended however to concentrate more on the doc than the dram, and my talk 'Acting Out Facts' (Radio 3, 28 December 1980) was intended to redress the balance. Extracts from the talk were published in the *Listener* and the *Stage*, and a rewritten and extended version – titled On Drama Documentary – in *Ah! Mischief: The Writer and Television* (edited by Frank Pike, Faber and Faber, 1982).

Ten Years of Political Theatre, 1968–1978

In 1967 there was one independent socialist theatre group in Britain: Cartoon Archetypical Slogan Theatre. There are now at least eighteen full-time subsidised socialist groups, in addition to perhaps as many unsubsidised or local groups who propagate revolutionary socialist ideas. In addition, socialist writers have penetrated the bourgeois theatre (of the eight new plays produced by the Royal Shakespeare Company over the last twelve months, five have been written by socialist revolutionaries) and television (the names that spring without much difficulty to mind include Jim Allen, Trevor Griffiths, Colin Welland, Alan Plater, and John McGrath).

However, while the scale of socialist theatre work is impressive, it is obvious that its intervention in the working-class struggle itself has been at best patchy and peripheral. Furthermore, socialist theatre has remained at a remove from revolutionary organisations. What follows is an attempt – from the uncomfortably interior perspective of a writer who has worked in socialist theatre for seven years – to explain why this should be so.

There are two reasons why 1968 can be taken as the starting date for the development of political theatre in Britain. The first was the general upsurge of revolutionary, or at least radical, consciousness among students and intellectuals, which affected young theatre workers just like anyone else (and also affected them in a particular way, as I shall argue in a moment). The second was the abolition of the institution of the theatre censorship, practised since the eighteenth century by the Lord Chamberlain. The most obviously irksome manifestation of censorship applied to sex (the writer Joe Orton suffering particularly and amusingly[1]), but political censorship was also involved and the very bureaucracy of script approval (which took several weeks) effectively pre-empted topical or improvised work.

Some groups, like CAST, had always merrily ignored the Lord Chamberlain, but for most theatre workers his abolition was a welcome release. The immediate reaction of the institutional theatre was to increase the sexual content of plays. A second development was a mush-rooming of small theatre spaces dedicated to 'experimental' work, much of it from America and the Continent. For the development of socialist theatre, however, two further happenings were more important.

The first was the growth of a group of university-educated writers (who formed a group, Portable Theatre, to tour their work), who drew much of their energy from the counter-cultural ideologies of the late 1960s. One such writer, Howard Brenton, described the making of his play *Fruit* as follows:

> In writing *Fruit* I was influenced by some French Situationist texts (the Situationists were very important to the May 1968 students). The Situationists describe our world as 'the society of the spectacle'. There is a screen called public life which is reported on the telly and in the newspapers. This version of public life is a spectacle, it operates within its own laws. It's a vast, intricate confidence game.[2]

Brenton outlined his theatrical response to the consumerist spectacle as follows:

> The theatre is a dirty place. It's not a place for rational analysis of a society – it's there to bait our obsessions, ideas, and public figures. A really great outburst of nihilism like *Fruit* ... is one of the most beautiful and positive things you can see on a stage.

The style and content of the Portable plays did not attract a working-class audience. Nor was it likely to: the theory of the capitalist spectacle was developed precisely to explain the lack of proletarian consciousness in the post-war western countries. For many radicals in the late 1960s (including Marcuse and some of the French student activists of May 1968), Marx's prediction that the working class would become ever more impoverished and so increasingly revolutionary as time went on had been disproved by history. The working class had been 'bought off' by a combination of material and ideological bribes. This did not, of course, make the capitalist system any less alienating and dehumanised: indeed, these thinkers saw alienation as a much more important phenomenon than exploitation. Revolutionary politics was seen as being much less about the organisation of the working class at the point of production, and much more about the disruption of bourgeois ideology at the point of consumption. The centre of the revolution had shifted from the factory-floor to the supermarket.

As Brenton makes clear, the Portable playwrights fitted neatly into this perspective. Their work was violent, anarchic and destructive, and had, as another Portable writer affirmed, 'a very bad record with working-class audiences'.[3] There was, however, another important development in socialist theatre at about the same time, which did not completely write off the working-class revolution. The revival of the street-theatre movement is described by Richard Seyd of Red Ladder (which started life as the Agitprop Street Players) as follows:

> Red Ladder Theatre emerged from the ferment of 1968. The Camden Road-based Poster Workshop – itself a product of that ferment – was at the time making posters with and for those involved in the Greater London tenants' rent fight. The Tenants' Action Committee asked the Poster Workshop whether anyone could get together a short sketch to put on at the beginning of their meetings to get them off to a lively start. A small group came together and made a fifteen-minute play.[4]

Red Ladder are now fairly scathing about their own early work (Seyd says of their second play that 'the title was its only redeeming feature'), and see their development in terms of their realisation that 'we had to relate to working people through their own organisations and not stay on the outside of the labour movement'. However, it is clear that the growth of a more class-oriented theatrical strategy was not merely an internal development, it was essentially a response to the greater militancy of the class itself, after the 1970 General Election. Some groups, indeed, are aware in retrospect of missing the boat, and remaining in the counter-cultural tradition long after it had become clear that reports of the death of working-class militancy had been much exaggerated. Roland Muldoon of CAST acknowledged recently that CAST remained committed to 'the alternative culture revolution' throughout the early period of the 1970-74 Conservative government, admitting that 'rich situations like Heath versus the miners went untouched by us'.[5]

The 1970-74 period saw a strenuous effort by a growing number of theatre groups, however, to create and then satisfy a demand for socialist theatre. For many, the paramount condition was that plays should be presented to people where they lived and worked, in community centres or pubs, in trades council halls or on the streets. The move towards a working-class audience took many forms, but it is possible to isolate three (with the reservation that, in many instances, the approaches overlapped).

The first approach was community theatre, which saw its function as the service of a particular geographical area, either from a (non-theatre) base, or touring. A good example of a group of this type is the Combination, who work for a community centre in Deptford, providing a number of services (including legal aid and educational advice) in addition to the presentation of theatre.

Secondly, there were groups who toured round the country, presenting shows of general political/industrial import (including Red Ladder itself, 7:84, North West Spanner and the General Will). A third approach was, in effect, a combination of the first two. Some groups sought to serve constituencies of people, bounded not by geography but common interest. Often these constituency-directed shows were in fact produced by political touring groups (an example is a show I wrote for the General Will about the Housing Finance Act, which was played to tenants' groups in 1972) until the later emergence of constituency groups like Gay Sweatshop and the Women's Theatre Group.

The dominant theatrical form of the work produced by community, political-touring and constituency groups alike was agitprop. Agitprop – the finest hour of which occurred immediately after the Russian Revolution – is one of a number of interventionist forms of socialist art that have been created in response to the perceived failures of social realism, the dominant radical form of the last 150 years.

In order to understand the reasons for the development of agitprop, it is necessary to define realism. John Berger has written a good definition in his book *Art and Revolution*.[6] He argues that, unlike the bourgeois form of naturalism (which attempts to portray a surface view of human behaviour as accurately as possible), realism is 'selective' and 'strives towards the typical'. The actions of people are presented within a 'total' context: the central character's actions are felt 'as part of the life of his class, society and universe'.

Realism, in other words, does not show people's individual behaviour as being somehow independent of the society in which they live; it relates people's recognisable activities to the history that is going on around them.

Many revolutionary artists have felt, however, that realism is an inadequate artistic tool in periods of heightened class struggle. The Marxist critic Terry Eagleton points out that Bertolt Brecht rejected realist novels as relating to 'a certain set of social relations', as a form 'appropriate to an earlier phase of the class struggle'.[7] Brecht turned instead to new forms, like Expressionism and Dadaism, that sought to expose capitalism in a much bolder and more aggressive fashion.

In the same way, socialist theatre workers in Britain responded to the increased militancy of the early 1970s by rejecting the social realism of writers like Arnold Wesker that had dominated radical theatre for fifteen years. They, like Brecht, sensed that realism was an inadequate form for a radical era; and they were also aware that the rise of mass-populist culture (notably television) had increased rather than decreased the problems of the realist approach.

The contradiction is put simply: the dominant form of television drama is naturalism, which shows people's behaviour as conditioned, primarily or exclusively, by individual and psychological factors. The socialist, on the other hand, requires a form which demonstrates the social and political character of human behaviour.

However, in the television age, the masses are so swamped by naturalism and, therefore, by its individualist assumptions, that the superficially similar techniques of realism are incapable of countering individualist ideology. The realist picture of life, with its accurate representations of observable behaviour, is open to constant misinterpretation, however 'typical' the characters, and however 'total' the underlying social context may be.

Faced with this barrage of bourgeois culture, the response of agitprop is precisely to eliminate the surface appearance of the situation it presents, and to portray instead what it regards as the political reality beneath. The capitalist, for obvious example, is shown as a Victorian, top-hatted archetype because the makers of the piece of theatre believe that, despite all the surface changes in the appearance, style, and attitudes of the employing class, the fundamental reality is still that of heartless exploitation.

There is no danger here of misinterpreting the actions of the capitalist in terms of his individual psychology; his class motivation is all too clear. The archetype is then presented acting within a series of non-realistic images which further define his class behaviour, as occurs classically in Red Ladder's show about the National Cake:

The 'National Cake' is a metaphor that is familiar to everyone. In 'The Industrial Relations Act' we use that metaphor visually. Inside that overall visualisation we then place further metaphors that express the ideas we want to get over: the workers are bakers who bake the national cake; the strike is seen as a knife which cuts into the cake; the myth of the 'national interest' is exploded visually because it is the capitalist who sits on top of the cake, the workers purchase cake to eat, the cake itself is a visualisation of the class structure in society, etc.

All these images can be concretised and made immediately comprehensible in seconds. Equally, because the image is so clearly defined, every time one of the actors changes position within the image a point is made visually: the 'union official' moves from the base on to the lowest rung of the ladder, the 'strike knife' held by one worker is too heavy, held by two it can be wielded as an effective weapon ... In this manner we attempt to explain, albeit simply, the concept of wage labour, inflation, and many other ideas of central importance to the tactics and strategy of the labour movement, and we try to explain them in a way that sticks firmly in people's heads.

The basic intention ... is to try and make the economic and social forces that so deeply affect our lives – which are usually invisible, hidden from our understanding – visible and tangible so that they can be grasped and hopefully acted upon.[8]

Functional agitprop of this type remained the dominant form of socialist theatre throughout the period of the Heath government, and then for a year or two beyond. Since then, however, a number of groups have moved away from this style, at least in its pure form. New directions have included, on the one hand, a return to forms of social realism (particularly among newer groups whose work deals with sexual politics), and, on the other, a much greater concentration on the entertainment value of performances, sometimes at the expense of overt political content.

These developments have been analysed and criticised in a detailed (but anonymous) article by a socialist writer and director in the magazine *Wedge*. The thesis presented is that recent developments have been a reformist retreat from the original revolutionary principles of socialist theatre, a retreat brought about by an increasing reliance on subsidy from the state.

(The facts on the growth of subsidy are simply stated: in

1971-72 the Arts Council of Great Britain gave two socialist theatre groups a total of £10,363; by 1973-74 it was paying eleven groups £41,490; and in 1976-77 eighteen groups were receiving a total of £421,093. This does not include locally financed groups, or groups in Wales or Scotland.[9])

The *Wedge* article defines the baleful consequences of subsidy as follows:

1. The 'professionalisation' of the theatre groups, through the achievement – in August 1974 – of Equity recognition and Equity wages for socialist theatre workers. This meant that 'revolutionary socialists who had started doing theatre as a political weapon, to create propaganda and agitation', were now joined by 'left-wing actors, active within their union, but with little or no other political work behind them'. The result was that 'once jobs had been created, people began to do the work as a job, and the possibility of careers within the theatre was created'. Finally, subsidy caused the 'rise of an administrative class' within the groups themselves.[10]

2. A move away from the principle of playing to workers in struggle, caused by (a) increased technical equipment, particularly musical equipment, which created the need to play 'venues that could accommodate the technology', i.e., arts centres and small theatres rather than pubs and clubs; (b) an increased reliance on the bureaucratic organisations of the labour movement as a source for bookings, when 'working-class' audiences *were* sought; and (c) the creation of internally democratic structures only among 'the arbitrary group of people who were the company at the time'. This internal democray, the *Wedge* article argues, had the paradoxical effect of cutting the companies even further off from the working class, by rendering them 'accountable to no one but themselves'.[11]

These factors, the article continues, have had a destructive effect on the form and content of the work itself. First, the influx of professional performers led to a stylistic regression:

> The professional actors, who basically wanted 'meaty parts', criticised the use of 'cardboard two-dimensional working-class caricatures' and argued for putting 'real people' on the stage,

people the audience could 'identify' with. This tended to mean lots of family scenes, emotionally fraught arguments and inner psychological motivations: all the clap-trap of British drama training was to be imported, uncritically, into a popular theatre tradition.

Furthermore, the move towards the labour bureaucracies as bookers of the shows tended to degrade the content of the plays:

> Many companies who once had militant things to say about the Tories became strangely silent in their plays about the Tory policies of the new Labour government ... The emerging administrative class within the theatre groups began increasingly to look for bookings and support, not to the mass of the working class, but to the bureaucratic layers of its workplace organisations ... Scenes in plays began to be altered so as not to criticise or offend the district officials and trades council secretaries who laid on the bookings.

This development, the article continues, occurred precisely because the very method of play-making had lost all contact with the people that the work was supposed to be created about and for:

> Revolutionaries would be unanimous in recognising that the ideas of the plays came from the most advanced sections of the class and that the particular skill of the theatre group is to turn these ideas into images, stories, scenes, and songs and give them back again to the class – and to learn from what goes down well, and what does not. A dialectical process, in other words ...
> The essence of the reformist illusion, however, is that radical intellectuals are the originators of ideas, the possessors of wisdom, and will set out to 'educate' their audiences, and 'raise their consciousnesses'. It is not enough to reject this position as being arrogant or élitist (which it is). It is necessary to discern that what has occurred is a degeneration from dialectical materialism into idealism, in other words the belief that ideas can change material reality, by themselves.

Despite its anonymity, the *Wedge* article is important because it is one of the few consistent critiques, written from within, of the socialist theatre movement. It seems, however, to contain several fundamental flaws.

The first is that, by defining the events it describes as 'a battle of political lines' between 'revolutionary socialist' and 'professional theatre workers' (also characterised as 'reformists' and occasionally 'Maoists'), the writer leaves out of account the relationship between developments within the theatre and the state of the struggle outside it. This omission, indeed, leads on to the thoroughly undialectical implication that socialist theatre can create a revolutionary working class on its own.

The movement towards 'workers in struggle' among socialist theatre workers in the early 1970s was, as I have shown, a response to and indeed only made possible by a heightening of the class struggle. In the same way, events of the post-1975 period can be understood in terms of what the *Wedge* writer himself acknowledges to be 'a period of class retreat'.

One of the major points made in *Wedge* is that the groups turned away from the advanced sections of the class, and began to rely on reformist bureaucracies. (It seems to be doubtful, by the way, that this is literally true: what certainly did occur was that the socialist theatre did not *increase* its penetration of the working class to the extent that one might have predicted in 1974.)

The *Wedge* article begs the question, however, of the organisational form in which such a relationship with rank-and-file advanced workers could occur. It seems to me obvious that this kind of relationship (if it is to move beyond the necessary but parochial business of dealing with specific struggles in particular workplaces) can only exist if socialist theatre is part of a mass revolutionary movement that has its roots deep within the advanced sections of the class.

It is no coincidence that the example of a satisfactory theatre/class relationship posited by *Wedge* is in a post-revolutionary society (the Peoples' Republic of China). In the absence of mass organisations of advanced workers, it is no surprise that theatre groups have found it impossible to relate in any consistent way to them. The organisational forms – even the geographical spaces in which to appear – are just not present.

Wedge may be correct to say that theatre groups are operating in a political vacuum; but the point is tautological. Groups are working in a vacuum because it is a vacuum in which they are working.

The objective state of class relations also has formal implications for socialist theatre. One of the clear consequences of the lack of a mass revolutionary perspective in the British working class has been the collapse of wage militancy in the post-1974 period (and the gradual realisation by revolutionaries that the *political* content of the class activity of the 1972-74 period had been over-estimated).

The move away from pure agitprop towards more complex theatrical forms seems to me satisfactorily explained in terms of a considered response by the groups to this failure of economism. Red Ladder, who have the authority of not a little experience, have found that agitprop, although a good weapon for confirming workers in their struggles and drawing practical lessons from their experiences (in other words, a form ideal to the subject-matter of economic militancy), is not suited to the tasks of a period of class retreat. As Richard Seyd wrote of the agitprop form: 'If people don't think that capitalism is an absurd and damaging way of organising society, then very little that one does is going to change their minds.'[12]

Furthermore, agitprop is formally 'unable to fulfill the artistic task of portraying and interpreting the way people operate, and why they operate in a particular way, revealing the contradictions as they grow out of the social, economic conditions of society itself '. Specifically, the techniques of agitprop are incapable of dealing with questions of consciousness, precisely because they portray only the assumed objective essence of a situation, rather than the dynamic between how people subjectively perceive that situation and the underlying reality.

The move towards the presentation of 'three-dimensional characters' might have been partly caused by the desire of performers for 'meaty parts', but even if the groups had been peopled entirely by vegetarians, it would seem likely that they would have found the agitprop form an inadequate tool under developing circumstances. Indeed, the *Wedge* article itself acknowledges that 'one of the weaknesses of the revolutionary left' was that 'they hadn't developed any theory of aesthetics – and had simply stepped into the shoes of an agitprop tradition, and tried to develop it from within'.[13] In an uncharacteristic fit of idealism, the article does not go on to enquire why this extraordinary omission should have occurred.

It seems clear to me that, in the same way that the absence of mass revolutionary organisations has prevented the building of a dialectical relationship between socialist theatre and class, the absence of a consequent mass revolutionary *culture* has obviated the growth of new theatrical forms. And in the same way that the lack of mass movement forces theatre groups into the arms of bureaucratic *organisation*, so the lack of a revolutionary culture forces them to relate to reactionary *forms*.

The work of Brecht did not drop off the trees, it drew on the existence of a working-class movement that was of sufficient cultural maturity, for example, to produce nearly 200 Social-Democratic and nearly twenty Communist *daily* newspapers.[14] The comparison with Britain today is odiously obvious.

Faced with this situation, socialist theatre workers have set out on a search for possible new forms, a process which has certainly been *allowed* by subsidy but not necessarily *caused* by it. It is, however, possible to analyse – and criticise – these attempts (which go far beyond the slide into rampant naturalism posited in *Wedge*), without explaining their limited success primarily in terms of reformist careerism.

One common experiment has been the attempt to draw upon traditions culled from popular culture, most notably the music hall and folk music, either as total formal structures, or at least as cultural reference points. The General Will is a case in point.

In our three chronicle plays about the Conservative government (*The National Interest, State of Emergency* and

The Dunkirk Spirit), we drew images and reference points from a number of sources, including what we saw as popular culture.

What became clear was that the images the audiences related to (in the sense of those that they remembered and commented on afterwards) were not those that were drawn from popular-cultural traditions. It was rather those images that we drew from bourgeois popul*ist* culture (films and television) that created the greatest resonances.

The Tory Cabinet portrayed as Chicago hoods and productivity deals related to *The Generation Game* were the metaphors that stuck, rather than those drawn from the music hall. When we made a whole show based round melodrama, we achieved some success; but this was due to the fact that the form naturally fitted the tasks we demanded of it, rather than any specific references the form had to our audiences' cultural experience.

The General Will was not the only group to realise that it was employing forms that had expired more than half a century ago. Further, the awareness grew that even those popular forms that had survived the electronic onslaught had degenerated into populism.

It is true, for example, that remnants of the music-hall tradition survive in club entertainment, but the grossly reactionary nature of the content of club acts is evidence that, though oriented towards the working class in form, the culture of the clubs has become bourgeois in essence (it is no coincidence that the uniform costume of club entertainers is the evening wear of the upper-middle class).

Some groups and companies have indeed drawn successfully on other popular-cultural forms, but it is interesting that they have achieved most when they have employed forms actually peripheral to the urban British working class. Joan Littlewood's *Oh! What a Lovely War*, for example, used the pierrot show (a basically Italian form, translated into British seaside entertainment), and 7:48 Scotland's use of the *celidh* form in *The Cheviot, the Stag and the Black Black Oil* succeeded precisely because it drew on a rural folk form, and, indeed, was directed at audiences in the rural highlands of Scotland.

Faced with the atrophy of popular culture, some revolutionaries have sought to move into enemy territory, and to inject socialist content into mass-populist forms. One example is the writer Trevor Griffiths, who explained his use of the drama serial (in *Bill Brand*) as follows:

> 'Strategic penetration' is a phrase I use a lot about the work of socialists and Marxists in bourgeois cultures ... I simply cannot understand socialist playwrights who do not devote most of their time to television. That they can write for the Royal Court and the National Theatre, and only that, seems to me a wilful self-delusion about the nature of theatre in a bourgeois culture now. It's just thunderingly exciting to be able to talk to large numbers of people in the working class, and I can't understand why everybody doesn't want to do it.

Griffiths then goes on to confront the formal problems of the medium, justifying his use of 'realistic modes as against non-realist alienating modes' in the following terms:

> I chose to work in these modes because I have to work now. I have to work with the popular imagination which has been shaped by naturalism ... One of the things about realistic modes is still that you can offer through them demystifying, undistorted, more accurate counter-descriptions of political processes and social reality than people get through other uses of naturalism. So that if for every *Sweeney* that went out, a *Bill Brand* went out, there would be a real struggle for the popular imagination.

Finally, Griffiths discusses the implications of the 'realist mode' for the treatment of characters, particularly those with whom he himself disagrees:

> I try to occupy the space of all the people I'm talking about. I have actually met almost nobody who goes around saying to people, 'Well the trouble with me is I'm a total shit. I tell lies all the time, and all I'm about is self-advancement; I don't give a fuck for anybody.' People don't seem to operate that way. But when I read about these people in *Socialist Worker* there is a sense in which the guy knows he's a shit. So that everyone who does not agree is in some way cynically distanced from his own reality, and wholly self-consciously so. I've never

found that to be the case. So when I write this way, it's with a feeling that it's kind of truthful.[15]

In order to assess how successful Griffiths has been in this project, it is necessary to distinguish between the inherent problems of the medium of television, and the further problems posed by the nature of the dramatic forms that television has developed. It seems to me that it is possible to counter the former only if one resolutely refuses to be bound by the limits of the latter.

The inherent problem with television as an agent of radical ideas is that its massive audience is not confronted en masse. It is confronted in the atomised arena of the family living room, the place where people are at their least critical, their most conservative and reactionary (the dwelling-addressed postal vote will always get a more reactionary response than any other form of balloted decision). The television audience, approached in the midst of their private and personal existence, are much more likely than collectively addressed audiences to take an individual, personalised (and therefore psychological rather than social) view of the behaviour demonstrated to them.

This problem is exacerbated, however, by the forms that television has developed (forms that are *suitable* to the medium, but not necessarily *inherent* to it). Format scheduling, for example, has the effect of dulling the audience's response to challenging material by placing it within a predictable and familiar framework of regular programme slots.

This can, of course, be countered by employing atypical techniques (the Battersby-Welland play *Leeds – United!* was made at unslottable length on black and white film), but *Bill Brand* itself was placed firmly within a conventional timing. Furthermore, it was written in a form – the drama serial – which demands that the audience identify uncritically with its central character or characters.

The degeneration of the serial *Z Cars* from a portrayal of working-class experience in which the linking factor happened to be involvement with the police to a soap opera about specific policemen (who, as they became more popular, could not be implicitly criticised to the extent that their audience could no longer identify with them; Watt and Barlow could behave in certain morally dubious ways, but not to the extent that they had to be taken out of the series) was a classic example of this process in action, on which John McGrath (one of the originators of the series) has frequently commented.[16]

The danger of a project like *Brand* is that, by the end of eleven episodes, the audience is identifying with Brand exclusively as the pivot of the story (my hero right or wrong), and sympathising with his views and actions only insofar as is necessary to a satisfactory dramatic experience.

In other words, identification with Brand's socialism is equivalent to the identification with certain chauvinistic ideas that it is necessary to share in order to enjoy Shakespeare's *Henry V*. The audience is prepared to share Brand's socialism for the duration of the play, but no longer.

Moreover, as has been pointed out, the countless other drama serials, series, and plays that are part of a television audience's experiential baggage will lead them to take an individual-psychological view of events if they are given any opportunity. (Griffiths in fact gave the audience ample opportunity to judge his central character's actions psychologically, by giving him a broken marriage and a feminist lover.)

Further, this experiential baggage will allow audiences to relate to Griffiths's concentration upon individual experiences ('I try to occupy the space of all the people I'm writing about') in an uncritical way. The writer no doubt wishes to present a realistic dynamic between the surface naturalism of his characters' represented behaviour and the political essence of their activities, but audiences will react only to the surface unless powerfully prevented from doing so.

This leads to a third problem with Griffiths's approach. He himself gives an example of how he tries to counter the surface with the essence, in a scene where a trade union leader used the moral pressure of his service in the International Brigade to counter Brand's argument that he is reneging on the interests of his class.

Griffiths seeks to undermine the emotional force of the union leader's speech by ending the scene with a shot of a portrait of Lord Citrine. What is immediately obvious (beyond the device's reliance on the audience knowing what Citrine looked like) is the lightness of this device compared with the power of what it has to counter.

As Griffiths himself admits, 'I don't know how you can prevent people getting out of the plays what they want,' and what they want is defined by the barrage of programmes surrounding *Brand* which use the *same* form to present an *opposite* view about human behaviour. (On commercial television, the problems of 'strategic penetration' are even more acute, as the experience is itself strategically penetrated back by raw capitalist propaganda at twenty-minute intervals.)

It might be true that 'if for every *Sweeney* that went out, a *Bill Brand* went out, there would be a real struggle for the popular imagination', but it is a 'wilful self-delusion' to think that such a struggle would be allowed to take place. In summary, therefore, television realism has all the problems of contemporary realism writ massively.

I have dwelt on what I regard as the limits of the contrasting approaches of Trevor Griffiths and the author of the *Wedge* article because of their theoretical exclusivity. In the absence of a mass revolutionary or popular culture, socialists will wish – and should wish – to exploit the opportunities presented by television, and to employ the techniques of agitprop in stage plays for the working class. However, the theoretical limits of these strategies seem to demand that theatre workers should consider whether new forms of – and even new roles for – socialist theatre can be found.

I believe that the germs of such new forms – and, more obliquely, of such new functions – are in fact present, though in a place that one would least expect to find them. Bertolt Brecht once remarked that 'the proof of the pudding is in the eating', a comment that might appear blindingly obvious until one observes that the major preoccupations of many socialist theatre workers are with the origins of the recipe, the cleanliness of the spoons, the decision-making methods employed by the chefs, and the address of the restaurant.

It seems to me demonstrably if paradoxically true that the most potent, rich, and in many ways politically acute theatrical statements of the past ten years have been made in custom-built buildings patronised almost exclusively by the middle class.

This is not to say that touring socialist groups have not produced acute and resonant images. The metaphor of the man's pint and the woman's half-pint in Red Ladder's *A Woman's Work Is Never Done*, for instance, does a great deal more than explain the difference between parity and equal pay.

But I have seen nothing in touring theatre to compare, in terms of memorable (and therefore *usable*) dramatic power, with the tearing down of the wall at the end of Edward Bond's *Lear*; the decision of the hideous Bagley dynasty to move into the Chinese heroin market in the last act of Howard Brenton and David Hare's *Brassneck*; and the sustained fury of Barry Keefe's *Gotcha*, in which a working-class teenager holds three teachers hostage in a school boxroom by threatening to drop a lighted cigarette into a motorcycle petrol tank.

There was also – significantly – nothing in the whole of *Bill Brand* to compare with the climax of the second act of Griffiths's stage play *Comedians*, where the white-faced, football-scarfed, totally unfunny stand-up comic Gethin Price screams at two upper-class dummies he is terrorising: 'There's people'd call this envy, you know. It's not. It's hate.'[17]

Nor is it easy to think of a series of images that says so much in so little time as those in the last half-hour of Howard Barker's *Claw*, the tale of a working-class boy who rejects the politics of his class, becomes a pimp to the aristocracy, and, after a scandal involving the Secretary of State for Home Affairs, is arrested by the Special Branch.

The last act here is described by the critic John Ashford:

> The third act opens with an even more extreme stylistic jolt
> than the second. Two waiters serve Claw breakfast. They do
> not speak to him. They speak to the audience about
> themselves.
>
> They are both men of violence. One tells the story of the
> first time he planted a bomb in Northern Ireland. The second
> tells of his experience as an apprentice hangman before the
> abolition of the death penalty.
>
> Both speeches are written with an extraordinary clarity and
> sympathy. The men also gossip about the grubby sexual
> origins of pop stars, and it gradually becomes clear that they
> are not waiters but warders. This is a mental institution of a
> very special nature, and they have been selected to work there
> because of their particular experience.
>
> Claw appeals to his warders but gets no response. He
> appeals to a vision of his father. Old Biledew, now dying,
> condemns Claw's individualism, regrets that he did not have
> the vocabulary necessary to pass on his experience, and
> advises Claw not to despise his class but to win them.
>
> Claw again appeals to his warders. They swiftly and
> efficiently drown him in a bath.[18]

I have quoted this description at length because it
demonstrates a vital element of the aesthetic that sets these
plays apart from most touring work. The ending of *Claw* is
a series of shocks, reliant on the audience's ignorance of
what is going to happen.

The same is true of *Gotcha*. The last scene of *Brassneck* is
nothing more than a build-up to the revelation that the
selling of lethal drugs is the purest form of the market
economy. And the whole of the first two acts of *Comedians*
builds up to Gethin Price's macabre performance, and
depends on the audience not knowing what he will do
until he does it.

This use of suspense and shock is, of course, a
fundamental break with the Brechtian tradition. Brecht's
concern was always to demonstrate *how* events unfold
(already having revealed *what* was going to happen in the
headings to the scenes).

On the other hand, the content of the plays I have

described is contained in *the fact that* the events occur. As in Brecht, the aim is to force the audience to respond analytically; but instead of distancing the audience from the occurrences, these writers involve the audience, provoking them into thought by the very surprise and shock of the images.

Conscious, perhaps, of the degeneration of Brecht's techniques to the condition of theatrical cliché, these writers are forging a style that uses opposite methods to the same end. The shock factor is not just a matter of internal dramatic effect. Another point to note is that these writers are employing given forms and structures, but they are not using them as a bridge into people's familiar dramatic experience; they are deliberately disturbing and disorienting the audience by destroying the form and denying expectations.

The motor of Bond's *Lear* is the way he *alters* and even reverses the original Shakespeare story. *Brassneck* is, in fact, the hoary old stand-by, the chronicle of a family through three generations; the shock element is provided by the fact that the generations are defined not by their domestic relations, but by their different methods of capitalist appropriation.

And Gethin Price's turn in *Comedians* depends completely on its denial of the basic principle of the form; Price is aggressively and deliberately *unfunny*.

This up-ending of received forms reveals the cultural heritage of these works, and, further, goes some way to explaining their revolutionary potency. Bond has never put his own work in the counter-cultural tradition, and Brenton feels himself to have moved on from the aesthetics of Portable Theatre.[19]

But the techniques I have described clearly arise out of the spectacle-disruptive, situationist era of the late 1960s, and, indeed, the success of Bond and Brenton's metaphors may well be explained by their place within a genuine (if politically misguided) revolutionary culture, a culture, furthermore, whose preoccupations with consciousness render it, in a revised form, eminently suited to confronting the gap between the objective crisis of the system and the subjective responses of the human beings within it.

The techniques of shock and disruption, therefore, serve the same function today as Brecht's methods performed 40 years ago: they pre-empt the degeneration of realism into naturalism, and preserve a genuine dynamic between the surface and essence of society.

It is, however, obvious that the form's exploitation of literary and theatrical sources (one might, but only might, except *Comedians*) renders it inaccessible to those without the dubious advantage of a university education. The writers I have mentioned are in fact much further from political activism than most touring socialist theatre workers.

The plays themselves are not, of course, performed anywhere near the working class: most of Bond's work has been premiered at the Royal Court, which has also produced two of Barker's plays; Bond and Barker have both recently written for the Royal Shakespeare Company; Brenton has worked and Hare is about to work for the National Theatre; *Brassneck* and *Comedians* were both premiered at Nottingham Playhouse, and the latter was transferred, via the Old Vic Theatre, into the West End.

To reject the contribution that these writers' discoveries might make to a socialist theatre on those grounds, however, seems to be a mechanical error, based on a false and one-dimensional view of the way in which artistic processes occur. I am not alone in this view. As Leon Trotsky warned a Communist Party cultural committee in 1924:

> One cannot approach art as one can politics, not because artistic creation is a religious rite or something mystical ... but because it has its own laws of development, and above all because in artistic creation an enormous role is played by the sub-conscious processes – slower, more idle and less subjected to management and guidance.
>
> Artistic creativity, by its very nature, lags behind the other modes of a man's spirit, and still more the spirit of a class. It is one thing to understand something and express it logically, and quite another thing to assimilate it organically,

reconstructing the whole system of one's feelings, and to find a new kind of artistic expression for this new entity. The latter process is more organic, slower, more difficult to subject to conscious influence.[20]

Furthermore, this analysis explains, for Trotsky, the apparent contradiction that as an artist grows in political sophistication, the quality of his work may actually regress; speaking of the work of the fellow-traveller Boris Pilnyak, he remarks:

> It has been said here that those writings of Pilnyak's which are closer to Communism are feebler than those which are politically farther away from us. What is the explanation? Why, just this, that on the rationalistic plane Pilnyak is ahead of himself as an artist.

What is obviously needed is a way of transforming the techniques that have been developed in metropolitan theatres into forms that are formally and geographically accessible to audiences directly involved in struggle against exploitation and oppression.

There are, I think, signs that such a transformation is beginning to occur – at least, that certain signposts on such a road are becoming visible. One group that is acting as a bridge between the Royal Court and a wider audience is the Monstrous Regiment, a company with a majority of women members.

Since their formation in 1976, they have produced a series of increasingly confident and powerful plays (presented largely but by no means exclusively in arts venues), and have done so at a time when many of the groups from which their members came (including, classically, 7:84 England) are racked with internal division and doubt.

The styles and techniques developed by socialists working in conventional theatres are clearly appropriate to the areas of experience with which Monstrous Regiment deals, and, indeed, the group has performed two plays written by Caryl Churchill, much of whose work has been premiered at the Royal Court. Further, and most importantly, the work of Monstrous Regiment can speak relevantly and *usefully* to the audiences that it is actually likely to gain.

It has been pointed out that socialist theatre has not built up a mass working-class audience. What it *has* done is to create substantial support among the socialist movement (by which I mean members of revolutionary parties, and non-aligned supporters of various left-wing organisations, causes and campaigns).

What groups like Monstrous Regiment have done is to acknowledge this audience (rather than pretending, despite all the evidence to the contrary, that they are not there) and to concentrate on the presentation of content that can speak appropriately, authoritatively, and also controversially to that audience: appropriately in the sense that the subject matter can speak directly and importantly to an audience that does not consist in the majority of manual workers (without, of course, excluding such an audience); authoritatively in that the plays draw on the direct experience of those who create them; and controversially in that sexual politics is an area of theory and practice on which socialists have tended to be at best woolly and at worst downright reactionary.

Finally, sexual politics is clearly an area of experience which can be much more illuminatingly and richly discussed in a representational rather than a purely descriptive medium of communication, precisely because it is at the interface of the personal and political.

It is this realisation that there are subjects with which theatre is uniquely fitted to deal that has led, I believe, to an increase in plays about various aspects of political consciousness, and explains, for me, the large number of plays presently being made or performed about race, a development recently quantified – not uncritically – by Sandy Craig in The *Leveller*.[21]

Craig himself concludes his piece by saying that socialist companies should 'come to a much fuller and more exact understanding of the function, purpose and effects of theatre'. It appears to me that, over the last ten years, socialist theatre workers have spent much time and energy discovering what they cannot do, to whom they are not appealing, and in what forms their work is least appropriately presented.

The seemingly modest aims of a group like Monstrous Regiment, to perform aesthetically and politically mature plays to an existing audience, are refreshing in themselves. But this is not, of course, the end of the story, and the realisation that socialist playmakers cannot themselves change the world may yet help them to discover ways of contributing, and in no small measure, to the work of those who can.

Notes

1. See, particularly, Joe Orton, *Loot*, London 1967.
2. Quoted in P. Ansorge, 'The Portable Playwrights', *Plays and Players*, February 1971.
3. Ibid.
4. Richard Seyd, 'The Theatre of Red Ladder', *New Edinburgh Review*, August 1975.
5. Roland Muldoon, 'Cast Revival', *Plays and Players*, January 1977.
6. John Berger, *Art and Revolution*, London 1969.
7. Terry Eagleton, *Marxism and Literary Criticism*, London 1976.
8. Seyd., op. cit.
9. From the *Annual Report of the Arts Council of Great Britain*, 1971-72, 1973-74, and 1976-77.
10. Anon., 'Grant Aid and Political Theatre', *Wedge*, Summer 1977.
11. Ibid., part two, unpublished.
12. Seyd, op. cit.
13. Anon., op. cit.
14. See Robert Black, *Fascism in Germany*, London 1975.
15. Interview with Trevor Griffiths, *Leveller*, November 1976.
16. See McGrath's Edinburgh Festival critique of television naturalism, reprinted in *Sight and Sound*, April 1977.
17. Trevor Griffiths, *Comedians*, London 1976.
18. John Ashford, review of *Claw* in *Plays and Players*, March 1975.
19. See the interview with Howard Brenton in *Plays and Players*, July 1973.
20. L.D. Trotsky, speech of 9 May 1924, reprinted as 'Class and Art', *Fourth International*, July 1967.
21. Sandy Craig, 'Scenes from the Anti-Racist Battle', *Leveller*, January 1978.

On Drama-Documentary

It's a truism that the one-off, original television play is always an endangered species; the irony of the early 1980s is that the target has shifted. The most poisonous darts are now aimed not so much at the 'obscure' Second City First or the 'obscene' Play for Today, but at manifestations of the only single-play television form that is unique to the medium: the form known variously as fiction, dramatic reconstruction, documentary drama or drama-documentary. This form has always had its critics, of course: Mrs Mary Whitehouse cut her teeth on *Cathy Come Home* and *Up the Junction*. But the debate over Anthony Thomas's *Death of a Princess* took matters on to a different plane. This was partly, of course, to do with the perceived threat to our trading and diplomatic links with Saudi Arabia, and most interesting it was, to see how those Conservatives who fervently believe in freedom of trade as a precondition of freedom of expression tend to support the former over the latter when the two conflict. But the importance of the affair to the makers of drama-documentary was that the film provoked many critics to express their strong reservations not just about *Death of a Princess*, but about the form as a whole.

Two extremely distinguished commentators expressed their reservations good and early: immediately after the Saudi storm broke, Sir Ian Gilmour, then the Lord Privy Seal, told the House of Commons that 'the so-called dramatisation or fictionalisation of alleged history is extremely dangerous and misleading, and is something to which the broadcasting authorities must give close attention.' His view was echoed by Lord Carrington in the Lords, who warned that 'it might be as well for those who are producing these programmes to have a good look at the consequences of what they are doing' (he was responding to a question about 'the tendency of some TV companies to present programmes deliberately designed to give the impression of documentary based on fact'). Others quickly entered the lists as well; reasonably representative were Geoffrey Cannon, writing in the *Sunday Times* and Richard Gott in the *Guardian*.[1] Cannon's basic argument against drama-documentary was that the 'known facts' of contemporary or recent history can and are subject to 'elaboration and embroidery', and, indeed, that 'TV drama-documentary may deliberately stray away from truth for dramatic impact, and to feed the audience's predispositions or prejudices.' Richard Gott's article began as follows:

> Well, what is it? Fact or fiction? History or current affairs? Scarcely a night goes by nowadays without Edward VIII, the Reverend Jim Jones, Winston Churchill, or some other famous or infamous figure from the recent past, appearing on the television screen. Significant episodes in their lives are then presented in fictitious form ('artificial, counterfeit, sham'), or, rather, in a mishmash of fact and fiction and producer's whim. It is a profoundly unsatisfactory development in the use of television.

Gott then went on to accuse television producers and writers of usurping the function of historians, claiming to explain 'what actually happened' in history, a role for which they are neither qualified nor competent, rather than pursuing their proper role of 'illuminating the human condition' through the creation of imaginary characters in invented situations.

These are serious arguments, which deserve to be taken seriously. They are, however, based on severe misconceptions about history itself and the playwright's relationship to it; and I use the word 'playwright' rather than producer or director deliberately, because it is my view that drama-documentary is, primarily, not a journalistic but a dramatic medium, like soap-opera, tragedy or farce, which has been developed by writers in response to the changing world about them, and that it should be defended as such.

The first and glaring problem with Gott's and Cannon's critiques of the form is one of definition. Richard Gott, for example, confines himself to the discussion of plays which present the actions of famous or infamous real people, living in the recent past, in fictional form. This definition would indeed take in most of the programmes which we would recognise as drama-documentary, but it would also encompass almost any biographical film set in the recent past, from *Lawrence of Arabia* and *The Dambusters* to *Funny Girl*. Geoffrey Cannon divides the form into two, distinguishing between faction (of which he gives *Roots, Holocaust* and *Washington behind Closed Doors* as examples), and drama-documentary, which he describes as a form dealing with 'matters of social and moral concern'. It is obvious that the latter definition could happily embrace almost every serious play ever written; but even the former group of plays have in common only that they deal with real historical events and use a mix of real and fictional characters – which might just about let out *Funny Girl*, if we define 'historical event' in a way that excludes the Ziegfeld Follies, but would include most biographical war films and stage plays as various as Brecht's *Galileo*, Rattigan's *The Winslow Boy* and Shaw's *Saint Joan*. And a third commentator, Robin Sutch, replying to Gott's piece in the *Guardian*, went so far as to give the historical plays of Shakespeare and Aeschylus as examples of ancient precedents of the drama-documentary form.[2] And it's worth pointing out that apart from Cannon's subjects of social and moral concern, none of the above definitions would cover programmes that most people would instinctively view as being drama-documentaries, but which do not include real people as characters, like *Law and Order*, two of the four episodes of Ken Loach's *Days of Hope*, and, indeed, *Cathy Come Home*.

It is of course true that drama-documentary makers themselves have extreme difficulty in defining the beast they are riding. But it is also clear that the above definitions won't do, and that pointing out that they won't do is more than a debating trick, because no definition of the difference between, say, *Churchill and the Generals*,

Three Days in Szczecin, Colditz and *Henry V* will do unless it takes into account the dramatic and ideological purposes of playwrights, and the artistic and social contexts in which they work.

It seems to me obvious that, however inspirational the process of literary creation may be, most playwrights draw most of their subject-matter from sources outside themselves, and when critics like Richard Gott complain that by recreating historical figures rather than creating imaginary characters writers are displaying a lack of creativity and imagination, they are themselves diplaying not a little ignorance about the process of making plays. It is, however, clear why this misunderstanding occurs; it is to do with the differences between writing plays about public and private life. When playwrights write about a private theme – about, say, domestic life or romantic love – their models in real life are cloaked in anonymity; the real families or couples on which the play is based are unlikely to be known to its audience. If, however, a playwright chose to write about a battle, it is likely that an intelligent audience would pick up pretty quickly whether the story was based on the Peloponnesian Wars, the Battle of Trafalgar or the Siege of Leningrad. Put another way, it is a shocking but true fact that, in France alone, literally millions of love affairs were commenced, enjoyed and concluded between 1958 and 1969, and the playwright interested in the sexual habits of the French during the first decade of the Fifth Republic would be able to base his plot on any number of them. The source material for a play about political leadership in France during that period is more limited, and it would be a perverse writer who did not consider including, in such a play, a tall, long-nosed statesman with a marked distaste for Anglo-Saxon countries, and a liking for grandiose political rhetoric. And similarly, if I wanted – and as it happens, I once did – to write a play about electoral malpractice in a large English-speaking democratic state possessed of sophisticated surveillance technologies, it would be pretty coy not to set that play in Washington DC during the Nixon presidency. It is true, of course, that some plays about public life have created their own allegorical world, or used an incident from the past to illumine the present (Max Frisch's *Andorra* is an example of the former technique, Arthur Miller's *The Crucible* of the latter). But by and large plays about public life have tended to be based on real and recognisable public events, either contemporary or historical. What sets drama-documentary apart from the mass of public plays is not the employment of facts but the theatrical use to which those facts are put. In drama-documentary, I believe, the factual basis of the story gives the action of the play its credibility.

Most good plays say things about human relationships and human society which are challenging and surprising and disturbing to their audiences; and all writers of such plays want to convince their audiences that they are right to be so challenged, surprised and disturbed. Sometimes – in absurdist or symbolic drama – the power of a playwright's metaphor will be proof enough that his or her bleak (or euphoric) view of the universe is credible. But, for most of us, it is necessary to establish a bedrock of material (or a dramatic style) which is recognisable to the audience, and gives what follows its legitimacy. For example, John Hopkins's classic quartet of television plays, *Talking to a Stranger*, presented an unwelcomely bitter view of family life. What gave those plays their power – to shock and to convince – was that the characters' day-to-day behaviour was terrifyingly recognisable, when set against our own lives and the lives of people we know. In the same way, Eugene O'Neill's *Long Day's Journey into Night* is incomparably superior in its perception, its power and its capacity to disturb to anything O'Neill had written before, precisely because the desperate and magnificent agony of the Tyrones is shown to us, initially at least, through the most trivial (but universal) of domestic conflicts: over meal-times, table-clearing and drinks before dinner. Similarly, the conclusions of the plays of Shakespeare are often more radical and challenging to our assumptions about the world than anything written before or since. But the fact that Shakespeare's plays employed recognisable forms – tragedy, comedy, historical drama – provided a bedrock of shared assumptions on which he could build his vision of the human condition. Without that bedrock, that sense that the writer has won his or her spurs, the audience can shrug off the playwright's conclusions as bearing no relationship to the real world.

Playwrights writing about public life in the contemporary world are in a different position, both from the writer of domestic drama and from Shakespeare. We all have experience of the subject-matter of domestic drama – we have all lived in families, grown up, fallen in love, and fallen out of it again; we can all judge our own experience against plays which present these activities to us. In public plays, however, there is no guarantee of any shared experience of the subject-matter. Plays about war are presented on British stages and British television to audiences who now, by and large, have no knowledge of soldiering. Plays about the workings of one particular political party will be performed or broadcast to audiences consisting, in varying and unpredictable proportions, of members of that party, members of opposing parties, or members of no party at all. Further, there are no longer any dramatic forms that retain the universally accepted power of, say, tragedy or the historical epic. And, of course, we live in an age in which any unifying belief or set of values – which means any generally accepted set of criteria for judging human behaviour – are absent.

I think that the theatre of fact, the documentary theatre, was created to give credibility to the playwright's analysis of the incredible happenings of our time. (The theatrical form of drama-documentary predated the television form, but, in my view, it is on television that the form has reached maturity.) One of the best examples of stage drama-documentary is Rolf Hochhuth's play *The Representative*, written in the early 1960s. Hochhuth wanted to write a play about men of power, and the terrible contradiction they face in balancing political expediency against moral principle. He decided to set his play not in the far or mythical past, but during the Second World War. The context of the play's story – the Holocaust – was then and is now well known. But Hochhuth's central incident – the refusal of Pope Pius XII to break the Vatican's Concordat with the Third Reich in protest against the mass-murder of the Jews – was not well known at all, and Hochhuth's representation of the Pope's actions provoked bitter controversy when the play was first staged. It's my belief that Hochhuth's statement on the Holocaust and the resistance to it would not have been nearly so powerful if it had not exposed an event of history about which his audience knew little or nothing. His act of documentary revelation performed, in his play, an equivalent function to that of the peripeteia of Greek tragedy: the sudden, unexpected and shocking reversal of fortune that captures and freezes the themes of the play, as if caught in a sudden shaft of bright light. The scene with the Pope in *The Representative* is in fact a reversal of *expectation*, both about the character and about the type of play we are watching; and the credibility it gives to Hochhuth's message is not about the following of agreed and accepted constructional rules, but about evidence.

This is a completely different use of historical fact in drama from that of Shakespeare in his history plays. Shakespeare drew stories from a variety of sources to explore the theme of kingship, including ancient Roman, recent British and mythological history. I don't believe, however, that the fact that the plots of *King Lear* and *Macbeth* were drawn from mythology, and those of *Henry VI* and *Richard II* from relatively recent history, makes Shakespeare's use of his source material substantially different. In all these cases he was writing tragedies; in no case was he revealing anything his audience couldn't have known. In one case, *Richard III*, he made a play of great dramatic power out of a set of facts that were almost certainly completely untrue.

In contrast, documentary drama relies on its facts being correct. The moral core of Rolf Hochhuth's second play (*Soldiers*, a critique of allied civilian bombing in the war) was undermined and destroyed by the historical *un*truth of an important though secondary incident in the play. Similarly, the power of *Cathy Come Home* depended on the fact that its thesis – that British cities suffered from wretchedly inadequate housing at a time of presumed general prosperity – was timely and true. Without that fact, *Cathy* would have been little more than a sad anecdote of an inadequate family destroyed by an indifferent bureaucracy. In reality, of course, the play changed the way we think about housing. I think it changed the way we think about other things too – like the inner-city, the role of the social services, and even the political system. Jeremy Sandford used his factual base in order to give dramatic force and credibility to a much wider theme.

It is of course precisely this *use* of factual material to sustain a thesis which provokes so much concern and criticism. As Leslie Woodhead of Granada Television's drama-documentary unit argued in his Granada lecture, 'the underlying assumption that television drama should seek not only to reflect but also to change society has informed much of the most interesting work in the field of documented drama over the past decade,' citing the work of Tony Garnett, Ken Loach, Jim Allen and G.F. Newman, and pointing out that 'the implied worry ... is that the forms and credibilities of documentary and news are being recruited to smuggle a political message.'[3] Certainly this worried Paul Johnson, in a piece commenting on *World in Action*'s reconstruction of the Cabinet debate over the 1981 budget: for him, drama-documentary deliberately blurs the fact/fiction distinction 'for tendentious purposes, often in pursuit of partisan political ends ... The object, quite brazenly, is to influence opinion on contentious matters.'[4] The same point was made by Geoffrey Cannon in his post-*Princess* piece in the *Sunday Times*:

> What I found disturbing about Ian Curteis's two recent dramatised reconstructions *Churchill and the Generals* and *Suez 1956* was that, in both cases, Curteis – as he stated openly and honestly – had a thesis about Churchill and about Eden (put simply, that they were liable to states of mind approaching dementia) and he used known facts to demonstrate his thesis ..... And while his thesis is – as far as I know – consistent with the facts, other interpretations are equally consistent.[5]

The problems with these arguments are several. While

few people would justify the deliberate falsification or invention of incidents to support a vacuous historical argument (it is right that the film *The Deer Hunter* was criticised for apparently inventing its central metaphor of a group of Vietcong guerrillas forcing their American captors to play Russian roulette), accusations of political bias have a tendency to be oddly selective (no problems, as Ken Loach points out, 'when Edward VII or Churchill's mother are romanticised and glorified'). Further, as Leslie Woodhead argues, even the makers of 'real' current affairs and news programmes are at last owning up about 'the inescapable subjective content in every camera movement and edit', and the fact that 'the manipulative presence of the director is as significant in *Johnny Go Home* as it was in *Cathy Come Home*.' But even more interesting, from the dramatist's point of view, is Richard Gott's unflattering comparison between the 'amateur' writer of drama-documentary and the professional historian.

In his witty and wonderful book *What is History?*, Professor E.H. Carr takes much pleasure in exposing the nineteenth-century view of history as a collection of objective facts that it is the historian's task merely to discover, separate from speculation, and reveal. In reality, as Carr points out, it is a subjective value-judgement that Caesar's crossing of the Rubicon is an important historical event, but that millions of other people cross and still do cross that petty stream – in both directions and for reasons doubtless important for them – is not a matter of any historical importance. Similarly, almost all our knowledge of Greece in the period of the Persian Wars is not objective knowledge at all, because it emanates exclusively from a small group of rich people in the one city of Athens. Further, our view that the medieval period was a time of great religious commitment might well have been influenced by the fact that almost all the contemporary chroniclers of that period were monks. And, finally, even those documents precisely designed to be pragmatically factual – minutes of meetings and so on – reflect the interests and prejudices and self-view of the person by whom or for whom the documents were written. Professor

Carr gives the example of the papers of Gustav Stresemann, the Foreign Minister of the Weimar Republic, which were published after his death in 1929 in three massive volumes, which concentrate almost entirely on Stresemann's successful diplomatic dealings with the West. This, as Carr points out, itself distorts history, as Stresemann in fact devoted a lot, even a majority of his time to the pursuit of a much less successful policy towards the Soviet Union. But the point is that, even if the published selection were complete or accurately represented the whole, then the minutes of Stresemann's meetings with, say, the Soviet Foreign Minister Chicherin would tell us not what actually happened, but only what Stresemann thought had happened, or what he wanted others to think, or wanted himself to think, or (most likely of all) what his secretary felt that he might want to think had happened. And Chicherin's records of the same conversation would doubtless look very different, but they would be strikingly similar in one respect: they would be highly contentious, tendentious and politically partisan.

But it is useful to take this example even further. Suppose, which is not the case, that historians had available to them both sets of minutes, Stresemann's and Chicherin's. I suspect – and I only suspect, because I'm not a historian – that they would look at those two accounts in two ways. First, the historian would set them against other facts, and if, for example, it was found that either statesman had said something he knew to be untrue, then he or she might conclude that the person was being either cunning, devious, or at least excessively cautious with the other. Second, the historian might set the documents against what could be discovered about the characters of the two men from other sources; what their relatives, friends and acquaintances said about them. What I suspect the historian would not do – because it would be a most unscholarly procedure – would be to set the recollections of these two men of this one event against the behaviour of the historian's *own* relatives, friends or aquaintances, or, even, against the behaviour of him or herself. It is *that* knowledge, knowledge not just of human behaviour but of the skills necessary to communicate that knowledge to others, which is the treasured possession of the creators of dramatic fiction. They do it all the time. And, in particular, they have throughout the ages developed ways of showing the kind of behaviour that tends to occur at meetings between the representatives of suspicious and hostile countries; of demonstrating the gap between what people say, and what they mean, and what they subsequently do. A historian can say, of course, and back up the assertion, that a king claimed to be wise, just and merciful when he was actually engaged in bumping off all his opponents. But only a dramatist can demonstrate how that hypocrisy manifests itself in the human soul: the self-deception, the paranoia, even the glorification of deceit, that go on in the minds of men and women whose public and private faces are at war. (And in this context, I have always thought it significant that the soliloquy and the aside have been such enduring devices in the playwright's armoury; they are, of course, devices precisely designed to show the gap between what someone says and what they think and feel.)

What I am saying is that dramatic fiction can uniquely illumine certain aspects of public life; and the dramatic power of drama-documentary lies in its capacity to show us not that certain events occurred (the headlines can do that) or even, perhaps, why they occurred (for such information we can go to the weekly magazines or the history books), but *how* they occurred: how recognisable human beings rule, fight, judge, meet, negotiate, suppress and over-throw. Perhaps the simplest example of the achievement of such an effect is in the actual physical reconstruction of a public event: trials, for example, can be comprehensively reported, but nobody who watched, say, the reconstructions of the *Gay News* blasphemy case, or the Chicago Conspiracy hearings, could fail to take away from those experiences not merely a richer sense of atmosphere, but a profounder understanding of the processes by which men and women advocate, defend themselves, give evidence and pass judgement. There are many other public processes ripe for such treatment: I have recently been involved (for the first time) in trade union negotiations, and was deeply impressed by the gap between the public image of such events and the reality. I am sure that when negotiators have behind them millions or thousands of manual workers (as opposed to our couple of hundred stage playwrights) matters feel a little different; but I'm equally sure that all negotiations ultimately come down to spatial relationships, the time of day, the length and structure of the meeting, and basic states of mind like tiredness, irritation and impatience (on the one hand), and confidence, bloody-mindedness and a functioning sense of humour (on the other).

The group of drama-documentary makers to have applied such principles to their craft with most consistency and rigour has been the Manchester-based Granada unit, under Leslie Woodhead. In one sense it is somewhat paradoxical that this group should have sought to apply what are (I have argued) essentially dramatic criteria to their work, because, as Woodhead explained in his Granada lecture, he entered the field at precisely the opposite corner:

> My own motive for taking up the drama-documentary trade was simple, pragmatic, and, I suspect, to some degree representative. As a television journalist working on *World in Action*, I came across an important story I wanted to tell, but found there was no other way to tell it. The story was about a Soviet dissident imprisoned in a mental hospital. By its very nature, it was totally inaccessible by conventional document-ary methods. But the dissident, General Grigorenko, had managed to smuggle out of mental prison a detailed diary of his experiences. As a result, it was possible to produce a valid documentary reconstruction of what happened to Gri-gorenko and tell that important story ... The basic impulse behind the drama-documentary form is, I suggest, simply to tell to a mass audience a real and relevant story involving real people. The basic problem is how to get it right after the event.

For Woodhead, the priorities have remained 'obsti-nately journalistic', with an emphasis on exhaustive research and cross-checking, 'and on high-grade source material such as tape recordings and transcripts'. But I would argue that the *results* of Woodhead's painstaking work have been increasingly dramatic, in the technical sense of that word. In the Grigorenko drama-documentary (titled *The Man Who Wouldn't Keep Quiet*, and scripted by Woodhead himself in 1970), the 'dramatic' element of the production consisted (by and large) of visual evocations of Grigorenko's protests, arrests, trials and incarcerations; hardly a word (apart from an explanatory commentary) did not originate in Grigorenko's own diary. In Granada's second drama-documentary treatment of East European resistance (*Three Days in Szczecin*, scripted by Boleslaw Sulik and broadcast in 1976), the main action (the historical meeting between Polish Party leader Gierek with striking shipbuilders in 1971) was based on an actual tape recording of the proceedings, but was amplified and fleshed out by the memories of strike leader Edmund Baluka (by then an exile in England). Baluka's reminiscences (as an openly acknowledged source) allowed Sulik and Woodhead to go much further in recreating not just the facts of what was said and who said it, but how the listeners reacted, inside and outside the meeting hall. *Three Days* was indeed a remarkable representation of an extraordinary historical event; it was also a peculiarly authoritative play about how meetings occur.

Woodhead's most recent drama-documentary (as I write: a further treatment of Polish worker resistance is planned for broadcast at the end of 1981) was *Invasion*, scripted by David Boulton and shown in 1980. The programme fitted neatly into Granada's drama-documentary criteria: it showed events (surrounding the Soviet invasion of Czechoslovakia) which could only be reconstructed; it was based on rigorous research. But for the viewer it was a play, in which recognisable human beings negotiated, discussed, argued, lost their tempers, kept their cool, supported and betrayed each other. Two examples may suffice: at one point in the play, a friend sends in beer and sandwiches for the Czech Politburo, by now effectively imprisoned by the Soviet invaders. After several moments of agonising indecision, the Czechs choose to offer part of their meal to the nervously polite Russian soldiers guarding them. Similarly, later on, another imprisoned Czech leader discovers that he and his Polish guard were members of the same unit in the International Brigade in Spain, and they swap reminiscences until the irony of the situation becomes too much for them. These are not just anecdotes, bits of what journalists call 'colour'. They may not be the usual stuff of historical scholarship, but they are absolutely the stuff of history.

No one would argue, however, least of all David Boulton, that his play was impartial. It was written from the point of view of the liberals on the Czech central committee, and doubtless the conservatives in the Soviet leadership would regard these events in a very different light. Further, the play was largely based on the recollections of one person: Zdenek Mlynar, part-author of the Action Programme of the Prague Spring. But, again, the programme makers were completely honest about this fact, and Boulton began his play with a shot of the real Mlynar, standing next to the actor playing him, on the Austro-Czech border, and reiterated the point frequently by using Mlynar's own recollections, in the past tense, as a commentary on the action. The viewers were therefore completely aware of the perspective from which the events were being seen; they could judge, for instance, Boulton's dramatisation of Mlynar's initial refusal, and subsequent agreement, to sign the Soviet-drafted communiqué that sold out the Prague Spring, against the fact that the scene was based on Mlynar's own recollections.

E.H. Carr argues that, in reality, the historian is a kind of protagonist in the history he or she is writing. In *Invasion*, the protagonist was Mlynar, with a little help from David Boulton. In other plays, however, the playwright him or herself becomes a central character. As I have pointed out, the writer Ian Curteis has been particularly berated for his treatment of Churchill and Eden; Geoffrey Cannon was concerned that 'millions of viewers will continue to see Churchill and Eden through Ian Curteis's eyes.' Now, I am sure that Curteis (who always insists that his works are firmly labelled as plays rather than drama-documentaries) feels that he has found the truth about his subjects, and hopes that others will agree with him. I'm not sure that I do, but I *am* sure that I find Curteis's vision revealing about both his and our attitudes, in our own time, towards these two important figures in our national mythology; in the same way as I find the novels of Evelyn Waugh perceptive, although I am not a High Tory, and the plays of Bernard Shaw instructive, although I am not a Fabian either. But the important point is that, like David Boulton, Ian Curteis writes plays, in which people are shown doing things that human beings do, and we are able to judge the quality of the writer's vision by the simple method that we unconsciously employ whenever we watch a piece of dramatic fiction – by asking the basic question as to whether it is credible that people should behave like this, setting what we see against our own experience of human affairs. And in the case of Curteis there are two bonuses: we have our own knowledge or even experience of the Suez crisis and the Second World War as yardsticks, and we can also judge Curteis's Eden and Churchill against other dramatic representations of the two men on stage and screen. With that armoury of weapons of judgement, one may respectfully suggest that if viewers do indeed continue to see the two statesmen through Ian Curteis's eyes, it is because they have judged his perception to be keener than the alternatives on offer.

And in this context, I can mention a case from my own experience. I can, perhaps, lay claim to having been the writer of the purest drama-documentary ever written, because, in 1974, during the Watergate crisis, I edited the White House tape transcripts into a 45-minute television play, in which every word spoken on screen had been actually spoken in reality, and we had the transcripts to prove it. But, in fact, of course, the play was bristling with impurities: the whole process of making it had consisted of value judgements, from my judgements about what to put in and leave out, to the director's judgements about what to look at, and the actors' judgements about pace and

inflection and gesture and mood. And those judgements –
about how the words were said, and why, and with what
relative significance – added up to an argument, which
was that Richard Nixon was progressively deluding
himself about what he was doing, and that when he said he
didn't know things that he did know, he wasn't pretending
but concealing the memory from himself. And although I
think we were right, it is equally possible to argue that
Nixon knew exactly what he was doing, and was deceiving
everybody *except* himself. But I'm sure that our act of
turning those documents into drama, of showing one way
in which those words *could* have been spoken by real
human beings, had the effect of deepening our audience's
understanding of those extraordinary events, and it may
even have proved, for those who disagreed with our
interpretation of the events, that they were right and we
were wrong.

The threat to drama-documentary does not just consist
of critical attacks from critics, pundits and Ministers of the
Crown. In November 1980, the Broadcasting Act became
law, and with it, the provisions for the setting up of a
Broadcasting Complaints Commission (BCC) came into
effect. Broadcasters had been acquainted with the baleful
nature of this body a few months earlier, when lawyer
Geoffrey Robertson had addressed the Edinburgh
Television Festival on the subject of the BCC:

> In the short space of three hours, the Commons Committee
> on the Broadcasting Bill approved the construction of a
> special court to judge radio and television programmes: the
> Broadcasting Complaints Commission. It will comprise 'three
> wise men' with no media links, appointed by the Home
> Secretary, to 'adjudicate upon complaints of unjust or unfair
> treatment ... or unwarranted infringement of privacy'.
> Replete with a staff of 'officers and servants' paid for by a
> special levy on broadcasting companies, it will sit in secret to
> consider complaints from individuals (alive or dead),
> companies, clubs and foreign countries. It will summon
> broadcasting executives, call for correspondence, and hand
> down judgements which must be published in any way it
> directs.[6]

Acting without even the right of appeal, the BCC has the potential of being a mighty force for censorship, particularly in the form of self-censorship before the event. As Robertson pointed out:

> The BCC, as it has emerged from this process, is no longer an exercise in accountability. It is an exercise in control. It will become another means of levering television and radio into a strait-jacket which could never be contemplated for newspapers, books or plays. It is not an effective method for securing a 'right of reply' for persons whose actions have been distorted, and its function is far removed from the desirable end of providing a speedy correction of untruths. It is, in effect, a court, whose case law will impinge on the way television programmes are made, the nature of subject-matter selected, and the techniques used for bringing history, drama and current affairs to life on the small screen.

The implications for historical plays and drama-documentary are indeed awesome. Even after the government amended the provision that would allow the relatives, friends and admirers of the dead to complain on their behalf (the Richard III Society?), the present procedure would allow the Saudi government to complain about *Death of a Princess*, the Soviet leadership to demand reparation for *Invasion*, and veterans of the ATS to prevent a second showing of Ian McEwan's *The Imitation Game*. Doubtless the social service ministries would have had a high old time with *Cathy Come Home* and *Spongers* (and the Police Federation with *Law and Order*) as well.

Not surprisingly, the BCC has the support of Mrs Mary Whitehouse,[7] and the ubiquitous Paul Johnson has applauded the Commission as 'an element of salutary terror' to be wielded against the 'new breed of young, radical producers and directors, some still in their twenties, who are without scruple in their pursuit of what they believe to be higher causes'.[8]

As long ago as 1951, drama-documentary maker Caryl Doncaster stated that 'the dramatised story documentary is one of the few art forms pioneered by television.' It is important that the form be defended for that reason alone; but there are wider implications. Through all the criticisms of drama-documentary runs a single thread of assumption: that, while clever, educated people are able to recognise and judge a thesis when they see one, ordinary television viewers can somehow be duped into accepting an argument as objective fact. As it happens, the so-called cheap, popular newspapers are full of letters from people who are highly critical of television programmes that do not live up to the virtues that their makers claim for them, whether those virtues are those of entertainment or of historical truth. But even if it could be proved (and I doubt it mightily) that the majority of viewers really will take at face value anything that is pumped out at them, then it is an extraordinary indictment *not of drama-documentary*, but of the rest of television, that it is so uniform, so uncontentious and so bland that it has bludgeoned its audience into a state of passive acceptance of everything they see.

As a writer about public life, I would defend drama-documentary as a form in which important things can be said in a uniquely authoritative and credible way. But the form also needs to be defended because the presence of drama-documentary in the schedules is an active encouragement to audiences to think critically and seriously about all the programmes they watch.

Notes

1. *Sunday Times*, 13 April 1980 and *Guardian*, 6 August 1980.
2. *Guardian*, 26 August 1980.
3. Typescript of lecture delivered at BFI, 19 May 1981.
4. *Listener*, 19 March 1981.
5. *Sunday Times*, 13 April 1980.
6. *Listener*, 11 September 1980.
7. Letter to the *Listener*, 15 January 1981, and elsewhere.
8. *Listener*, 1 January 1981.

On the Right

The British left's line on the British right has often been characterised by imprecision. When I began studying the extreme right (initially for my play *Destiny*), I realised that there was such a thing as fascism; that it was alive, not unwell, and living in England; and that it did no service to the fight against it to fling the words 'Nazi' and 'fascist' around like rhetorical confetti. Similarly, when Mrs Thatcher was elected, it seemed important to emphasise the distinction – and indeed, potentially, the contradiction – between the libertarian and authoritarian elements of her ism. 'Racism, Fascism and the Politics of the National Front' was written for the Institute of Race Relations' journal *Race and Class* (Autumn 1977), and subsequently published as a pamphlet; 'The Free or the Good' developed ideas first outlined in *New Socialist*, and was written as a chapter of *The Ideology of the New Right* (edited by Ruth Levitas, Polity, Cambridge 1985).

More recently, the British New Right mounted a sustained critique of what it sees as the central tenets of the left-liberal agenda, including the 'proletarianisation' of the culture, and the campaign to redress racism in education. I looked at the former in a review of Auberon Waugh's *Another Voice* ('Let Them Eat Dirt', *New Statesman*, 26 September 1986) and the latter in a piece on Frank Palmer's *Anti-Racism – an Assault on Education and Value* ('Dreams of the Volk', *New Socialist*, January 1987).

In response to the latter piece, Conservative polemicist Roger Scruton called my piece 'an incontrovertible instance' of 'guilt by association, and the presumption of evil' in its description of the allegience and ideology of the book's authors. I continue to think it significant that two-thirds of them had contributed or do contribute to

Scruton's *Salisbury Review*, but are still unable to resolve the contradiction (between liberal individualism and authoritarian collectivism) which continues to cleave contemporary Conservative thought.

Racism, Fascism and the Politics of the National Front

Next April 20 is the 89th anniversary of the birth of Adolf Hitler. Coincidentally, but perhaps more significantly, it will be ten years to the day since the Rt Hon J. Enoch Powell seemed, like the Roman, to see the River Tiber foaming with much blood.

During the decade since Powell's speech, against a background of the worst economic crisis since the war, there's been an Immigration Act and a brace of Race Relations Acts. Unemployment has risen to high levels for whites, higher for blacks. Police harassment of blacks has become systematic. And there's been the National Front.

There has also been anti-racist activity. Much of it (on the predominantly white left) has been directed against the NF and other racist organisations, as the embodiment, in its most blatant and brutal form, of the racist nature of society. Some black organisations have responded by arguing, with justice, that white socialists have tended to ignore institutional, state racism. Conversely, this has led to the view that the NF is significant only as a rabidly racist organisation, as an awful warning of what excesses lie further along the continuum of immigration control, cessation and, finally, the deportation of Britain's black population.

Anti-fascists have, of course, pointed to other elements in the NF's stated and implied programme, and have identified the NF as fascist, a designation which has stuck, at least as a slogan. But in the public mind, and in the minds of not a few on the left, the NF has been seen, none the less, primarily as the organisational expression of anti-black prejudice in Britain, as a pressure-group for racist legislation and, in so far as their demands have not been met, as propagandists for even harsher legislation in the future. For those who accept the 'fascism' tag, the NF's anti-black racism has been regarded as equivalent to the German National Socialists' scapegoating and persecution of the Jews.

It is possible, however, to interpret the history of the last ten years in a rather different way. It can be argued that the National Front's influence as an anti-immigration pressure group has been almost negligible; that its racial politics are fundamentally out of accord with those of the state; that its propaganda on immigration is not so central to its ideology as might appear; and that the direct identity of Jews in Germany in the 1930s with blacks in Britain now is incorrect and misleading.

Theory

The classic model

'Fundamentally,' Joachim Fest wrote, 'National Socialism represented a politically organised contempt for the mind.[1] But because fascist ideology is irrational, that doesn't mean it's non-existent; the contradictions of its dogma do not make it arbitrary. Far from it: the very contradictions of the doctrine, and their irrational resolution, are at the core of its functional effectiveness as a mobiliser of support.

It's not the purpose of this essay to present a detailed definition of the function of fascism, partly because there is, and should be, much controversy about it, particularly on the nature of its relationship with the ruling class.[2] I hope, however, that the following is broad enough not to beg too many questions.

Fascism is the mobilisation of a counter-revolutionary mass movement during a period of capitalist crisis in which the conventional forces of the state are seen to be incapable of resolving the contadictions of the system. The participants in this mass movement tend to be drawn from those sectors of society – notably the lower middle class, unorganised workers, the peasantry and backward sections of the ruling class – which are facing a relative and progressive worsening of their economic and social position, but who nonetheless see no future in an alliance with the organised proletariat. The role of fascism, both in power and on the road to it, is the destruction of the independent organisations of the working class, sometimes in collusion with and always in the broad interests of the employing classes.

The central problem of fascist ideology – the purpose of which is to mobilise the mass movement – is that the real interests of their various potential supporters are, in many cases, opposed. In advanced capitalism, for example, it is often literally true that government policies to assist the small saver and businessman by reducing the inflation of the currency result directly in the increase in the number and the misery (by cutting expenditure on benefits) of the unemployed.

However, these groups do have two things in common: a profound disillusion with the present ordering of society, and nostalgia for a previous age in which their lot, relative to other sections of society, was supposedly better. Fascism seeks to exploit this by providing a programme which calls for radical, even revolutionary change, not towards a new future, but backwards, in the reactionary direction of the past. Thus fascist ideology opposes the more unpleasant symptoms of the development of capitalism – the development of joint-stock monopolies, speculation and the internationalisation of the economy – while retaining a commitment to the private ownership of the means of production, a private ownership which, it's argued, monopolisation and internationalisation have destroyed. As Hitler wrote:

> A grave economic symptom of decay was the slow disappearance of the right of private property, and the gradual transference of the entire economy to the ownership of stock companies, thus robbing the enterprises of the foundations of a personal ownership.[3]

Elsewhere, Hitler referred to the 'difference between this pure capital as the end result of productive labour and a capital whose existence and essence rests exclusively on speculation'.[4] The political conclusions are clear:

> The sharp separation of stock exchange capital from the
> national economy offered the possibility of opposing the
> internationalisation of the German economy without at the
> same time menacing the foundation of an independent
> national self-maintenance by a struggle against all capital.[5]

This absurd division of capitalism into good (productive) and bad (financial, speculative) lies at the core of
fascism's pseudo-radical posture, seen at its most blatant in
the early programmes of the Fascist parties. The Italian
Fascist movement called for 'Suppression of limited
liability companies and shareholding companies, suppression of all forms of speculation, suppression of banks
and stock exchanges.'[6] However, it saw no contradiction in
also 'supporting every initiative of those minority groups
of the proletariat who seek to harmonise the safeguarding
of their class interests with the interests of the nation',
these minority groups graphically defined as 'the
bourgeoisie of labour'.[7] Even clearer is the first
programme of the NSDAP (*Nationalsozialistische Deutsche
Arbeiter Partei*, the Nazi Party), whose eleventh to fifteenth
clauses state:

> We demand therefore: Abolition of incomes unearned by
> work. Abolition of the thraldom of interest ... The ruthless
> confiscation of all war profits. We demand the nationalisation
> of all businesses which have been amalgamated. We demand
> that there shall be profit sharing in the great industries. We
> demand a generous development of provision for old age.[8]

The sixteenth clause, however, reads: 'We demand the
creation and maintenance of a healthy middle class.'[9]

Fascist doctrine thus sets 'national' against 'international'
capitalism. It also sets 'national' working-class activity
against the internationalist aims of Marxism. Mussolini
said: 'Socialist theories have been disproved; internationalist myths have crumbled. The class struggle is a fairy tale,
mankind cannot be divided.[10] And Hitler had this to say of
workers' organisations:

To call the trade-union movement in itself unpatriotic is nonsense and untrue to boot. ... The trades union in the National Socialist sense does not have the function of grouping certain people within a national body and thus gradually transforming them into a class, to take up the fight against other similarly organised formations. We can absolutely not impute this function to the trade union as such; it became so only in the moment when the trade unions became the instrument of Marxist struggle.[11]

Later in the same passage, Hitler hinted at his real plans for trade unions: 'The strike is an instrument which may and actually must be applied only so long as a National Socialist volkish state does not exist.'

The ideological alternatives to the internationalised economy varied from country to country. For Mussolini, the national form was the state – 'Everything inside the State, nothing outside the State, nothing against the State'[12] – and the creation of the vertically organised industrial corporations, a caricature of the medieval craft guilds. For the German National Socialists, the national idea was further developed, and the internationalisation of both bourgeoisie and proletariat was seen in terms of a racial conspiracy theory, which served to combine in one theoretical model the wide varieties of enemy that faced the potential support-groups of the Nazi Party. This theory posited a conscious, covert alliance between the international banker and monopolist on the one hand, and the international Marxist on the other. It sought, further, to racialise the plotters, so that the foe could be more readily differentiated from the friend. The unemployed worker's oppressor could be thus identified as the 'finance capitalist' rather than his own boss; the small businessman was threatened not by all workers but only by 'alien subversives'. There was only one racial candidate for the role of arch-conspirator. As Hitler said, 'Only an anti-semite is a true anti-communist,' an equation completed by Goebbels in his statement that 'It is because we want socialism that we are anti-semitic.'[13]

The classic text on the Jewish conspiracy is, ironically, a supposed example of it. The *Protocols of the Learned Elders*

of Zion purport to be the minutes of a series of meetings of
Jews, the purpose of which is to plan the take-over of the
world. The actual document is forgery, written by the
Tsarist secret police in the early years of this century.[14] It
is difficult to overestimate their impact throughout
Europe between the wars, but, particularly, in confirming
the Nazi *Weltanschauung*.

In their schemes to destroy all that is good, true and
noble in man, the Elders are nothing if not industrious.
Through their control of money, and, particularly, gold,
they have destroyed the aristocracy, led the French
Revolution, gained control of the press, provoked
inflation, created the doctrine of liberalism, corrupted
youth and undermined the family. Not content with that,
however, they now plan for world revolution:

> Nowadays, with the destruction of the aristocracy, the people
> have fallen into the grips of merciless money-grinding
> scoundrels who have laid a pitiless and cruel yoke upon the
> necks of the workers. We appear on the scene as the alleged
> saviours of the worker from this oppression and we suggest
> that he should enter the ranks of our fighting forces –
> socialists, anarchists, communists, to whom we always give
> support ... We shall create by all the secret and subterranean
> methods open to us and with the aid of gold, which is all in
> our hands, a universal economic crisis whereby we shall
> simultaneously throw upon the streets whole mobs of workers
> in all the countries of Europe.[15]

And, having created the final conflagration, the Elders
will, they inform us, institute a world-wide dictatorship,
'distinguished by a despotism of ... magnificent proportions'. (It is worth remembering that, despite the
transparency of the fantasy, the *Protocols* were widely
believed. A British government White Paper – Russia No. 1,
1919 – described Bolshevism as being 'organised and
worked by Jews ... whose object is to destroy for their own
ends the existing order of things'; and Winston Churchill,
writing in the *Illustrated Sunday Herald* – 8 February 1920 –
referred to a 'world-wide conspiracy for the overthrow of
civilisation' as a 'movement among the Jews'.) Hitler put it
more simply:

While Moses Kohn sits in the director's meeting, advocating a policy of firmness ... his brother, Isaac Kohn, stands in the factory yard, stirring up the masses.[16]

The National Front version

The most cursory glance through the pages of *Spearhead*, the National Front journal, or *National Front News*, its paper (or, indeed, the National Party equivalents), will reveal that the conspiracy theory runs through contemporary British fascist ideology like Blackpool runs through rock. In *Spearhead*'s 100th edition, for instance, there are four articles on supposed sectors of the conspiracy – the Bilderberg Group, the Round Table, the Trilateral Commission and the Zionist movement itself – and none, specifically, on race.[17] Much of the NF's booklet output is concerned with the exposure of the machinations of international financiers and the advocacy of economic protectionism. Of the seven books on *Spearhead*'s present booklist,[18] four are concerned with supporting the conspiracy theory. And the only book actually written by a leading NF member – *The New Unhappy Lords* by A.K. Chesterton, first chairman of the Front – is wholly concerned with proving the existence of a world conspiracy, whose organs include the UN, the IMF, the World Bank and NATO, and whose aim is to destroy the white nations and impose a One-World dictatorship.

The theory does, however, suffer somewhat in translation. Often the word 'Jewish' appears in various coy disguises, such as 'Zionist', 'cosmopolitan', 'alien', 'international' or even 'ersatz'. At its most covert, the doctrine of a capitalist/communist axis appears thus in the NF Statement of Policy:

> The NF recognises that International Monopoly Capitalism is as great a menace to the freedom of the nations as International Communism, and that in fact the two represent different means to the same end: a world tyranny.[19]

Spearhead, the NF journal, is rather less euphemistic about defining this alliance (indeed, as a general rule, the lower the circulation of a piece of literature, the more specific does it become). For instance, Richard Verrall, now its editor, describes 'our principal enemy' thus:

> 1) International Finance, the parasite that feeds on nations and on free-enterprise industrial capitalism by the process of debt-creation, and which is predominantly Zionist in composition and Zionist in its global aims. 2) Marxism, a conspiracy fostered by the former.[20]

And Chesterton's *New Unhappy Lords*, referred to above, is brazenly specific:

> Are these master-manipulators and master-conspirators Jewish? Because of the power of the purse afforded by the control of credit and the preponderant participation in America's most powerful industries and commercial firms, and because of commercial preponderance in the economies of the so-called 'free world', the answer must certainly be 'yes'.[21]

Not surprisingly, the division of 'finance' and 'productive' capital is as central to the NF version of the conspiracy theory as it was to Hitler's. It will be seen lurking behind Verrall's definition of 'international finance' quoted above. *The Money Manufacturers*, a NF booklet, openly states that 'capitalism' is 'a term which is loosely used to cover two very different systems and it is important not to confuse one with the other'. These two systems are 'Free Enterprise Capitalism' on the one hand, and, on the other, 'Loan Capitalism (Finance Capitalism, Monopoly Capitalism, International Finance)',[22] a list so comprehensive that no one can be forgiven for missing the point.

The same pamphlet contains an example of the way in which the NF have taken over a number of pre-war anti-semitic forgeries. One persistent myth is that Jewish Wall Street bankers financed the Russian Revolution: 'International bankers ... supplied the money, and then men for the Russian Revolution ... Jacob Schiff, a partner in the Wall St banking firm of Kuhn Loeb and Co., contributed $12 million.'[23] This particular story, often backed up by quotations from the actual forged document on which it was based, reappears time and again in NF and National Party literature.[24] The *Protocols* themselves tend to be cited more circumspectly (the British edition of the book has slithered in and out of their booklists over the years). However, the Front's continued commitment to them was made clear by the NF's chairman John Tyndall, in March 1976:

> So long as Jews are to the fore in promoting Communism and World Government, fuel is going to be given to those who maintain that there is a Jewish conspiracy for world power as outlined in the *Protocols of the Elders of Zion*. If evidence of such a conspiracy is to be refuted ... there has got to be, I would maintain, a change of heart on the part of Jewry ...
> 'The Jewish Question' consists of the fact that Jewry hitherto has been unprepared to do this, and 'anti-semitism' as a doctrine is nothing more than a natural Gentile reaction to this fact.[25]

Its belief in the conspiracy theory allows the NF, like the Nazis, to indulge in much pseudo-radical demagogy. One extreme example is the journalism of the NF's erstwhile newspaper *Britain First* (before it, and its editorial staff, split from the Front to form the National Party in January 1976). The December 1974 edition, for instance, led with the following stirring call, beneath a picture of the Jarrow marchers and the headline 'Must the Slump Come?':

> As world-wide slump looms before us, the Labour, Tory and Liberal parties are asking the British people to tighten their belts by the imposition of either the so-called Social Contract, or some other 'prices and incomes' fraud. When did we ever cause inflation, and why should we suffer a drop in our standard of living?

These extremes of demagogic cynicism (a more recent example from the post-split *Britain First* is the headline of the March 1976 edition: 'Seize the Right to Work') are not reflected in the rest of NF literature. But even the staid old Statement of Policy 'upholds as a principle the right of all to work' and 'advocates stronger, not weaker trade unions'.[26]

Of course, like the German Nazis, the NF's real plans for the unions are very different. The Front is careful on this (after all, Hitler issued a proclamation guaranteeing the freedom of trade unions under his regime the day before he abolished them), but a hint is given in this quotation from Tyndall:

> We would apply government legislation which *compelled* all unions to adopt a secret ballot for all elections and all major union decisions. The same legislation would *establish* one union for one industry. (My emphasis, D.E.)[27]

And there is nothing too impenetrable about Tyndall's demand that 'water cannon, tear gas and rubber bullets' be used against trade union pickets.[28]

Racism and the conspiracy theory
A major dynamic of any racist theory of society is bound to be an obsessive fear of miscegenation – it is unfortunate, but significant, that there is no less pejorative word for inter-racial breeding. One obvious example is the centrality of the Immorality Acts in the repressive apparatus of South African apartheid, and it is also present in the ideas of Hitler. In *Mein Kampf* he acknowledges specifically his debt to the ideas of Count Arthur de Gobineau, a nineteenth-century French aristocrat, who believed that 'All civilisations derive from the white race, that none can exist without its help, and that a society is great and brilliant only so far as it preserves the blood of the noble group.'[29]

It will be obvious that this fear of 'racial pollution' cannot, if the ideology is applied strictly, be a component of anti-semitism: that it tends *not* to be applied strictly is a point made below. Gobineau himself cites the Jews as an example of a race that has preserved its 'purity', and the National Front, too, express a grudging admiration for the Jews, though within a critical context: *Spearhead* writes that 'Loyalty to kith and kin beyond territorial boundaries is something for which the Jews should be admired.'[30] The place of this 'admiration' in the conspiracy theory is clearly shown in this quotation from *Britain First*:

Zionists believe that while the gentile nations of the world will all become internationalised, the Jews will enjoy a national state based on Jerusalem which will be the seat of a World Government. This helps to explain the seeming contradiction prevalent in Zionist circles which simultaneously demands fanatical support for the survival of Israel, but race-mixing for everybody else.[31]

The argument is thus quite simple: among the dastardly schemes of the Elders of Zion is the destruction of the white races from within, by the encouragement of inter-breeding with 'inferior' groups. Hitler put it clearly when he spoke of the Jewish aim of

> breeding a general inferior human mishmash, by way of a chaotic bastardisation and which ultimately would no longer be able to do without the Jews as its only intellectual element ... His ultimate goal is the denationalisation, the promiscuous bastardisation of other peoples.[32]

That this kind of racism is bound up closely with imperialism is made clear by Hitler: 'Aryan races – often absurdly small numerically – subject foreign peoples ... In the end, however, the conquerors transgress against the principle of blood purity.'[33] For the German National Socialists, the most immediate 'inferior' threat was the Slav races of Eastern Europe, though Hitler was also concerned with the presence of African soldiers of the French army on German soil:

> It was and is the Jews who bring the negroes into the Rhineland, always with the same secret thought of their own of ruining the hated white race by the necessarily resulting bastardisation ... to deprive the white race of the foundations for a sovereign existence through infection from lower humanity.[34]

A direct comparison can be made between that passage and the following from *Spearhead*:

> It may well be that the masters of the campaign for world government know very well the truth concerning the cause of racial differences. If so, it would certainly explain why

internationalist elements of all types are at the forefront of all
attempts to encourage people of different races to interbreed
and produce half-caste offspring. The reason for this is
obvious. If separate races can be eradicated by the process of
miscegenation and the whole of humanity submerged into a
single slant-eyed khaki-coloured lumpen, then racial
differences will have disappeared – along with any sense of
national identity – and a world government system will be
much more easy to impose.[35]

In earlier, less cautious days, *Spearhead* was able to put the
same idea more simply: 'If Britain were to become
Jew-clean she would have no nigger neighbours to worry
about.'[36]

It's been my purpose to show that the National Front's
ideology is classically National Socialist, and that, within
this context, the slogan 'Hitler blamed the Jews, the Front
blames the blacks' is an oversimplification, in that, strictly,
the NF blames the Jews *for* the blacks. However, it would
be grossly foolish to follow this abstract model through
schematically, and to ignore the essential opportunism of
the ideology in practice. First of all, it's demonstrably true
that many if not most NF supporters *do* blame the blacks
for bad housing, poor education and declining services.
It's conversely true that many if not most of Hitler's
stormtroops treated the Jewish proletariat as an 'inferior'
racial group. Much Nazi-supporting propaganda concerned accusations of miscegenation against Jews, and it's
arguable that the very lack of a substantial non-'Aryan'
population in Germany, apart from the Jews, created the
need to treat the Jewish working class as an 'inferior' goup,
while retaining the doctrine of a controlling, exclusive
'superior' caste of Jewish financiers.

Secondly, there are, of course, many objective differences between the two social situations which render
anti-semitism less potent as an ideological weapon; notably
the diminution of an independent petit-bourgeoisie
(reduced in comparative size by the growth of monopolisation and by the dramatic increase in white-collar
unionisation) who could be seen as directly threatened by
Jewish monopoly capitalist institutions. This has created

the need for the National Socialists to penetrate much more deeply into the working class, and, consequently, for the concentration of their propaganda on an out-group which can be seen as directly threatening workers.

But against this must be set the fact that there is a limit to the level of responsibility for the national crisis that can be laid at the door of an almost exclusively working-class minority of the population; that if they are serious about achieving power the fascists have to provide a more comprehensive world-view; and that their own use of conspiratorial anti-semitism indicates that they at least think this is the case.

Finally, one needs to look closely at the influence on the National Socialists' practice of the increased racism within the main political parties, and the consequent growth of harsh state controls on the very presence of the black population, an institutional racist apparatus that is not, in that form, paralleled at all in Weimar Germany.

Practice

Since 1945, there have been fascists active in Britain, whose aim has been to revive Hitler's ideas and to create a National Socialist state. They have faced the obvious problem that, after the war and particularly since the discovery of the death-camps, their ideology has been viewed by the vast majority with revulsion and horror. They have sought to resolve this problem in two ways. The more overt Nazis have tried to rehabilitate Hitler's regime, particularly by denying that many of the atrocities took place. But the mainstream has attempted to combine a denial of Nazi associations with a vigorous campaign on the one racial-populist issue that has gained support in this country: opposition to black Commonwealth immigration.

However, the level of support for anti-immigration measures has not been reflected in a corresponding commitment to the National Socialist parties. There have been three main reasons for this: first, the alacrity with which the state has responded to racist demands; secondly, the faith that racists felt able to place in the Conservative

Party as an organisational forum for their ideas, at least until 1972; and, thirdly, the fascists' own use of the immigration issue not as an end in itself but as a means to attract people towards a National Socialist ideology. This last, particularly, has prevented the Front and its predecessor parties from taking full advantage of popular racist opinion. In relation to the first of these reasons, the influence of public opinion on the development of the immigration laws was clearly considerable; though, certainly, from the Labour Party's commitment to the Common Market onwards, the shift from settler to contract-worker migration was also an economic decision.

National Socialists, state racism and the Conservatives
In the late 1950s, the British ultra-right was in a right old mess. Most of the people who were to dominate the movement in the years ahead – Colin Jordan, John Tyndall, Martin Webster, Andrew Fountaine, John Bean – had left A.K. Chesterton's League of Empire Loyalists (founded in 1954 to protest against decolonisation, but also to propagate the conspiracy theory) and formed a variety of miniscule organisations, including the White Defence League (Jordan) and the National Labour Party (Fountaine and Bean). Years of economic boom, and the prospect of more to come, seemed to consign the National Socialists to the most lunatic of lunatic fringes.

The Notting Hill and Nottingham 'race riots' of 1958 must have seemed a gift from the gods. Here, at last, was an indigenous racial-populist issue, on which the major parties seemed inclined to take no action (the then Conservative Home Secretary, R.A. Butler, said as late as July 1960, 'It is very unlikely that this country will turn away from her traditional policy of free entry'), and which the National Socialists could use as a wedge into the minds of millions.

The sorry saga of the next few years demonstrated, and not for the last time, the inability of the National Socialists to take full advantage of racial conflict. In 1960 Jordan and Fountaine brought their organisations together to form the British National Party (other members included

Tyndall and Webster), whose policies included the freeing of Britain from 'domination of the Jewish-controlled money-lending system'. In 1962 Jordan, Tyndall and Webster decided to take an even bolder step, and formed the overt National Socialist Movement, which hosted the even more grandiose founding conference of the World Union of National Socialists. Later that year Jordan, Tyndall and two others were jailed for organising a paramilitary body. Apart from one successful electoral intervention – when the old BNP gained 9 per cent at Southall in 1964 – British National Socialism had shot its bolt and spent the next five years in a spate of internal dogfighting, creating ever-tinier splinter groups (each with their very own individual Führer) and, periodically, making the headlines by attacking synagogues.

What, then, was happening in the loftier reaches of national politics, as the National Socialist leaders split, reformed, failed and failed again? Despite Butler (and Gaitskell) the foundations of the racist state were being laid. As Tyndall faced jail in 1962, the Commonwealth Immigration Act was being passed. As Webster sat in prison for assaulting President Kenyatta, the country was voting in the 1964 general election, in which Peter Griffiths (with a little help from the fascists, but much more from local Tories) was to win Smethwick from Labour on an openly racist ticket. And as John Bean was being convicted of unlawful assembly in October 1965, the Labour Party conference was approving the government's August White Paper, which limited immigration to 8,500 new work vouchers a year. And in 1966 the extreme right gained more than 5 per cent in only two constituencies (Deptford and Leicester North-East), and the BNP, whose Southall vote fell to 4.9 per cent, received a derisory 1.5 per cent in Smethwick.

The lessons of the past had not been lost on the ultra-right, however. In 1967 the National Front was formed under the Chairmanship of A.K. Chesterton, with the specific aim of presenting a 'respectable' facade. (The component groups of the NF were, initially, the League of Empire Loyalists, the British National Party and bits of the

Racial Preservation Society. Tyndall and Webster's Great Britain Movement – which, despite its less Teutonic image, still called for compulsory sterilisation of 'all those who have hereditary defects, either racial, mental or physical', joined a little later.) And after a year spent wallowing in gloomy obscurity, the new party was granted yet more manna from heaven, this time in the shape of one Enoch Powell.

In fact, however, the only significant intervention by the ultra-right in the 1968 pro-Powell demonstrations was that of Mosleyite Danny Harmstone in Smithfield Market. The NF was outflanked by a combination of government action – the Kenyan Asians Bill had in fact just pre-dated Powell and in 1969 the government announced restrictions on the entry of dependants – and Powellite agitation within the Conservative Party itself. The Front as an organisation gained little direct benefit, and its then stated policy of 'crashing our way into the headlines'[37] did not bash it into the polling booths. In 1970 it gained an average of 3.6 per cent of the vote in the ten constituencies it fought, its highest vote being 5.6 per cent in North Islington.

However, two years later, the situation changed radically. The Conservatives' 1971 Immigration Act was the final link in the chain of what was by then a bipartisan state strategy on race, which combined the ending of all new permanent black settlement with legislation to promote 'integration' of those already here.[38] There were only two remaining commitments – to dependants and East African British passport-holders. It was the latter commitment that created the Front's great breakthrough. The Tories' admittance of the Ugandan refugees in the autumn of 1972 demonstrated that the state had concluded – for economic rather than philanthropic reasons – its restriction of immigration, and the continuum had broken. Those racists who had hitherto placed faith in the Tories were rudely awakened. The National Front's own 1968-72 policy of infiltrating the Conservative Party, not to gain members so much as to influence grass-roots opinion, was dropped in favour of an open policy of recruitment, particularly from the Monday

Club, and the Front could claim, at last, leadership of the campaign against the entry of the refugees. (For instance, O.C. Gilbert, a pre-war member of the Imperial Fascist League, wrote to *Spearhead* in December 1969: 'I believe that the Conservative Party can be made much more right-wing by the infiltration tactics now operated by men like myself who for years have been members of the Conservative Party.') The Front confirmed its success by saving its deposit in West Bromwich, with a 16 per cent by-election vote that bit hard into the Conservative share of the poll.

Events over the next two years followed the established pattern. The Front put up 54 candidates in the February 1974 election, and polled an average of 3.2 per cent. At the October election, its share of the vote had fallen to 3.1 per cent (although, with 94 candidates, its vote was obviously much higher), despite the intervening Jenkins amnesty for those immigrants who had been retrospectively criminalised by the 1971 Immigration Act. Internally, too, the Front became engaged not in the consolidation of its new support, but in a mighty internal dogfight about how far and how fast to move towards what sort of more overt National Socialist programme.

The battle for the soul of the National Front – which lasted from October 1974 to January 1976 – can be interpreted in a number of ways. Some – notably Martin Walker in both the *Guardian* and his recent book – have seen it as a struggle between the old-guard hard-line Nationalists (led by Tyndall and Webster) and ex-Conservative, more 'moderate' populists.[39] Under the latter's influence, 'the NF had moved not only to the left, but towards a coherent populist programme', and NF members 'had begun to wonder whether Tyndall and Webster were not a liability'.[40]

But, in fact, the NF leadership was faced with two opposing groups, attacking on two fronts. One group, certainly, was composed of men like Roy Painter, who had defected from the Conservative Party to stand for the NF in Tottenham. This group was indeed worried by the direct association of the leadership with overt National

Socialism and, particularly, anti-semitism. The other group, however, which controlled the NF's newspaper *Britain First*, had no objection to anti-semitism. (The classic world-government conspiracy theory quote above (p.78) was printed as part of a series of anti-semitic articles by *Britain First* at the height of the internal dispute.) What it objected to was Tyndall's authoritarianism, both internally within the Front, and as an element of doctrine. We saw above an example of the wholesale hijack of left-wing rhetoric employed by *Britain First* in this period. This is their view of the NF:

> We believe that such compromises and betrayals as have been made by the traditional 'left' and 'right' have been the inevitable product of rule by an authoritarian oligarchy. For this reason we are irrevocably committed to a belief in *democratic* nationalism, and reject all forms of authoritarianism.[41]

The reference to betrayals of the right is interesting, and is explained: 'Hitler ... was backed by International Financiers and eventually liquidated those inside his Party whose radicalism he had earlier tolerated and used.'[42] For the doctrine that the pseudo-radicals were propagating, with its anti-authoritarian stance and 'left-wing' rhetoric, was more or less identical to that of the Strasserites in the German Nazi Party who, while remaining fervently anti-semitic and chauvinistic, expanded the Nazis' attack on 'international capitalism' to embrace capitalism as a whole. This historical analogy was not lost on the leadership faction of the NF. In an article in December 1975 Richard Verrall mounted a lengthy assault on the controlling group of *Britain First*:

> The emergence of these ideas within the National Front represents, in fact, the perennial heresy of Nationalist politics; it was preached before by the National Bolsheviks and National Syndicalists, by the Strasser faction of the early Nazi party and by syndicalist groups on the Italian Right. It is Marxism in the guise of Nationalism.[43]

The end of the dispute in January 1976 (the two dissident groups broke off to form the National Party) was shortly followed by a series of events that gave the NF the chance to regroup its battle-weary forces. Tyndall's long knife was hardly back in its sheath when the Malawi Asians story broke, Robert Relf was jailed for defying the Race Relations Act, Enoch Powell leaked the Hawley Report on future sub-continental immigration and the BBC obligingly gave 30 minutes of free air-time to Jim Merrick, a Bradford National Front candidate and Chairman of the 'British Campaign to Stop Immigration', in its 'Open Door' series.

Once again, the Front saw the consequent racial violence – in Southall and elsewhere – as an opportunity to push out more overt propaganda.[44] Tyndall's resurrection of the *Protocols*, referred to above, occurred in March. In June, at the height of the hot summer, *Spearhead* printed an article claiming that the Nazi death camps did not exist.

This article, in the form of a book review, claimed that 'the extermination charge' was 'manufactured from the persistent propaganda of the World Jewish Congress and its agencies' and that the exterminations of Auschwitz were 'a tissue of lies'. The article concluded by asking: 'Can anybody believe such a story?'[45]

The electoral performance of the Front in the 1976 and 1977 local elections revealed strong areas of support, but not a significant mass breakthrough. In 1976 the showcase was Leicester, in which the NF was supported by 15,340 voters. The following year, when London voted, the Front achieved percentages of 19 (Hackney South), 19.2 (Bethnal Green) and 16.4 (Stepney). The NF is presently seen as taking more votes from Labour than from the Conservatives, which, in a time of high unemployment, an unpopular Labour government and (then) relative control of the inflation rate, is what you'd expect.

However, there are indications tht the NF's strategy is, once again, to move on from its proven bases of support. Tyndall told last year's NF Annual General Meeting:

Let us remember that only certain areas are touched by immigration. Let us also remember that on the questions of the economy the British electorate does not consist of experts or specialists; it is difficult for them as ordinary men and women to sort out one economic argument from another. But there is one thing that the great majority of the electorate can immediately recognise – and they recognise it by instinct rather than by any form of intellectual understanding: that is a party which has the strength and the will to govern and to rule.[46]

An indication of the kind of rhetoric the NF may employ over the next months was given in June 1977 in an article by Tyndall in *Spearhead*. Here Tyndall, with his 119,000 largely working-class votes secure in his back pocket, deals out a running flush of monetarist demands, for 'the ruthless trimming down of labour forces in many industries' and 'proper control of the money supply'; for compulsory secret ballots in the unions and legislation to 'establish one union for one industry'; and 'for the Welfare State in a drastically revised form' in which 'for able-bodied people in the prime of life there should be the inducement to rely much less on the Welfare State and much more on personal initiative and hard work';[47] demands, in short, designed to undermine the interests and standard of life of those very people who, in the main, gave him their support in May.

I have tried to argue that, in practice, the NF's desire to exploit anti-black racism as part of a National Socialist campaign has limited its effectiveness until recently. There has, however, been another way in which the National Front's racism has been fundamentally out of accord with the racial strategy pursued by the state and advocated, in a different way, by Enoch Powell.

The National Front and black militancy
One of the most remarkable facts about the 'rivers of blood' speech was how tardy Enoch Powell was about making it. 20 April 1968 post-dated the control of immigration by six years, and the Labour government's restriction of vouchers by three years. It even followed – by a month – the passing of the Kenyan Asians Bill. Part of the reason for Powell's extraordinary reticence was, no

doubt, his own political opportunism.[48] Another reason, however, lies within the choice phrases and the pedantic rhetoric of the speech itself.

For, read as a whole, it is clear that although Powell's background, his context, is the presence of Britain's black population, his target is black militancy. Not for nothing does he refer to 'that tragic and intractable phenomenon which we watch with horror on the other side of the Atlantic'.[49] And here is the kernel of his thesis:

> We are on the verge here of a change. Hitherto it has been force of circumstances and of background which has rendered the very idea of integration inaccessible to the greater part of the immigrant population ... Now we are seeing the growth of positive forces acting against integration, of vested interests in the preservation and sharpening of racial and religious differences, with a view to the exercise of actual domination, first over fellow-immigrants and then over the rest of the population ... For these dangerous and divisive elements the legislation proposed in the Race Relations Bill is the very pabulum they need to flourish. Here is the means of showing that the immigrant communities can organise to consolidate their members, to agitate and campaign against their fellow-citizens, and to overawe and dominate the rest with the legal weapons which the ignorant and the ill-informed have provided.[50]

In short, the dynamic of Powell's protest was not against the feebleness of the immigration laws but the strength of the Race Relations Bill. In other words, it was not, primarily, an attack on the presence of a black sub-proletariat, conveniently situated in the 'Mother Country', and which Powell as Minister of Health had done so much to attract. It was the demand of the sub-proletariat for equal treatment in housing, education and jobs, that in fact aroused the ire of the then shadow Minister for Defence.

The American experience was not lost on the British government either, although it drew opposite conclusions from it. In July 1967 Roy Jenkins' commitment to the Race Relations Bill had been made at the height of the Detroit riots; and a speaker at the October 1967 Labour conference had pointed out that, were the Bill not enacted, 'the coloured population in this country will have no alternative but to take its remedy in the way it has been taken in some cities of America'.[51]

The difference between Powell and the state lay in the former's pessimism at the possibilities of containing the growth of black militancy. But Powell was not in government; the state could not indulge in luxurious fantasies about 'voluntary repatriation'. It had to preserve the existing sub-proletariat, to effect the delicate transfer from settler to contract-worker immigration, and to keep the blacks quiet. As Sivanandan writes, the state found it 'more profitble to abandon the idea of superiority of race in order to promote the idea of the superiority of capital'.[52] For the National Socialists, however, the model has been fundamentally different from that of the state or Enoch Powell. Listen to these two homilies, the first from the NP's *Britain First*, the second from the NF's *Spearhead*:

> Many aspects of immigration are, to say the least, distasteful to the British population. Our anger, however, should not be directed towards immigrants but to the politicians who allowed or encouraged the problem. Race hatred is counter-productive and no sympathy can be extended to those who incite it.[53]

> Our magazine, though it believes in racial differences, opposes race-hatred. All those who oppose multi-racialism should attack the politicians who promote it, not the immigrants, who are merely its victims.[54]

Now on one level, of course, both these statements are nothing more than cynical hypocrisy. But there is a deeper, ideological truth contained, nonetheless, in the casting of immigrants in the role of 'victim'. For another cursory glance, this time through the more popular NF and NP literature, reveals a vision of blacks not as actors but as essentially passive and objectified. Black people – overwhelmingly black men – are portrayed in a politically or socially inactive way: as the carriers of disease, as creatures of blind instinct (muggers and rapists) or as 'innocent' victims of forces of which they are unaware.

Evocative evidence of the limits of this stereotype and the Front's consequent inability to cope with conscious black self-activity is shown whenever they are forced to confront black industrial militancy. In its summary of the Imperial Typewriters dispute, for instance, *Spearhead* was concerned primarily (and obsessively) with the trans-ference of responsibility for the dispute away from the strikers themselves and towards 'professional agitators', who were said to view the Asian workers as 'poor, misunderstood strikers' and who 'led week after week of Asian strike, picketing, violence, disturbance and dis-order'.[55] But even this transference of impetus was not enough for *Spearhead*, which concluded its article by shifting the 'blame' away even from outside 'agitators' and towards the mysterious world of the super-conspirators:

> The industrial action by Britons at Imperial ... is the struggle of a united British people fighting to preserve their freedom and identity against the forces of Communism and International Capitalism which seek to destroy the British nation and which *use as their tool* the immigrant minorities *placed by them* in our midst. (My emphasis, D.E.)[56]

A further example is the inability of *Spearhead*, in its July 1977 issue, to take *any stand whatsoever* on the substantive issues of the Grunwick dispute, which is described as 'not in itself ... of great historical importance' precisely because it involves 'one gang of Asian Trotskyites trying to force another lot of Asian immigrants to stop working or join a trade union'.[57]

For the National Front, therefore, the whole panoply of state repression, immigration restriction, and race relations legislation is not merely too 'moderate' or, in the case of the latter, a threat to 'free speech'. It is irrelevant. Their view of black people as an essentially static and passive mass, incapable of the very self-activity which the state has expended so much energy and time attempting to control, is the direct practical consequence of their

primary fear of black people as the consciously-directed
agents of miscegenation and destruction of the race.

The Front's demand for the compulsory repatriation 'of
those coloured immigrants already here, together with
their descendants and dependants' is not, therefore, a
more extreme point on a continuum of controls, each one
harsher than the last in degree.[58] It is the function of a
racism in many ways different in kind to the bipartisan
strategy of the state.

Conclusions

One of the differences between the Nazis' campaign
against the Jews on the road to power, and the harassment
of the British black population by contemporary fascists,
is, as stated above, the extent and character of British state
racism. On the other hand, modern British fascists, unlike
the Nazis, cast their most public victims in an ideologically
symptomatic rather than causative role.

It's not my aim to draw any detailed political conclusions
from this dual perspective. However, tentatively and
generally, its consequences would seem to be two-fold.
First, the fact that the fascist strategy on race is not a
continuum but an alternative to the strategy of the state
suggests that a defeat for state racism will not of itself
represent the defeat of fascism; on the contrary, the
failure of the state's racist strategy will make the threat to
blacks from the fascists themselves acute. Conversely, it is
also clear that defeating National Socialism will of itself
hardly dent the racist apparatus of the state itself. An
anti-racist strategy which concentrates solely or primarily
on defeating the NF will thus have little practical or
ideological effect on the racist attitudes of the population
at large or the state apparatus that enshrines them.

In this context, it is possible to argue, for example, that
the debate as to whether the primary or immediate enemy
of black people is the forces of the state or the shocktroops
of the National Front may be posing the wrong question.
Paradoxically, the fact that defeating one does not
necessarily undermine the other may mean that the united

and contemporaneous struggle against both is made more and not less urgent by an understanding of the differences between them.

Finally, that urgency itself should not be underestimated. Until now, National Socialism has been fettered by its own ideology. But there are signs that the distance that the NF has kept from the state may work to its advantage in the longer term. The crisis may well recede as the economy floats for a year or two on a sea of North Sea oil; bit when the oil is gone the frustrations and despair of vast sections of British society will be exposed once again. The Nazis know that; so should we.

Notes

1. Joachim C. Fest, *The Face of the Third Reich*, Munich 1963.
2. For a cogent and concise analysis of various theories of fascism, see Martin Kitchen, *Fascism*, London 1976.
3. Adolf Hitler, *Mein Kampf*, London 1969.
4. Ibid.
5. Ibid.
6. 'The Founding Programme of the Italian Fascist Movement', adopted March 1919.
7. 'Postulates on the Fascist Programme', May 1920.
8. 'The Founding Programme of the National-Socialist German Workers' Party', adopted 1923.
9. Ibid.
10. Benito Mussolini (November 1921).
11. Hitler, op. cit.
12. Quoted in Ernst Nolte, *Three Faces of Fascism*, New York 1969.
13. Quoted in Daniel Guerin, *Fascism and Big Business*, New York 1973.
14. The definitive work on the *Protocols* is Norman Cohn, *Warrant for Genocide*, London 1967.
15. Victor E. Marsden, *World Conquest through World Government: Protocols of the Learned Elders of Zion*, London 1972.
16. Adolt Hitler (28 July 1922).
17. *Spearhead*, 100, December 1976.
18. *Spearhead*, 107, July 1977.
19. National Front Statement of Policy, *c*. 1974.
20. *Spearhead*, 90, December-January 1976.
21. A.K. Chesterton, *The New Unhappy Lords*, London 1972.
22. Clare MacDonald, *The Money Manufacturers* (National Front).
23. Ibid. For details of the Schiff forgery, see Cohn, op. cit.

24. For recent examples, see *Spearhead*, 103, Februaryu 1977, and *Beacon*, 2, May-June 1977 (National Party).
25. *Spearhead*, 92, March 1976.
26. Op. cit.
27. *Spearhead*, 106, June 1977.
28. *Spearhead*, 107, July 1977.
29. Quoted in Gobineau, *Selected Political Writings*, London 1970.
30. *Spearhead*, 81, March 1975.
31. *Britain First*, May 1975.
32. Adolf Hitler, *Hitler's Secret Book*, New York 1961.
33. Hitler, *Mein Kampf*.
34. Ibid.
35. *Spearhead*, April 1971.
36. *Spearhead*, October 1964.
37. Quoted by Martin Webster in *Spearhead*, 103, March 1977.
38. See A. Sivanandan, 'Race Class and the State: the black experience in Britain'. *Race & Class* Vol. XVII, No. 4, Spring 1976.
39. Martin Walker, *The National Front*, London 1977.
40. Ibid.
41. *Britain First*, December 1974.
42. Ibid.
43. *Spearhead*, 90, December-January 1976.
44. See 'Editorial' and 'UK Commentary' in *Race & Class*, Vol. XVIII, No. 1, Summer 1976.
45. *Spearhead*, 95, June-July 1976.
46. Quoted in *Spearhead*, 99, November 1976.
47. *Spearhead*, 106, June 1977.
48. See Paul Foot, *The Rise of Enoch Powell*, London 1969.
49. Quoted in Bill Smithies and Peter Fiddick, *Enoch Powell on Immigration*, London 1969.
50. Ibid.
51. Both cited in Dilip Hiro, *Black British White British*, London 1973.
52. Sivanandan, op. cit.
53. *Britain First*, January 1977.
54. *Spearhead*, 107, July 1977.
55. *Spearhead*, 79, September-October 1974.
56. Ibid.
57. *Spearhead*, 107, July 1977.
58. Statement of Policy, op. cit.

The Free or the Good

The Assault on the 1960s

In the month immediately preceding the Argentinian invasion of the Falkland Islands (March 1982), a number of British ministers made speeches about the declining moral fabric of the nation. The context of these speeches was the continuing debate on the causes of, and responsibility for, the urban riots of the summer before – a debate that was revitalised by the publication of police figures purporting to expose the extent of the involvement of young blacks in London in violent street crime.[1]

On 17 March, for example, junior Home Office minister Timothy Raison laid the blame for 'crime and hooliganism' on a pot-pourri of environmental factors: from inadequate schools and broken homes to a lack of 'meaningful work' and 'sour media and mores which may set the tone'[2]. While ten days later, the Prime Minister herself placed responsibility for the breakdown firmly on ideas sown some years before: 'We are reaping what was sown in the 1960s,' she announced: 'The fashionable theories and permissive claptrap set the scene for a society in which the old virtues of discipline and self-restraint were denigrated.'[3]

In blaming the sins of the 1980s on the whims of the 1960s, Mrs Thatcher was echoing an earlier speech made by another junior minister, Dr Rhodes Boyson of the Department of Education. On 5 February, Dr Boyson had told Conservatives in Lougborough that:

The permissive age, which blossomed in the late 1960s, bringing in its wake such intense suffering, has created a pathless desert for many of our young people ... Tradition – the cement which helps to hold society together – has been scorned as restrictive and replaced in most cases by a destructive, naive arrogance ... We have created our own plagues by the break-up of stable families, with a malignant effect on many of our children, while many of our city streets and entertainments flaunt debased morals and false values. We have undermined the authority of parents and have had to take more children into care as a result. Similarly, the authority of head teachers and their staffs has often been attacked and society has reaped dragons' teeth in the form of juvenile revolt.[4]

The demonisation of the 1960s has been a characteristic of the New Right on both sides of the Atlantic. Indeed, the New Right phenomenon itself can be seen as a backlash against the social radicalism of the decade, as well, of course, as a reaction against the eonomic reformism of the 1930s and 40s. If, in their first terms of office, Margaret Thatcher and Ronald Reagan set out to demolish the extant works of the New Deal and the welfare state, then it is fair to say that they are now being encouraged to confront the social libertarianism that characterised public policy and attitudes in the 1960s, from anti-militarism to anti-racism, from the liberalisation of sexual life and the liberation of women to the protection of the environment and the privacy of the individual.

For many New Rightists – and for most commentators as well – the manifest inadequacies of John Maynard Keynes were on a natural continuum with the manifold iniquities of John Winston Lennon. But the contradiction between the libertarian rhetoric of those mainly concerned with the roll-back of the welfare state, and the growing authoritarianism of those primarily interested in the reimposition of traditional social values, has become increasingly obvious. Conflict between the economic liberals and the social authoritarians is a relatively new phenomenon in Britain, where long draughts of refreshing power have slaked the Conservative thirst for theory. In the USA on the other hand, the right's long dark years of intellectual opposition tended to encourage ideological introspection, and led both factions to nail their colours firmly to the mast.

One of the most succinct statements of the social authoritarian position was made in 1962 by Brent Bozell, speech writer to Republican Senators Joseph McCarthy and (later) Barry Goldwater. For Bozell, 'the chief purpose of politics' was not to succour freedom but 'to aid the quest for virtue'. Indeed, he went on, 'The story of how the free society has come to take priority over the good society is the story of the decline of the West.'[5] It is in the arena of that dichotomy that the real battle within contemporary conservatism is being joined.

Libertarians against Traditionalists

As George H. Nash points out in his monumental history of *The Conservative Intellectual Movement in America since 1945*, the years after Pearl Harbor were not encouraging for the American right. Not only had traditional conservative isolationism been routed, but the consequence of Roosevelt's interventionism was that America was fighting in alliance with Communism against a regime universally regarded as being on the extreme right (the barbarity of whose practices were becoming daily more apparent), and was doing so, furthermore, on the back of an economy rescued from near-collapse by governmental action on a hitherto unprecedented scale.

Strangely, it was the publication of a short book by a mid-European economist, then living in London, which gave the American right new heart. From its first appearance in 1944, Friedrich A. Hayek's *The Road to Serfdom* had an extraordinary impact on an American right, which had hitherto seen itself, half-proudly but half-despairingly, as a kind of Calvinist 'remnant', a tiny group aware that history and the masses had passed it by. With the publication of *Serfdom* however, it could take new heart, and by 1947 the 'remnant' was able to mount a major international conference, at Mont Pelerin in Switzerland, to promote its ideas. In the words of a young Chicago economist, Milton Friedman, 'The importance of that meeting was that it showed us that we were not alone.'[6]

But although indeed no longer alone, the 'we' referred to represented only part of the American right. The sigificant characteristic of the political philosophy of both Hayek and Friedman was, and is, not so much their advocacy of laissez-faire economics *per se*, as the belief that the free market is a necessary *and sufficient* condition for the just society. As *Serfdom* has it, 'We have progressively abandoned that freedom in economic affairs without which personal and political freedom has never existed in the past,' a freedom which consists primarily in 'the respect for the individual man *qua* man, that is the recognition of his own views and tastes as supreme in his own sphere, however narrowly that may be circum-scribed'.[7] Similarly, Friedman argues strongly in *Capitalism and Freedom* that the major problem with governmental intervention in the economy is that it conflicts with 'one of the strongest and most creative forces known to man – the attempt by millions of individuals to promote their own interests, to live their lives by their own values'.[8]

It was on the question of values that the individualists parted company most dramatically with traditional conservatism. As Hayek himself put it in his essay *Why I am not a Conservative*, it is only 'the co-existence of different sets of values that makes it possible to build a peaceful society with a minimum of force'. Indeed, for Hayek, 'The most conspicuous attribute of liberalism that distinguishes it as much from conservatism as from socialism is the view that moral beliefs concerning matters of conduct which do not directly interfere with the protected sphere of other persons do not justify coercion.'[9]

Such views were anathema to a significant group of American conservatives, most of them surrounding the journal *National Review* (the motto of which, according to its founder William F. Buckley, was that it 'stands athwart history yelling Stop').[10] As arch-traditionalist Russel Kirk argued: 'Once supernatural and traditional sanctions are dissolved, economic self-interest is ridiculously inadequate to hold an economic system together, and even less adequate to preserve order.'[11] While for Richard Weaver – who saw the model of the virtuous society in the Old

South – 'Capitalism cannot be conservative in the true sense as long as its reliance is on industrialism, whose very nature it is to unsettle any establishment and initiate the endless innovation of technological "progress".'[12]

As Michael W. Miles argues in *The Odyssey of the American Right*, the principal divisions between the economic liberals and the social traditionalists were religious as well as ideological, the 'libertarians' deriving from 'the old Protestant Right', the traditionalists, often Catholic, less concerned with individualism and freedom and more with 'God, family and order'.[13] What both factions had in common, in the 1940s and 50s, was an alienation from, and deep distrust of, the majority, a prejudice darkly expressed by German émigré Peter Viereck, who argued in 1949 that 'We don't need a "century of the common man"; we have it already, and it has only produced the commonest man, the impersonal and irresponsible and uprooted mass-man.'[14] The American right, then, watched with some distaste as its post-war standard-bearers sought to court a plurality for their views. For most libertarians, Senator Joseph McCarthy's anti-Communist crusade of the early 1950s represented a basic challenge to freedom of conscience (and few traditionalists were happy with his rabble-rousing style). But, conversely, Senator Barry Goldwater's subtle compromise between 'southern' traditionalism and 'western' individualism (in his 1964 presidential platform) led merely to electoral ignominy.

It was not until the late 1960s that the 'revolting masses' of right-wing demonology were transmuted into the new 'silent majority' of Nixonian myth, a majority of whom were either southern traditionalists or northern workers, neither of which groups was particularly attracted by liberal economic theory, but both of which shared what one chronicler of the New Right described as a profound revulsion against the ideologues of the 1960s, particularly those promoting affirmative action, 'unilateral disarmers slashing Pentagon budgets' and 'radical feminists, students and homosexuals repudiating and assaulting traditional values', in association with 'a burgeoning "knowledge elite" turning increasingly hostile to capitalism'.[15] Thus, after all the debates and arguments in the post-war years, it was the social issues that finally came to dominate the right's political agenda.

Powell and his Allies

Because of the slacker grip of party loyalties in the USA, American conservatives could cast themselves in an oppositional role during the Eisenhower, as well as the Truman and Johnson years. In Britain, the Tory Party's thirteen uninterrupted years of power kept its ideologues under firm control, while the leadership retained its commitment to the post-war settlement and its belief 'in Keynes, in the welfare state as we have come to know it, in high government spending, in government's ability to create full employment and encourage growth'.[16] It is true that even during the thirteen years there were flashes of what might now be called monetarist or Friedmanite strategy – in the first years of the peacetime Churchill government with its 'bonfire of controls', and during the early Macmillan period, when the then Chancellor of the Exchequer and two of his junior ministers resigned over their belief in a tighter fiscal and monetary policy. And there were groups – like Aims of Industry (founded in 1942) and the Institute of Economic Affairs (1957) – which advocated economic liberal ideas, and others (like the Monday Club, founded in 1960) which proselytised the more ancient and venerable conservative traditions of paternalism, imperialism and racism.

But the major change came, predictably, with the loss of power in 1964, and it was one of the two ministers who resigned with Peter Thorneycroft who came to represent the breaking of the consensus most powerfully. Enoch Powell was probably the most senior committed economic liberal in the Conservative Party. Echoing the libertarian rhetoric of Hayek and Friedman, he wrote in 1966 that 'When a society's economic life ceases to be shaped by the interaction of the free decisions of individuals, freedom is in a fair way to disappear from other sides of its existence as well.'[17] And, indeed, in the 1960s Powell clearly saw the advocacy of such ideas as the *primary* purpose of his political life:

> Whatever else the Conservative Party stands for, unless it is the party of free choice, free competition and free enterprise, unless – I am not afraid of the word – it is the party of capitalism, then it has no function in the contemporary world.[18]

The fact that Powell's commitment to market forces was always tempered by a fair deal of old-fashioned welfare paternalism (the National Health Service, for instance, being justified on the grounds that 'a civilised, compassionate nation can do no other',[19]) does not completely obviate the sense that his later views on race represent a significant disjuncture with his opinions on the economy. As Paul Foot exposes, Powell in his early days attested that he would always 'set my face like flint against making any difference between one citizen of this country and another on grounds of his origin'.[20] It is surely fair to see no little contradiction between Powell's oft-expressed belief that labour should be free, and indeed encouraged, to move between regions but not between countries; that freedom of movement should apply internationally only to capital. Powell himself, perhaps aware of the problem, has addressed himself to the relationship between his nationalism and his liberalism, and came up with an explanation that is really no more than a tautology:

> It is not for the sake of a dry-as-dust theory, or because of the academic beauty and precision of a market economy, or from materialist calculation ... that we are called upon to commend the test of competition to the nation, and to submit our politics and actions to that test first. The demand comes passionate and direct from the heart of national pride itself. Britain today needs desperately for its own sake, for the sake of self-respect, to regain the confidence and the conviction that it can hold up its head in competition with all comers in the world.[21]

The idea that nationalism can only exist when a nation is economically competitive, is not only dubious in the sense that nationhood is tested most strongly in times of war when such conditions cannot by definition apply. The concept of a people finding itself through equivalent facility in the market-place, contrasts starkly with Powell's own definition of national consciousness as 'a sense of difference from the rest of the world, of having something in common which is not shared beyond the limits of the nation'.[22]

Whether or not Powell's change of course in the late 1960s was a genuine conversion or an act of opportunism, change it was. The economics of Adam Smith might seem 'dry-as-dust' to Powell's electors in Wolverhampton: the issue of immigration was anything but. Laissez-faire economics has usually been a minority obsession. Powell's three major anti-immigration speeches of the late 1960s were a bid, over the heads of the flaccid consensualists of both parties, for a new majority. As Powell put it, with a typical combination of grandiosity and dry impishness, 'the greatest task of the statesman ... is to offer his people good myths'.[23]

The importance of Powell's majoritarianism has been acknowledged both by commentators on, and adherents of, Thatcherism. In the wake of the 1979 election, Andrew Gamble noted that 'without "Powellism", "Thatcherism" would not have had the same opportunity',[24] a point echoed by the *Sunday Telegraph*'s Peregrine Worsthorne, in the immediate aftermath of June 1983:

> It was Enoch Powell who first sowed the seeds whose harvest Margaret Thatcher reaped last Thursday ... and to his great voice should credit go for shattering the Butskellite glacis, the dissolution of which led to the avalanche.[25]

But there is a huge irony contained within the career of Enoch Powell – an irony that goes beyond the fact that by the time his party embraced his philosophy, he was no longer a part of it. The paradox is that between 1974 and 1979 it was Powellism Mark I – economic rather than nationalist Powellism – which came to gain an increasing hold over the Conservative Party. Following Edward Heath's defeat at the February 1974 General Election, the Conservative Party fell increasingly under the influence of a mushrooming number of campaigns, organisations and groupings proselytising free market economics – from academic study groups like an increasingly prestigious and influential Institute of Economic Affairs (joined in 1974 by Sir Keith Joseph's Centre for Policy Studies), to populist movements like the National Association of Ratepayers' Action Groups, the Association of Self-Employed People and the National Association for Freedom. Electoral failure is almost bound to increase ideological voltage: what was significant about the post-1974 upsurge was the singular magnetism of the libertarian pole of the Conservative right.

There were both political and economic reasons for this phenomenon. Politically, the years following Powell's 1967-68 speeches had demonstrated the risks involved in playing the racist card. The growth of fascist groups like the National Front made any organisation presenting a militant anti-immigration line vulnerable to infiltration – which was precisely what happened to the Monday Club during the two years following the Heath government's admittance of 30,000 Asian refugees from Uganda in 1972. As a number of people have pointed out, the ideology of the National Association for Freedom was in large part built around a political model that set it at the greatest possible distance from the National Front.[26] As NAFF founder Norris McWhirter argued:

> In the west the internal struggle is that between the libertarian elements and the corporatists. The nationalisers, the neo-Keynesians and the advocates of universal welfare with their cohorts of index-pensioned civil servants are ranged against the advocates of market economics.[27]

By placing the political fracture line between 'individualism' and 'collectivism', the NAFF was able to pit itself against both the left and what it acknowledged to be the fascists of the National Front, frequently making the point that 'The abbreviation "Nazi" ... actually stands, of course, for National *Socialist*.'[28]

Far from wishing to promote the communal oneness of the nation, then, the NAFF was careful to base its highly successful propaganda 'upon the presumption of the value of the human being as an individual, and not on the concept of men and women as mere units within the collectivist state'.[29] The NAFF was also aware of the increasing prestige of free market ideas in the intellectual and academic worlds (Milton Friedman and F.A. Hayek received Nobel Prizes for economics in the early 1970s). But perhaps most important of all was the growing economic desperation of the Tory grass roots, faced with what they saw as an exponential increase in trade union power on the one hand, and an equally ratchet-like growth in the power of government to constrain, direct and regulate, on the other. It was the image of the self-employed small businessman, harassed by restrictive practices all day, dripping midnight oil on his VAT return, which inspired NAFF ideologues like David Kelly:

> I consider that history will see the period of the Heath government as one of the most crucial in cementing the acceptance of socialism in Britain. It was at this time that the self-employed came to feel most abandoned ... their so-called own kind turned on them.[30]

So on 3 May 1979 the Conservative Party, the party of order and government and rule, went to the country with a manifesto that committed the incoming government to redress a balance that 'had been increasingly tilted in favour of the state at the expense of individual liberty'. Four and a half years later, at the Tory Conference following another crushing victory, a delegate from Bristol stated in the law and order debate: 'We are paying the price for too many years of free expression and freedom.' What had changed?

USA: Neo-Conservatives and the New Right

In March 1952, the American Jewish magazine *Commentary* ran a piece by a young intellectual called Irving Kristol, a graduate of City College New York, and, like many such, also a graduate from militant Trotskyism. 'There is one thing that the American people know about Senator McCarthy', Kristol wrote, 'he, like them, is unequivocally anti-Communist. About the spokesmen for American liberalism, they feel they know no such thing.' Nine years later, *Commentary*'s new editor, Norman Podhoretz, a well-known radical and accepted spokesman for the 'beat' generation of American novelists and poets in the fifties, wrote an article railing against

> all the white liberals who permit Negroes to blackmail them into adopting double standard of moral judgement, and lend themselves – again assuming a responsibility for crimes they never committed – to cunning and contemptuous exploitation by Negroes they employ or try to defend.[31]

While in October 1970, Podhoretz published an article by another former radical, Nathan Glazer of Harvard, which charted Glazer's progression from being 'a radical' – a mild radical it is true, but still someone who felt closer to radical than to liberal writers and politicians in the 1950s – to that of believing that the position he formerly espoused was 'so beset with error and confusion that our main task ... must be to argue with it and to strip it ultimately of the pretension that it understands the causes of our ills and how to set them right'.

The process of defection from Marxism to liberalism, followed by an equally stark shift from liberalism to conservatism, is a common trajectory for almost all the eastern intellectuals collectively dubbed 'neo-conservative' in the late 1970s, a group led by Kristol, Podhoretz and Glazer (and articulated by their journals *Commentary* and *The Public Interest*), and also including academics Daniel Bell, Samuel P. Huntingdon and Robert Nisbet, and politicians like Senator Daniel Patrick Moynihan and UN Ambassador Jeane Kirkpatrick. Following as said a remarkably common path of political defection (Kristol enjoys remarking that he has been 'moving consistently to the right since 1942'), the present position – and, just as importantly, the tone – of American neo-conservatism was well defined by Adam Meyerson of the *American Spectator*:

Neo-Conservatives are liberals with a sense of tragedy. We wish it were possible to live without defence budgets, but realize that it is not. We'd like to campaign for comprehensive national health insurance, but are afraid that its costs would interfere with other humanitarian ends ... And Neo-Conservatives are conservatives with a liberal attachment to the common man. We think that, for all its many, many injustices, the United States has given more freedom and more opportunities both for self-rule and for economic advancement to more people over a longer period of time than has any other political system in the history of the world. So we think that our institutional traditions and constitutional heritage should be modified only with the greatest caution and deliberation.[32]

'Caution' and 'deliberation' are key neo-conservative words (another is 'prudence'), and in that way the neo-conservatives are considerably removed in style from the network of organisations and campaigns jointly defined as the 'New Right' in the run-up to the 1980 Presidential election, when it acted as a marriage-broker to a coalition of anti-abortionists, gun-owners, tax-reducers, John Birch Society stalwarts and Protestant preachers which was later to call itself the 'Moral Majority'. (In *Back to Basics*, Burton Yale Pines describes how leading New Right organisers Paul Weyrich and Howard Phillips assembled the components of the Moral Majority, in collaboration with its most public spokesman, the Reverend Jerry Falwell.)[33]

The strength of organisations like the National Political Action Committee, the Committee for the Survival of a Free Congress and the Conservative Caucus (all founded in the 1974-75 period), lies in their use of sophisticated direct mail technology. All three of the above organisations are closely linked with Richard A. Viguerie, the first executive director of the Young Americans for Freedom in the early 1960s, and fund-raiser for George Wallace's 1972 Presidential campaign. Viguerie's technique is to build up computerised mailing lists of supporters of single-issue right-wing campaigns, and either to lease them out to other conservative groups or to use them in his own campaigns. By 1980, Viguerie was reported to have 10,000,000 names on twenty-five lists, variously in receipt of letters and appeals like the following:

> Dear Friend, I think you will appreciate, more than most Americans, what I am sending you. I have enclosed two flags: the red, white and blue of Old Glory – and the white flag of surrender. I want to show you, by these two flags, what is at stake for America under the SALT II treaty with Russia ...[34]

The luridness of the New Right's propaganda (a Viguerie letter signed by New Right Senator Jesse Helms stated unequivocally that 'your tax dollars are being used to pay for grade school courses that teach our children that cannibalism, wife-swapping and the murder of infants and the elderly are acceptable behaviour')[35], has perhaps obscured the similarities between its ideological bias and that of the neo-conservatives. For, despite what New Right biographer Burton Pines calls the neo-conservative discomfort with 'the direct, insistent and studiedly unsophisticated manner of the social issues crowd',[36] the two groups share an ideological commitment to the socially authoritarian rather than the economically liberal end of the spectrum when the two conflict. The New Right's house journal *Conservative Digest* admits that 'attention to so-called social issues – abortion, busing, gun rights, pornography, crime – has ... become central to the growth of the New Right', because 'the New Right is looking for issues that people care about, and social issues, at least for the present, fit the 'bill'.[37] Richard Viguerie has admitted that 'I'm willing to make concessions to come to power ... We're going to have to be willing to use the government to stimulate the economy more than I think we should in order to get the votes.'[38] And, for at least one mainstream Republican (George Bush's campaign manager David Keene), these compromises 'go right to the core of what we consider conservatism – our dedication to preserving the free enterprise system'.[39]

The neo-conservative case against economic liberalism is both more sophisticated and to a certain extent more opaque. Irving Kristol writes for the *Wall Street Journal* and he and many of his fellows are, or have been, employed by the American Enterprise Institute, which is as its name implies. But the theme of much of Kristol's writing – encapsulated in the title of his essay collection *Two Cheers for Capitalism* – is a serious questioning of 'the original liberal idea that it is possible for the individual, alone or in voluntary association with others, to cope with the eternal dilemmas of the human condition'. The reason why Kristol is unable 'to celebrate the unqualified virtues of individualism'[40] is that while Adam Smith's hidden hand 'has its uses in the market place, which is the domain of "economic men" rather than of citizens, and where the specter of bankruptcy does impose a kind of self-discipline', the results of the 'emancipation of the individual from social restraints' are disastrous when 'extended to the polity as a whole, which can go bankrupt only once, and whose destiny is finally determined by the capacity of its citizenry to govern its passions and thereby rightly understand its enduring common interests'.[41] And the paradox is that, by encouraging the pursuit of 'self-seeking, self-indulgence and just plain ... selfishness',[42] the untrammelled free-marketeers like Friedman and Hayek might unwittingly promote the destruction of the economic system they so fervently espouse:

> The idea of bourgeois virtue has been eliminated from Friedman's conception of bourgeois society, and has been replaced by the idea of individual liberty ... (But) what if the 'self' that is 'realised' under the conditions of liberal capitalism is a self that despises liberal capitalism, and uses its liberty to subvert and abolish a free society? To this question Hayek – like Friedman – has no answer. And yet this is *the* question we now confront, as our society relentlessly breeds more and more such selves, whose private vices in no way provide public benefits to the bourgeois order. Perhaps one can say that the secular, 'libertarian' tradition of capitalism – as distinct from the Protestant-bourgeois tradition – simply had too limited an imagination when it came to vice ... It could refute Marx effectively, but never thought it would be called upon to refute the Marquis de Sade.[43]

It is clear that in this key passage, Irving Kristol has a particular period of recent history in mind. As he told *Newsweek* (19 January 1976), 'if there is only one thing that Neo-Conservatives are unanimous about, it is their dislike of the "counter-culture" which has played so remarkable a role in American life in the last 15 years'. Or, as commentator Elizabeth Drew has written, the neo-conservatives 'are on common ground against what they see as the spoiled children and their indulgent elders of the late 1960s and early 1970s'.[44] Or, again, as neo-conservative Robert Nisbet argued:

> I think it would be difficult to find a single decade in the history of Western culture when so much barbarism – so much calculated onslaught against culture and convention in any form ... passed into print, into music, into art, and on to the American stage as the decade of the 1960s.[45]

Nisbet then proceeded to define the central, primary heresy of the 1960s as a massive 'revolt against authority' and 'consecration of disorder', an analysis echoed by Samuel P. Huntingdon in his article 'The Democratic Distemper', in which he described the 1960s as a time in which:

> people no longer felt the same obligation to obey those whom they had previously considered superior to themselves in age, rank, status, expertise, character and talents ... the democratic principle was extended to many institutions where it can, in the long run, only frustrate the purpose of those institutions.[46]

For the problem was not merely confined to the behaviour of college students in the 1960s, because, of course, it was by no means certain that upon graduation they would grow out of what Kristol dubbed their 'phase of infantile regression'.[47] Indeed, perhaps the most important ideological construct developed by the neo-conservatives is the notion that a significant proportion of the 'Vietnam generation' of college students now forms the core of a 'New Class' of 'scientists, teachers and educational administrators, journalists and others in the communications industries, psychologists, social workers, those lawyers and doctors who make their careers in the expanding public sector, city planners, the staffs of the larger foundations, the upper levels of the government bureaucracy and so on', a class which, while 'not much interested in money' is 'keenly interested in power', a power which it wishes to transfer from business to government, where the new class itself will 'have a major say in how it is exercised'.[48]

And in a situation where, as Kristol argues, 'to see something on television is to feel entitled to it';[49] in a time, further, when (as Nathan Glazer sees it) 'our systems of communications are such that everyone is aware of the level of goods and services that prevails in some places, and the deficiencies that still obtain in others';[50] then, as Robert Nisbet claims, the uses of that power become the satisfaction of the appetites of the poor:

> Expectations cannot do other than increase exponentially. Envy ... quickly takes command, and the lust for power with which to allay every fresh discontent, to assuage every social pain, and to gratify every fresh expectation soon becomes boundless.[51]

Or, as New Rightist William S. Rusher put it, in less elegant but more electorally practical terms:

> A new economic division pits the producers – businessmen, manufacturers, hard-hats, blue-collar workers, and farmers – against the new and powerful class of non-producers comprised of a liberal verbalist elite (the dominant media, the major foundations and research institutions, the educational establishment, the federal and state bureaucracies) and a semi-permanent welfare constituency, all coexisting happily in a state of mutually sustaining symbiosis.[52]

For Rusher, then, a 'vast segment of society' (the welfare class) is being 'carefully tended' and indeed 'forever subtly expanded' by the New Class 'as a justification for their own existence and growth'.[53] And thus the New Class becomes, as Burke wrote of the 'political men of letters' of the

French Revolution, 'a link to unite, in favour of one object, obnoxious wealth to restless and desperate poverty'.[54]

In summary, then, the neo-conservative case is that liberal capitalism, unlimited by bourgeois constraints, encouraged the post-war generation in the belief that it has a right to the instant satisfaction of all appetites, regardless of effort. In the late 1960s, this conviction shifted from the purely economic into the political arena, with the consequence that a whole new class of people entered the distributive sectors of government, there encouraging its clients to believe in turn that they were entitled, as of right, to the full benefits of a consumer society, whether or not they could afford them. Thus liberal capitalism gave permission to the post-war boom generation to pursue its appetite for moral self-satisfaction regardless of the political consequences; allowing this new class in its turn to foster in a new underclass the notion that it had the right to satisfy its physical appetites without economic restraint, to the point where liberal capitalism itself is threatened by social violence on the one hand or financial collapse on the other.

Just as important as the bones of the argument, however, is the vocabulary chosen to express it. Drew's 'spoiled children', Kristol's 'infantile regression', Nisbet's 'revolt against authority': all speak of the neo-conservative belief that above all else they are the proselytisers of 'adulthood – the things you learn when you grow up'.[55] And the notion that the radicalism of the 1960s was no more than a peculiarly virulent outbreak of juvenile dementia runs through neo-conservative polemics against the movements of the time: from the student movement itself ('what the dissatisfied students were looking for were adults – adults to confront, to oppose, to emulate');[56] to the demographic causes of crime ' "there is a perennial invasion of barbarians who must somehow be civilised" ... that "invasion" is the coming of age of a new generation of young people');[57] to feminism (the women's liberation movement demands on behalf of women 'a freedom demanded by children and enjoyed by no one: the freedom from all difficulty')[58] and, in the company of Norman Podhoretz, beyond:

In the case of the white young, the contemptuous repudiation of everything American and middle-class was mistaken for a form of idealism when it really represented a refusal to be who they were and to assume responsibility for themselves by taking their place in a world of adults ... But if the plague seems for the moment to have run its course among these groups, it rages as fiercely as ever among others: among the kind of women who do not wish to be women and among those men who do not wish to be men ... there can be no more radical refusal of self-acceptance than the repudiation of one's own biological nature; and there can be no abdication of responsibility more fundamental than the refusal of a man to become, and to be, a father, or the refusal of a woman to become, and be, a mother.[59]

It is an extraordinary passage. From it, it is clear that, for Podhoretz at least, the enemy is no longer merely the infantile, or even just the barbarian: he wrestles with plague-carriers, he jousts with demons.

UK: The Peterhouse School

The main intellectual challenge to the hegemony of the economic liberals in the Conservative Party in Britain in the 1970s has been centred not round an organized faction so much as a loose grouping of graduates from a particular Cambridge college. In 1978, Maurice Cowling, fellow of Peterhouse, Cambridge, edited a selection of *Conservative Essays*, in which the essayists included Peterhouse graduates Roger Scruton, Peregrine Worsthorne and George Gale and the college's present dean, Edward Norman. Other Peterhouse men prominent in the advocacy of social-authoritarian positions include John Vincent (like Scruton, a *Times* contributor), Colin Welch (like Worsthorne, a regular writer for both the *Spectator* and the *Telegraph* group), novelist Kingsley Amis and Patrick Cosgrove, Mrs Thatcher's biographer.

The project of *Conservative Essays* was to attack the rhetoric of freedom with which the economic liberals in the Conservative Party sought to promote their aims. In his introduction, Cowling attacked the economic liberals for 'lending themselves too readily to the idea that in some exclusive way "freedom" is the ultimate value', arguing instead that 'it is not freedom that Conservatives want: what they want is the sort of freedom that will maintain existing inequalities or restore lost ones'.[60] (In this view, he was to be echoed by fellow-contributor Roger Scruton, who in his book *The Meaning of Conservatism* claimed that liberalism, economic or otherwise, was no less than 'the principal enemy of conservatism', adding that democracy itself can be 'discarded without detriment to the civil well-being as the conservative conceives it'.)[61] Indeed, the keynote essay in many ways was that of the *Sunday Telegraph*'s Peregrine Worsthorne, who insisted that:

> If one were to probe into the hearts of many potential and actual Tory supporters – and others besides – one might well discover that what worried them most about contemporary Britain was not so much the lack of freedom as its excessive abundance ... The trouble about Labour on this view is that it has set too many people far too free.[62]

But perhaps the most striking thing about *Conservative Essays* as a volume is its obsession with ideas of nationhood and race. Thus T.E. Utley ('massed immigration has saddled [the nation] with a "racial problem" to which it has still given no systematic thought'),[63] John Biffen (the 'scale of immigration that has transformed the heartland of many English cities ... has not been willed by the British people'),[64] and George Gale ('in rejecting Powell, the Conservative Party ... ignored the instincts of the nation, and chose instead the modish hypocricies of Hampstead about immigration'),[65] joined Cowling himself in a call for a reassertion of national identity, and the manufacture thereby of 'a spiritual glue that would bind down the elite and force it to use a language that would bind it to everyone else'.[66]

It might be cynical to argue that it is the assumed electoral potency of the race issue that led not only Maurice Cowling's social authoritarians to evoke the mystic oneness of nationhood, but also a number of key figures on the libertarian right. Despite the National Association for Freedom's strenuous (though not always totally successful) attempts to evade the issue in the late 1970s, two fully paid-up libertarians seemed perfectly content with the Powellite position that it is perfectly possible to argue for the full play of market forces on the capital side of the equation, while strenuously resisting the free flow of labour.

On 8 September 1976, the Director of the Centre for Policy Studies, Alfred Sherman, wrote in the *Daily Telegraph* that 'nationhood can neither be ignored or wished away' as 'man's main focus of identity', quoting in support Edmund Burke's 'partnership between those who are living, those who are dead, and those who are to be born'. Less loftily, in the same paper the following day, he wrote that 'the imposition of mass immigration from backward alien cultures' was just one symptom of a generalised attack by person or persons unknown on 'patriotism, the family, and ... all that is English and wholesome'. While four months later, no less a person than Hayek himself, who in *The Constitution of Liberty* had bitterly criticised the Conservative 'hostility to internationalism and its proneness to a strident nationalism',[67] wrote to the *Times* in support of strict immigration control, on the grounds that the

> ordinary man only slowly reconciles himself to a large increase in foreigners among his neighbours, even if they differ only in language and manners, and that therefore the wise statesman, to prevent an unpleasant reawakening of primitive instincts, ought to aim at keeping the rate of influx low.[68]

Such instincts were rudely shaken from slumber by events in the early 1980s, which effectively concluded the pure libertarian phase of Thatcherism, and substituted a new authoritarianism that owed much more to Peterhouse than to the Institute of Economic Affairs. There was more than a hint of 'I told you so' in Peregrine Worsthorne's immediate response to the riots of the summer of 1981:

> More violence there is certain to be. If it is not in the inner cities, then it will be on the picket lines. It was always Utopian to expect the body politic to suffer the pains of economic

retraction without violent convulsions. One suspects that those who voted Mrs Thatcher into office did so in the belief that a Tory government would know best how to control them; that having willed the economic ends it would have the courage and determination not to shirk the necessary social means.[69]

What was particularly instructive about the instant analysis that proceeded from the pens of conservative commentators in the wake of the riots, was how closely it was modelled on the constructs developed by the neo-conservatives in the USA. On the very morrow of Toxteth, George Gale blamed the riots on a 'revulsion from authority and discipline' which reached its zenith during the 'permissive revolution' of the 1960s;[70] not long after, Edward Norman argued that the rioters had been 'nurtured in a society which offered them seemingly endless expectations to personal and social satisfaction',[71] a society furthermore in which (according to Colin Welch) 'all fidelity, restraint, thrift, sobriety, taste and discipline, all the virtues associated with work, with the painful acquisition of knowledge, skill and qualifications' have been undermined.[72]

Present too was the concept of the New Class – albeit described as the 'liberal establishment' (by Peregrine Worsthorne, commenting on the 'sheltered lives' that had been led by 'the likes of Lord Scarman' before the Brixton riots confronted them with the reality of 'Enoch Powell's increasingly urgent reiterated warnings about the inevitability of racial violence'),[73] or indeed as the 'radical establishment, founded in the 1960s' (by Ronald Butt of the *Times*).[74] Like their American counterparts, the British conservatives see the New Class as a potent tool for the mass brainwashing of the public, by which technique, according to Powell himself as early as 1970 'the majority are reduced to a condition in which they finally distrust their own senses ... and surrender their will to the manipulator'.[75] And, like the American New Class, the British version is accused of inspiring, if not creating, an underclass. Thus, Paul Johnson, with characteristic lightness of touch, writes of a 'mercenary army' consisting of 'the burgeoning bureaucrats of expanded local and central government; the new breed of "administrators" who control schools and hospitals and even the arts; sociology lecturers and others on the fringe of the higher education afflatus; so-called social workers with their glib pseudo-solutions to non-problems,'[76] who have in common 'an interest in exciting public demands, real or imaginary'.[77] While for the *Spectator*'s Richard West, writing after the first Brixton riots of April 1981, the conspiracy theory applied directly to the question of the urban uprisings:

> Here, as formerly in the United States, the champions of the black cause are middle-class, well-meaning or radical whites ... They see in the grievances of the blacks a weapon for use against all bourgeois society.[78]

So thus, as US neo-conservative Midge Dector continued, in an article glowingly quoted in the *Daily Telegraph* days after Toxteth, the purveyors of 'enlightened liberal attitudes' had 'given permission' to the rioters to 'go on their spree of looting', by promoting the idea among young blacks that 'race and poverty were sufficient excuses for lawlessness'.[79]

And, like their American counterparts also, British conservatives are concerned to point the finger of blame for urban disorder at a cult of youth and youthfulness, initially promoted and developed in the 1960s, but now being transferred by that decade's graduates to a new generation. As Colin Welch writes:

> The decade of the 1960s (or perhaps more precisely of '65-'75) is often remembered ... as a horrendous episode which ended in tears, after which reason resumed her sway and wiser counsels prevailed. This is but a comforting illusion. The poisons then injected into our system, though doubtless diluted, course still through its veins ... The revolting students of the 1960s are the revolting teachers of today, reproducing themselves by teaching as received wisdom what they furiously asserted against the wisdom received from their own teachers.[80]

Welch goes on to name the received wisdom in question as a form of 'puerilism' or 'adolescent barbarism', having earlier defined it as a variety of 'poison'. In this of course, he echoes Norman Podhoretz's definition of feminism and homosexuality as a form of plague. And he is not alone: the language of demonology is now *de rigueur* for the discussion of the social reforms of the last twenty years, as Christopher Booker demonstrates:

> Looking back over what has happened we may be put in mind of one of those fairy stories or myths where someone is told that a certain box or bottle or door must not be opened, because they will regret the consequences ... And the point of the story is always that once the demons are unleashed they can never be put back again. Many people must feel the same about what has happened in our society over the past 25 years – that ... the demons of drugs, pornography, violence and permissiveness in all its forms, are now raging out of control.[81]

No wonder, then, that the Tory libertarians have fallen silent. No wonder that even the National Association for Freedom (renamed the Freedom Association), heralded 1983 by announcing that it was no longer primarily concerned with 'the political forces currently threatening our freedom', but rather with 'rising crime, sexual permissiveness and family breakdown'.[82] How could they not be, with the devil himself stalking the land?

Family and State

In all crucial aspects, then, the New Class model has been recast in British terms, and in terms, furthermore, that have united an extraordinarily wide variety of British conservative, from self-styled libertarians like Alfred Sherman and Paul Johnson, via reluctant wets like Ronald Butt, to High Tory traditionalists like the Peterhouse trio of Norman, Worsthorne and Welch. One reason for the attractiveness of the model may well be that it goes some significant way towards squaring the circle between an intellectual adherence to the free market and the emotional attachment to authority and imposed tradition. To talk of the new class as the donor not just of welfare payments but of 'permission' – indeed to attest that a state that cannot of course be 'compassionate' can nonetheless be 'permissive' or otherwise – is to speak the language of parenthood. And it is worth noting that, in the British context, the metaphor of the disadvantaged as children demanding rights of the beneficent state, has wider application than it does in the USA, by virtue of the greater size of the public sector. As Powell himself argued, the 'translation of a want or need into a right is one of the most widespread and dangerous of modern heresies',[83] a concern reiterated by Alfred Sherman when he berates 'armies of social workers' not only for 'recruiting armies of welfare claimants', but also for 'encouraging them to press for what they call "rights".'[84] While for Kenneth Minogue, LSE political scientist and *Conservative Essays* contributor, the 'politics of compassion' have turned not just the poor and the recipients of welfare, but the entire British population, into 'a collection of noisy corporate children crying "it's not fair" as they roll up their sleeves, not to do something for themselves, but to display their sores and scars' – encouraged, naturally, by 'a sizeable army of bureaucrats, counsellors and managers of the lives of the needy who constitute a major corporate interest in our political life'.[85]

In this context, the contradiction between the anti-statism of free market ideology, and the authoritarianism of the traditionalists, suddenly appears less acute. Indeed, in this sense, it's possible to see Thatcherism not as a libertarian ideology, calling for the dismantling of the state, but as the articulation of demands for the reassertion of the paternal authority of the state over its pampered and infantilised subjects, for the firing of the indulgent nanny and the hiring of the no-nonsense martinet. From this perspective, the crucial role of the free market is not to emancipate the entrepreneur but to chastise the feckless, an instrument not of liberation but of discipline. Hence, perhaps, the extraordinary recommendations of the Government's 'Family Policy Group' (leaked to the

Guardian on 18 February 1983), which sought to transmit free market values to the young via the family, not least by 'training children to manage their pocket money'. And hence also, some more recent pronouncements by Mrs Thatcher herself, including an interview in which she compared governing the country to bringing up a child ('you don't get the best out of them unless you are really rather firm'),[86] and a speech in which she sought to reduce a whole series of social conflicts and tensions to the ethical scale of the nursery moralism:

> Young people are impressionable. How we behave – whether as parents, teachers, sportsmen, politicians – is bound to influence how our children behave. When teachers strike and cause disruption – that's a bad example. When football idols play foul – that's a bad example. When local councils refuse to set a legal rate – that's a bad example. And when some trade union leaders, yes, and some politicians, scorn the law and the courts and the police – these are bad examples. So too is picket-line violence. And who can help but worry about some of the violence we see on our television screens? The standards of society are set by what we tolerate, by the discipline and conventions we set.[87]

Or, as Paul Johnson put it, in a hostile review of former Thatcher aide Ferdinand Mount's book *The Subversive Family*,[88]

> Civilised societies require institutions which restrain our passions and supplement our shortcomings. The three principal ones are the family, organised religion and the state ... In my view, family, church and state are complementary institutions, both of control and charity.[89]

'Control and charity'. What more suitable slogan could there be for an ideology that seeks to reimpose the values of the soup-kitchen and the workhouse?

Squaring the Circle

In the search for that elusively silent majority that would transform the American right from a remnant into the trumpet of the age, a Nixon aide is reputed to have pointed out that the majority of the American people were 'unyoung, unblack and unpoor'. The achievement of both Reaganism and Thatcherism has been to weld together the instincts of individual greed and collective self-righteousness into a coherent model of the world, in which the rhetoric of freedom can co-exist with the reassertion of virtue. Put crudely, the new authoritarianism allows people to vote in their own, narrow self-interest, but yet to feel good about doing so. One might say, it gives them permission.

Notes

1. The Metropolitan Police's 'racial' crime statistics were published on 10 March 1982.
2. Quoted in *Daily Telegraph*, 18 March 1982.
3. Quoted in *Guardian*, 28 March 1982.
4. Dr Rhodes Boyson, speaking to the Loughborough Conservative Association, 5 February 1982.
5. L. Brent Bozell, 'Freedom or Virtue?', *National Review*, 11 September 1962, quoted in George H. Nash, *The Conservative Intellectual Movement in America since 1945*, New York 1976, pp. 176-7.
6. Nash, op. cit., p. 26.
7. F.A. Hayek, *The Road to Serfdom*, London 1976, pp. 10-11.
8. Milton Friedman, *Capitalism and Freedom*, Chicago 1962, p. 200.
9. F.A. Hayek, *The Constitution of Liberty*, London 1976, p. 402.
10. Nash, op. cit., p. 151.
11. Ibid., p. 81.
12. Ibid., p. 204.
13. Michael W. Miles, *The Odyssey of the American Right*, New York 1980, p. 254.
14. Nash, op. cit., p. 65.
15. Burton Yale Pines, *Back to Basics*, New York 1982, p. 268.
16. David Howell, *The Conservative Tradition and the 1980s*, London 1980.
17. Quoted in Neill Nugent and Roger King (eds), *The British Right*, Farnborough 1977, pp. 107-8.
18. Quoted in Andrew Gamble, *The Conservative Nation*, London 1974, p. 116.
19. Nugent and King, op. cit., p. 105.
20. Quoted in Paul Foot, *The Rise of Enoch Powell*, Harmondsworth 1969, p. 66.
21. Nugent and King, op. cit., p. 117.

22. Ibid., p. 111.
23. Gamble, op. cit., p. 115.
24. Andrew Gamble, 'The Decline of the Conservative Party', *Marxism Today*, November 1979.
25. *Sunday Telegraph*, 12 June 1983.
26. R. King and N. Nugent, *Respectable Rebels*, London 1979, pp. 186-7.
27. Norris McWhirter in K.W. Watkins (ed.), *In Defence of Freedom*, London 1978, p. 61.
28. *Free Nation*, 5 August 1977.
29. Viscount De L'Isle in Watkins (ed.), op. cit., p. 17.
30. Quoted in King and Nugent, op. cit., p. 56.
31. *Commentary*, February 1963.
32. Quoted in *Listener*, 17 July 1980.
33. Pines, op. cit., pp. 294-5.
34. *The Conservative Caucus*, direct mail leaflet, *c.* 1979.
35. Quoted in *Guardian*, 14 November 1978.
36. Pines, op. cit., p. 329.
37. *Conservative Digest*, June 1979.
38. Quoted in *Nation*, 29 January 1977.
39. *Nation*, 29 January 1977.
40. Quoted in Nash, op. cit., p. 340.
41. Irving Kristol, *On the Democratic Idea in America*, New York 1973, pp. vii-xiii.
42. Ibid., p. 27.
43. Irving Kristol, *Two Cheers for Capitalism*, New York 1978, pp. 67-8.
44. Quoted in Peter Steinfels, *The Neo-Conservatives*, New York 1979, p. 10.
45. *Encounter*, August 1972.
46. *Public Interest*, February 1975.
47. Kristol, *Democratic Idea*, p. 104.
48. Kristol, *Two Cheers*, pp. 27-8.
49. Kristol, *Democratic Idea*, p. 26.
50. *Commentary*, October 1970.
51. Steinfels, op. cit., pp. 243-4.
52. William S. Rusher, *The Making of the New Majority Party*, Green Hill, Illinois, 1975, p. 14.
53. Ibid., p. 33.
54. Edmund Burke, *Reflections on the Revolution in France*, New York 1961, pp. 124-5.
55. *Esquire*, 13 February 1979.
56. Kristol, *Democratic Idea*, p. 125.
57. Norman B. Ryder, quoted by James Q. Wilson, *Thinking About Crime*, New York 1975, p. 12.
58. Midge Dector, 'The Liberated Woman', *Commentary*, October 1970.
59. Norman Podhoretz, *Breaking Ranks*, New York 1979, pp. 362-3.
60. Maurice Cowling (ed.), *Conservative Essays*, London, 1978, p. 9.
61. Roger Scruton, *The Meaning of Conservatism*, Harmondsworth 1980, p. 16.

62. In Cowling (ed.), op. cit., pp. 147-8.
63. Ibid., p. 49.
64. Ibid., p. 156.
65. Ibid., p. 183.
66. Ibid., p. 19.
67. Hayek, *Constitution of Liberty*, p. 405.
68. *Times*, 1 March 1978.
69. *Sunday Telegraph*, 12 July 1981.
70. *Daily Express*, 7 July 1981.
71. *Sunday Telegraph*, 19 July 1981.
72. *Spectator*, 17 December 1983.
73. *Sunday Telegraph*, 29 November 1981.
74. *Times*, 2 June 1983.
75. Enoch Powell, *Powell in the 1970 Election*, London 1970, p. 108.
76. Paul Johnson, *The Recovery of Freedom*, Oxford 1980, p. 72.
77. Ibid., p. 8.
78. *Spectator*, 18 April 1981.
79. *Daily Telegraph*, 27 July 1981.
80. *Spectator*, 20 October 1983.
81. *Daily Mail*, 10 November 1983.
82. *Free Nation*, January 1983.
83. Enoch Powell, *Still to Decide*, London 1972, p. 13.
84. *Daily Telegraph*, 30 May 1977.
85. *Daily Telegraph*, 8 February 1977.
86. *Evening Standard*, 11 April 1985.
87. Speech to Conservative Central Council, Newcastle-upon-Tyne, 23 March 1985.
88. Ferdinand Mount, *The Subversive Family*, London 1982.
89. *Observer*, 10 October 1982.

Let Them Eat Dirt

In one of his diverting *Private Eye* diaries, Auberon Waugh announced that he'd been asked to chair a meeting of British revolutionary leaders, to be held, if memory serves, in the Hyde Park Hotel.

As the world knows, Waugh's diary was in fact a work of semi-fiction, in which the articulation of the author's views was both alternated with and expressed through a narrative often, though not necessarily, involving real people, which purported to consist of actual episodes culled from day-to-day life. This use of private chronicle as a medium for polemic had precisely the opposite effect from that, say, achieved in Swift's *Modest Proposal*: far from the fiction intensifying the passion of the argument, the mendacity of the annal served to diminish the credibility of the opinion, not least via the reader's understandable fear of being caught out twice. And, if both story and sentiment are suspect, then the diarist himself becomes ontologically dubious, not Waugh but 'Waugh', a thing of wisps, an optical illusion.

This problem shouldn't arise with Waugh's weekly column in the *Spectator*, a little under a hundred of which are now anthologised. But, even here, it's hard not to feel the presence of invisible quote-marks hovering impishly over the elegant logo. Not for nothing are both column and book called *Another Voice* and the latter subtitled 'An Alternative Anatomy of Britain': both clearly evoke *Private Eye*'s own 'Alternative Voice', the 'fearless and outspoken' Dave Spart, who expresses the dreariest of left-wing commonplaces in the most crassly incoherent terms. Similarly, Waugh's familiar blend of bucolic spite and ultramontane prejudice has, for the most part, long since ceased to be remotely controversial (as he himself unhappily admits) and it's now only the chosen manner, the constant flavour of pastiche, which remains even faintly individual. Perhaps, indeed, both column and book could be more aptly titled 'Another Tone'.

All of which makes it hard for even a conscientious reviewer to do much more than shrug, smile and wave. (Waugh himself advises him or her merely to read the introduction, which summarises the rest of the book in the manner of a theatrical dumbshow.) But, in fact, Waugh's view of the world is more important than it appears to be, in that, whether he likes it or not, his angle on things represents an increasingly significant trend in the New Conservatism. It is not the now somewhat passé cocktail of disciplinary and libertarian attitudes that makes Waugh an ideological market leader (indeed, he's retreated from all that a bit and his polemic against the Waffen-FCS line on heroin is not only rather well argued but could apply equally well to his position on drunk driving, particularly for a man so adept at ad absurdity). No, Waugh's importance lies in his best known clutch of opinions, those which appear to be most obviously affected by a touch of the only-doing-it-to-annoys: his attitudes to class.

The initial strategy of Thatcherite Conservatism toward the working masses was a strange refraction of the Marxist doctrine of false consciousness. The theory was that the proletariat had been blinded to its true interests by a combination of collectivist propaganda, corrupt if not Bolshevik leadership and material pressures (the best example being the way council house rental inhibited the free movement of labour). And the solution was equally simple: disarm and isolate the militants, sell off the council houses (and shares in the telephone company) and the natural, capitalist consciousness of the working class would emerge, blinking, into the light of day.

In order to bring off this trick, it was necessary to make an important conceptual distinction. One of the many problems of the false consciousness theory is that it has to cope with those sections of the working class whose commitment to the status quo cannot be entirely explained by even the subtlest machinations of the craven reformists in the Labour bureaucracies; similarly, the Tory Turn to the Class had somehow to sidestep those sections of the oppressed masses who were obviously too alienated to be susceptible to even the most tempting entrepreneurial blandishments. Hence the highly successful Thatcherite endeavour to Americanise people's conception of the working class: to detach the full-time employed proletariat from the part-time or unemployed section and invent (or, rather, import) a new vocabulary – 'the inner cities', 'the underclass' – to define the latter. And, again as in America, this construct could be given a covertly racial twist, since the inhabitants of this newly discovered country seemed (well, most of them) to be foreign, or to be living with foreigners, or too old, tired and miserable to move away.

What threatened this model was not just the fightback of the miners (fully employed, far from even the outer reaches of the towns), but also the alliance between them and elements of the urban culture in the Miners Support Groups. Further, the fact that the GLC's support for feminism and the black struggle appeared at the very least not to reduce its working-class appeal raised the spectre of a labour movement culturally and politically revived by the energies of the underclass – a development confirmed by the Labour Party's own electoral revival. Worst of all, the wave of public sympathy for the defeated miners as they trooped back to the pitheads indicated that the hold of traditional loyalties and empathies was a great deal stronger than it had looked in 1979 or 1983; that the Unmaking of the British Working Class was going to take a lot more than the humiliation of a few TUC bureaucrats, the odd cut-price mortgage and a share or two.

One of the most striking features of the last two years has been the revival of a kind of blatant, rancorous class contempt unseen in most of our lifetimes, directed not just against the blacks, the single parents or the unemployed (always fair game) but against the proletariat as a whole. In a piece too recent for inclusion in this book, Waugh himself drew what he saw as the vital lessons of the events at Heysel football stadium in May 1985:

Neither the 'workers', nor their sycophants on the sensitive
fringes of the middle class have any alibis on this occasion. It
was not the blacks who chased 31 terrified Italians to their
deaths, nor was it the National Front, nor was the group
hooliganism sanctified by being in furtherance of an
industrial dispute. None of these Merseyside 'animals' was
poor and few, apparently, were unemployed. They were
quite simply our wonderful, overpaid 'workers' on a spree.
(*Spectator*, 8 June 1985)

What is remarkable about the last couple of years is the
way in which such ideas – albeit not always so
unambiguously nor so gleefully expressed – have
themselves become commonplace. What is striking about
Another Voice is that Auberon Waugh has held, and has
been expressing, such views for so long. On the book's
cover is a drawing of the author, standing with a glass of
wine in a sort of pillared folly, in front of what at first sight
appears to be a domed Town Hall, its windows smashed,
its roof burning, its broken cupola crazily skewed and its
windows festooned with the political emblems of urban
life, from the National Front to Socialist Workers, from
'Wimmin' to 'Punks' and 'Yobs'. But the drawing is
misleading on two counts. First, as is clear from the book,
Waugh's main target is really none of these trends or
manifestations (try as he might to indulge in fashionable
misogyny, or modish racialism, his heart is really not in it).
Second, as the American edition reveals, the classic pile is
not really a public building at all. There, the book is called
Brideshead Benighted and, over that title, the cover
illustration appears in a whole new light. It is nothing less
than Waugh's own country seat, his birthright, his private
inheritance, occupied and squatted by his hated working
class, or, put another way, the majority of his fellows, of all
colours and both sexes.

Had Waugh actually taken the chair at an assemblage
attended by Tony Cliff, Ted Grant and Gerry Healy (for
these were happier and more innocent days), he could
have given them a simple message: that an element at least
of the impetus behind Thatcherism was to be nothing to
do with the release of vital new entrepreneurial energies,

but was all about the reassertion of the most ancient of privileges, the most crude and atavistic of class hatreds. That the restitution of seignorial authority is not the *whole* of the New Conservatism shouldn't blind us to the fact that it's a part and we should, I suppose, be grateful to 'Bron' for so consistently reminding us.

Dreams of the Volk

One of the exceptional characteristics of Thatcherism as a populist movement is that its concepts have tended to trickle down rather than up, from the intellectuals rather than to them. This was true of the clutch of ideas collectively dubbed 'monetarism'; it's also true of the revival of 'family values' now being articulated so fulsomely by Norman Tebbit. And even though its cutting edge appears to be the yellowest section of the gutter press, it's true now of the assault on anti-racism.

Hardly a day passes without another exposes of race commissars in Brent, or headlines in the *Mail* and the *Sun* of the 'Barmy Bernie Blasts Biassed Books' or 'Loony Lefties Lop Library Lists' variety. But nonetheless, the attack on anti-racism and multiculturalism began with the New Right intellectuals, and they've now produced a book (*Anti-Racism – An Assault on Education and Value*) to explain why.

As its authors spent a lot of time exposing anti-racists as sinister revolutionaries (so obsessed are they with the powers of Institute of Race Relations Director, A. Sivanandan, that they've granted him an honorary doctorate), it's legitimate to ask who they are. In fact, as editor Frank Palmer acknowledges, the idea and inspiration for the book came from none other than Roger Scruton, professor at Birkbeck College and editor of the ultra-conservative *Salisbury Review*. And nine of Palmer's fourteen contributers have written for the *Review*, in some cases (like that of Bradford's Ray Honeyford and former Monday Club activist David J. Levy) not infrequently.

The *Salisbury Review* itself is an outgrowth of the Salisbury Group and the overlapping Conservative Philosophy Group, both of which emanate (in large part) from present or past members of Peterhouse, Cambridge. Like Thatcherism, the Peterhouse Persuasion has sought to challenge the post-war political consensus, and, in Scruton's words, 'to express concepts which have long been forbidden of expression' (*Guardian*, 1 March 1983). But unlike Thatcherism, the tendency is highly suspicious of the idea that economic liberty is a sufficient condition of the good society. As Maurice Cowling wrote in his introduction to the Salisbury Group's *Conservative Essays* (published in 1978), 'It is not freedom that conservatives want: what they want is the sort of freedom that will maintain existing inequalities or restore lost ones.' And as recently as April 1986, Scruton confirmed that the purpose of the *Salisbury Review* was 'to separate conservatism from the economic liberalism with which it has recently been confounded'.

What Scruton means by conservatism was simply summed up in the *Review*'s inaugural statement: 'The consciousness of nationhood is the highest form of political consciousness.' This belief has resulted in an obsession with the baleful effects of immigration – *Conservative Essays* is riddled with plaintive references to the erosion of 'national identity', and *Salisbury Review*'s first edition contained John Casey's notorious call for compulsory repatriation. It also accounts for the tendency's belief that there are certain values – and indeed *opinions* – which should not be questioned. In *Conservative Essays*, Cowling criticised the assumptions of the then notorious Gould Report into Marxist infiltration of the universities, on the grounds that its assumptions consecrated 'the unthought-out pluralism in which we live'. And in his essay in *Anti-Racism*, Roger Scruton argues that it is the primary duty of the schools to 'transmit the common culture of Britain' and the 'high culture that has flowed from it'.

It's therefore superficially surprising that much of the rest of the book proceeds on what appear to be liberal assumptions. Throughout, the advocates of anti-racism and multiculturalism (only one essayist realises that the terms aren't interchangeable) are presented as dour totalitarians, with pejoratives like 'McCarthyite' and 'witch-hunt' joining the 'commissars', 'race spies' and 'big brothers' of the popular press. In his introduction, Frank Palmer firmly asserts that 'Suppression of intellectual inquiry is not a healthy foundation for any educational policy, or for living in a society that wishes to remain a liberal democracy.' Palmer's view flies in the face of his mentor Scruton's now quite famous view that liberalism is in fact no less than 'the principal enemy of conservatism', and indeed that even democracy 'can be discarded without detriment to the civil well-being as the conservative conceives it'. (In fact, Palmer himself appears to rethink the rampant liberalism of his introduction; his own chapter is full of volkish stuff about education as 'the medium through which the generations of the dead can speak to the living, and through which we enact our duty to the yet unborn'.)

To point out that there is a contradiction between the pluralist assumptions of the book's critique of anti-racism and the authoritarianism of its authors' views is not just an academic matter nor a debating trick. It is important for educationalists who might be attracted or influenced by the book's libertarian rhetoric to be aware that while one section is devoted to condemning censorship *by* anti-racists, another demands censorship *of* them. (Baroness Cox is particularly disturbed that the Institute of Race Relations' cartoon book *How Racism Came to Britain* is 'on sale in shops such as W.H. Smith where anyone could buy it and read it without the safeguard of having a teacher who would put the "other" view'.) It is equally important for anti-racists to understand that the project of *Anti-Racism* is to individualise the concept of racism, to detach it from the social arena, and to relocate it in the realm of personal morality.

In most chapters, the conviction that racism is the consequence not of unjust social arrangements but 'a defect in human nature' is asserted rather than argued. The exception is 'Clarifying the Concepts' by Professor Anthony Flew, which is in fact a rewrite of his Centre for Policy Studies pamphlet *Education, Race and Revolution*, which was itself a version of an article published in the Winter 1984 issue of *Salisbury Review*, from which he borrowed material for a piece in the *Times*. His arguments are thus nothing if not practised, and one of the most frequently used arises out of a document circulated by the Advisory Committee for Multiracial Education in Berkshire. From this document Flew draws the conclusion that anti-racists believe that

> if there are n per cent of blacks and m per cent of browns in the population as a whole, then there have to be n per cent of blacks and m per cent of browns in every profession, class, team, area or what have you,

or, as Ray Honeyford puts it, that anti-racism 'assumes that inequality of outcome proves inequality of opportunity'. Flew then goes on to enjoy himself with the over-representation of blacks in American basketball teams, and Jews among Nobel prizewinners (sometimes, he substitutes string quartets). But the fact is that, on the basis of the Berkshire document, Flew tilts at straw men. What the document actually says (and what Flew actually quotes) is that

> there are certain routine practices, customs and procedures in our society whose consequence is that black people have poorer jobs, health, housing and life-chances than do the white majority ... These practices and customs are maintained by relations and structures of power, and are justified by centuries-old beliefs and attitudes which hold that black people are essentially inferior to white people – biologically, culturally or both.

To draw from that the message that Berkshire is demanding racial parity within assemblages of sports-players, musicians and Nobel laureates – or that the absence of such parity of itself implies racism in their selection procedures – is to go beyond caricature. It just ain't so.

The concept of institutional racism having thus been disposed of, the authors of *Anti-Racism* can go on to explore the implications of racism as a matter of individual personal morality. The first effect is simultaneously to downgrade racism in importance, and if not to justify then at least to show some indulgence towards it. Thus, for Palmer himself, 'racism can only be an object of moral evaluation if considered as a failing', or rather a set of failings (the thing that's wrong with racial victimisation is the victimising not the grounds), and if all whites are inevitably racist, then racism can hardly be considered a failing in the moral sense. Now, for a Christian, we are all victims of original sin, but that doesn't stop clergymen attempting to discourage us from envy, gluttony and sloth. Palmer is softer on sin: having claimed that what is 'irrational' about racial prejudice is the prejudice not its object, he commissions an article from Dennis O'Keeffe which asserts that: 'To prefer one's children ... to marry people of the same race as oneself is an acceptable preference.' Above, Palmer argued that 'no reasonable or decent person could condone racial discrimination or racial victimisation.' But it's OK not to want your daughter to marry one.

A further consequence of the individualisation of racism is, of course, that by detaching it from notions of power or privilege in society, racism ceases to be principally, or even primarily, a white phenomenon: both the editor of the *Sun* and the editor of the *Sunday Telegraph* believe (to quote the latter) that 'The most flagrant and blatant examples of racial discrimination apply to white people.' But the most important consequence of the redefinition, the one that goes to the heart of the anti-racist project, is that it transfers responsibility for a manifest social evil from those who promote it to its victims.

One of the most striking contrasts between Thatcherism Mark I (the pre-Falklands phenomenon) and Mark II has been the relative importance given to economic and social issues and policies. Under Thatcherism Mark I – Friedmanite Thatcherism – almost every political question was, as it were, 'economised', from the decline of education (which would be solved by the 'market place solution' of educational vouchers) to the malaise of the inner cities (which would be cured by 'free enterprise zones'). Even issues like the protection of the environment were translated into questions of 'over-regulation'. But under Thatcherism Mark II the rhetorical process has been almost entirely the reverse. Issues that appeared to be economic or industrial were 'socialised'. The miners' strike became an issue of law and order. The welfare state was no longer just an economic drain (indeed, the Tories went rather quiet about the need to carry on cutting it); the principal problem was that 'welfarism' was *socially* draining and debilitating. And most importantly of all, unemployment ceased to be an economic problem, located in the ministry, the boardroom and the bank, but a social problem, located in the personality and character of the unemployed person. Suddenly – but, like Richard III, with a full set of teeth – the concept of 'unemployability' was born. And this new condition was a consequence of a set of interlocking pathologies which included unstable families, lax education, 'sour' social mores spread by the media and overheated expectations encouraged by political extremists. And while such pathologies could be applied to the young unemployed of all colours (particularly after the too easily conflated events at Orgreave and in Heysel football stadium), they applied most obviously and easily to young blacks.

So, now that institutional racism no longer needs to detain us, Anthony Flew asserts that we can and should 'look for most of the explanation of under-achievement in any under-achieving group'; in the case of West Indians the prevalence of single parent families 'might be sufficient to explain the present scholastic under-achievement of our British Caribbeans'. Similarly, Roy Honeyford is impressed by research which indicates that

> If there is a sufficiently rigorous attempt to control all relevant variables, including IQ, there is little evidence that West Indian children are doing less well than their overt ability would predict.

None the less, Honeyford has written elsewhere (in *Salisbury Review*, as it happens) that 'The roots of black educational failure are, in reality, located in West Indian family structure and values, and the work of misguided radical teachers whose motives are basically political.'

The virtues of the attack on anti-racism for apologists for the Conservative government are clear. On one level, the issue can bring together in a neat package the currently fashionable issues of education, local government, law and order and personal morality; it's possible to throw in a few goodies like the defence of the British Empire (a good half-dozen of the chapters in *Anti-Racism* reiterate that blacks participated in slavery and whites abolished it); but most centrally of all, anti-anti-racism provides a means to transfer responsibility for the most visible and threatening sector of the young unemployed (and thereby responsibility for the problems, including civil unrest, connected in the public mind with that unemployment) away from the state and towards the black community itself, aided and abetted by the sinister forces manipulating it. The irony, of course, is that while they deny the existence of institutional racism, the anti-anti-racists are happy to blame its consequences on the social character of the West Indian family and the uses (or misuses) to which local government and the school system are put.

How should anti-racists – and particularly, anti-racist councillors, borough officers and teachers – respond to this attack? How can they avoid being demoralised by the kind of craven retreat under fire demonstrated by sections of the Labour front bench over the McGoldrick affair? Are there ways in which anti-racist and multicultural education policies should be changed?

First, and despite the achievements of the GLC, there does appear to remain a resistance on the part of some Labour authorities to the idea that their policies can and need to be sold. It is clear that the Brent NUT and the Board of Governors of Ms McGoldrick's school behaved suspiciously to say the least, particularly at the point where they overlapped. And while it is equally clear that a local authority must retain the right to investigate complaints against its employees, it is surely also obvious that Brent's public relations on this issue have not been so much maladroit as non-existent, leaving the press an empty canvas on which to daub lurid pictures of classroom commissars, banned books and green sheep. It takes a rare genius to present multi-cultural education in terms of restriction and censorship, as opposed to being what it is – the opening up of a limited and in some ways dusty and decaying culture to the bright rays of the world, and the press should not be allowed to get away with it any longer.

One of the reasons the press has been able to construct its 'race gulag' fantasies is because debate within and between anti-racists and multi-culturalists is threatened by an atmosphere of paranoia which is understandable (in terms of the barrage of misrepresentation emanating daily from the gutter press) but is nonetheless invidious and self-destructive. Socialists experienced in transforming their personal practice in the realms of gender relations should be able collectively to suppress the essentially Stalinist tactic of accusing of racism those with whom one disagrees on aspects of anti-racist policy.

On this, it is particularly pleasing to be able to cite the case of the much-maligned Institute of Race Relations (dubbed by *Anti-Racism* contributer David Dale as no less than 'Railton Rd's political wing') which has entertained a refreshingly wide variety of views in the columns of its quarterly *Race & Class*, including a piece by Chris Searle in defence of the teaching of standard English as a tool of black and Third World emancipation; and an article in its forthcoming issue, written by George Ghevarughese Joseph, rigorously and wittily dissecting the Eurocentricity of conventional mathematics. No doubt the *Sun* and the *Mail*, if they spot it, will have a field day ('Now Silly Siva Slams "Slanted Sums" '). But the debate on the future of education in our cities – particularly at a time when the government seems determined to wrest it away from locally elected socialists – is too important to fall victim to the laager mentality.

Finally, it is incumbent on anti-racists to demonstrate that institutional racism does indeed exist, not least because such a demonstration will bring the arguments of the anti-anti-racists fluttering down like a house of cards.

This means not only the rehearsing of the history of immigration, the colour bar of the 1950s and early 1960s, the consequent concentration of West Indians, Indians and Pakistanis in the worst houses and the worst jobs, and the efforts (often undertaken by the institutions of local government) to keep them there; it means also the reiterating of the lived experience of being black in the inner city, and the collective victimisation of young blacks by the police. And last but not least, there is the mighty institution of racially motivated immigration control, the institution which enabled and gave permission to so many other organisations to institute those practices which have kept black people artificially concentrated on the lowest rungs of everything, not least by its reaffirmation that the black communities are not secure, are here on sufferance, are constantly under threat from those like the *Salisbury Review*'s John Casey, who speculate in Cambridge colleges how best to remove them.

There is in several of Anthony Flew's articles a little construction, which, as it happens, doesn't appear in *Anti-Racism – An Assault on Education and Value*, but does in pieces for the Centre for Policy Studies and the *Salisbury Review*. In the former case, Flew argues that the object of teaching English to the children of immigrants 'is, or ought to be, as fast as we can so to assimilate our non-white immigrants that they become English or Scots or Welsh who just happen to have skins of a minority colour', and in the CPS pamphlet he leaves it at that. For the readers of *Salisbury Review* however, he goes on to remark that 'Those who want to remain – say – Bangladeshi ought to be planning later, if not sooner, to be returning to Bangladesh.'

Professor Flew may well have erased that last, chilling sentence from his computer's memory. That doesn't mean we should delete it from ours.

Theatre and Fiction

After a decade of ascetic minimalism, the early 1980s saw a significant revival of the spectacular and the celebratory in the theatre, a development which I addressed in a piece on John Osborne ('The Diverse Progeny of Jimmy Porter', *New Society*, 6 January 1983). One of the more obvious examples of this phenomenon was my own adaptation of *Nicholas Nickleby*, the history of which was told in 'Adapting *Nickleby*' (written as a talk, the piece was published in the Spring 1983 number of the *Dickensian*, and also in *The Changing World of Charles Dickens*, edited by Robert Giddings, Vision, 1983). In the same period, I wrote a more general talk on the state of the play and the playwright – 'Public Theatre in a Private Age' – which was published in edited form in the *Times Literary Supplement* (10 September 1982) and completely by the British Theatre Institute (Autumn 1984).

The Diverse Progeny of Jimmy Porter

John Osborne's autobiography, *A Better Class of Person*, begins as follows. It's a good, strong, opening:

> May 8th is the one unforgettable feast in my calendar. My father, Thomas Godfrey Osborne, was born in Newport, Monmouthshire, on May 8th. Had he lived, he would now be the age of the century. The Second World War ended on 8 May 1945, a date which now passes as unremembered as 4 August 1914. On 8 May 1956, my first play to be produced in London, *Look Back in Anger*, had its opening at the Royal Court Theatre. This last particular date seems to have become fixed in the memories of theatrical historians.

I was eight in May 1956, and so I can't judge if Osborne was right in saying (in a 1981 interview) that *Look Back in Anger* was far from being an instant triumph. From reviews quoted in John Russell Taylor's *Anger and After*, it seems to have been about an instant a success as can be expected for a serious play in the post-war English theatre (liked by the *Sunday Times*, loved by the *Observer*, and rubbished by Milton Shulman in the *Standard*). What does seem clear is that it was perceived as a *watershed* with remarkable speed. It's hard to conceive, for instance, of a book called *Widowers' Houses and After*, *The Vortex and After*, or even *The Birthday Party and After*. The matter of the play was discussed by school debating societies, anatomised in leading articles, and worried in the pulpit. Surely no British play of the twentieth century can have so assuredly and rapidly taken its times by the throat.

I appear to have bought my paperback copy of *Look Back in Anger* on or about the year MCMLXII, for 4s 6d. For an additional six shillings, I could have purchased 'another and more durable edition, strongly bound in cloth'; but despite repeated readings, the book has held together remarkably well. And as an additional bonus, there is a selection of Faber paper-covered editions, listed on the inside back and back cover, reminding us of a forgotten world in which *An Invitation to Chess* and *Romping through Mathematics* rubbed shoulders (on the well stocked bookshelf) with eight Lawrence Durrells, six T.S. Eliots, four William Goldings, two William Saroyans, a solitary Samuel Beckett and F.C. Hoppold's *Everyone's Book about the English Church.*

By MCMLXVII, when I bought my copy of *Inadmissable Evidence* (6s 6d), Durrell was down to two titles, and both Golding and Saroyan had disappeared completely, to make way for five Becketts, four Genets and three Osbornes; while chess, mathematics and the English church had been elbowed out by Ann Jellicoe, David Halliwell and George Steiner's *The Death of Tragedy.* And instead of only five plays out of a list of 60-odd titles, the proportion had risen (in only v years) to over a third.

Apart from the fact that I have never written a full-length play for the Royal Court (not, I may say, for want of trying), I suppose I am an average-to-good example of the 'left agitprop troglodytes' who have apparently hijacked the theatre Osborne loved. Nonetheless, I don't think I would now be writing for the theatre had it not been for *Look Back in Anger* (or, had Osborne fallen from the window of his digs in 1954, the play that would have had to be invented in its stead). As Faber's list shows, the play made the theatre a respectable forum, even *the* respectable forum, for a literary person to engage in; and it did so because, with one bold gesture, the play rewrote the agenda of the British stage, placing our own times and our own country firmly at its centre, and making the medium, in Balzac's phrase, the secretary for the age.

The date, 8 May 1956, was the last great U-turn in the British theatre (or perhaps not quite, but of that more later). Certainly, whether Osborne likes it or not (and he probably doesn't), all the subsequent 'waves' of the new British theatre follow the agenda he set. Despite a brief flirtation with new forms (inspired by the new European and American theatre, admitted in a rush after the 1968 abolition of theatre censorship), the new British theatre remained remarkably conservative as to form (as *Look Back in Anger* is), relying either on the tried, trusted and three-acted structures of social realism, or borrowing (as Osborne was subsequently to do) Brechtian or Living Newspaper techniques from the radical theatre of the 1930s. More importantly, the play defined ways of looking at the relationships between the author, the medium and the audience which were new. It also created a type of dissident hero that was to crop up again and again.

Osborne's own political development since the late 1950s – even more so, that of his contemporaries, Kingsley Amis and John Braine – perhaps removes any sense of surprise at the realisation, when re-reading the play, that Jimmy Porter is far from being a revolutionary. He is, by trade, a very small shopkeeper (he runs a sweet stall). When he isn't enjoying himself slumming around with his Welsh working class oppo, Cliff, he's calling the workers 'yobs' for being noisy at the flicks. True, he admires and envies the 'revolutionary fire' he senses in others, but he confesses he cannot share it. 'If the revolution ever comes,' he says, 'I'll be the first to be put up against the wall, with all the other poor old liberals.' When Osborne speaks, in a stage direction, of Porter's, 'rabble-rousing instincts', it begs a question. Rousing he may be, but one suspects that if faced with an actual rabble, all he'd do would be to tell it to shut its face, or sell it a Crunchie.

Further, it's clear that what vision Porter has of the good society (or of good times) is drawn exclusively from the past. There is, for a start, all that Edwardian nostalgia ('pretty tempting', says Porter, 'all home-made cakes and croquet, bright ideas, bright uniforms'), evoked twice in the play by the sound of church bells, one of Osborne's two Chekhovian off-stage sound effects. The other is Porter's jazz trumpet, itself literally an attempt to recapture something lost ('He had his own jazz band once,' his wife Alison tells us, 'that was when he was still a student, before I knew him.')

But trad jazz possesses a wider symbolism, of course, recalling the 1930s, the time Porter harks back to in his famous, wistful 'no good brave causes left' speech, itself interestingly placed, not in the middle of some great, furious peroration, but in the quietest, gentlest and in a way happiest scene of the play.

For Porter, indeed, the 1930s are the bourne from which, and by implication to which, no traveller can return. 'For twelve months,' he says, 'I watched my father dying – when I was ten years old. He'd come back from the war in Spain, you see. And certain God-fearing gentlemen there had made such a mess of him, he didn't have long left to live.' As Alison herself realises, Jimmy Porter was not born before his time, but after it: 'There's no place for people like that any longer – in sex, or politics, or anything – that's why he's so futile.'

Watching old people die happens twice in *Look Back in Anger*: Porter watches his own father dying, and also Hugh's mother (Hugh, the unseen Other-Jimmy, who got out, to bum around the world in search of an undefined 'New Millennium'). Albert Camus' Outsider, too, reacts with pain and confusion to a parent's death. On the surfce, Porter's craggy passion is a million miles removed from Camus' distanced anomie. But, as Osborne puts it, to be as vehement as Porter 'is to be almost non-committal'.

In short, Jimmy Porter is an existential hero, angry but helpless, at odds with the present but faithless in the future, incapable of starting with himself without also ending there. And thus Porter is the Daddy and the Mummy of all the anti-heroes of the 1960s and the 1970s faced with similar demons, from Simon Gray's Butley to Tom Stoppard's George Moore.

But what interests me is the notion that Jimmy Porter also gave birth to the protagonists of many of the much more overtly political, even revolutionary, plays to emerge from the next generation of new British writers, in the 1970s. Susan in David Hare's *Plenty*, Jed in Howard Brenton's *Magnificence*. Fish in Pam Gems's *Dusa, Fish, Stag and Vi*, Gethin Price in Trevor Griffiths's *Comedians*, Howard Barker's Claw, even Edward Bond's Lear: for all of these characters, political change is an existential matter, part of the business of personally feeling right with the wrongness of the world, of setting an individual clock in accordance with out-of-joint time.

It is an irony that the major flowering of radical drama in Britain took place, not in the revolutionary 1960s but in the atomised 1970s when, in the outside world, all that appeared to remain of the political energy of the previous era was an individualised inclination to do it if it felt good: in this sense, Jimmy Porter was the first hero of the Me Decade.

But in another sense, perhaps the most significant of all, Jimmy Porter was nothing of the kind. Throughout Osborne's writing career, reading its climax in *A Sense of Detachment*, he has written about men (largely) and women alienated from their worlds, to an extent unimaginable (for example) in the plays of Shaw. But Osborne's most enduring legacy, it seems to me, has been the extension of that alienation into the realm of his own relationship (and that of his plays) with the audiences to which he and they are performed.

I remember, when discussing the dissatisfying ending of a play of mine with a New York director (the play could have ended, ten minutes before it actually did, on a note of triumph), the look of blank incomprehension on her face when I suggested that quite the best reason for keeping the last couple of scenes was that the preview audiences clearly disliked them so much. It was literally impossible for the American theatrical mind to conceive that the customer might be wrong.

For the last 26 years in England, however, it has been more than possible to believe that it is the proper function of playwrights to 'piss in the audience's eyeballs' (the phrase is Howard Brenton's), and that exercise has defined the higher calling of the craft ever since John Osborne first opened his fly at the Royal Court Theatre on 8 May 1956.

I think it's possible that this is beginning to change, or perhaps has already changed. Over the last couple of years (from, in fact, on or about the 25th anniversary of *Look Back in Anger*), the phrase 'celebratory theatre' has begun to creep into the critical vocabulary. Usually it is applied to large-scale spectaculars, performed at the great institutional theatres, which have sought to comfort rather than to agitate, to confirm rather than to disturb. But celebration is also at the heart of the altogether tougher arena of the new women's theatre and alternative cabaret, where, however distanced they may be from much of the world outside, performers and performees share a common identity and a common project, expressed with an enthusiasm and energy as far removed from the alienated impotence of Jimmy Porter as he himself is from the protagonists of the plays of Noel Coward – or of Bernard Shaw.

Last year, John Osborne commented that it was a mistake to treat *Look Back in Anger* as a period piece. For the first time, now, he might be wrong in that opinion. In many ways, of course, it's a healthy and positive development, that the British theatre now wants to run with the grain of its audience, rather than against it. There *is* something arrogant and elitist (and irredeemably male) about the desire to rub an audience's face in the mire of its own subconscious. But there remains a nagging doubt as to whether being healthy and positive is always a good thing for the theatre: as John Nott so often tells us, the nuclear bomb cannot be uninvented, and, by the same token, *Look Back in Anger* cannot be unwritten, and I think I'm very pleased that is so.

Adapting 'Nickleby'

I have discovered in recent years that there is nothing more snobbish and élitist than the view of even the most liberal thinkers as to the correct and proper hierarchy of art. In the performance sector, the so-called 'interpretative' arts – musicianship, acting – have struggled for years for their status as equal to and complementary with, rather than secondary and inferior to, the 'primary' arts of composition and playwrighting. Even worse is the position of what one might call 'transformation artists', those primary artists whose source material is other primary art. Translators, who transform other people's work from one language to another, are beginning – and not before time – to be viewed as creators in their own right. Adaptors, who transform other people's work from one medium to another, are still viewed as mere technicians, and pretty low-grade mere technicians at that.

When I started adapting books for the stage, I came up against the full force of this prejudice. My work had ceased to be 'original'. It was assumed I was only doing it for the money, or that I was 'marking time' while I developed a 'proper idea'. Maybe I had 'dried up' completely. Or perhaps I hadn't, and would soon return to the fold, and start writing 'real plays' again.

Well, I think all three adaptations I've done are real plays, and should be judged as such. They were very different. One, *Mary Barnes*, was a version of an autobiographical book by two people, a psychiatrist and a schizophrenic woman whom he'd helped through madness in a radical therapeutic community in the 1960s. The second, *The Jail Diary of Albie Sachs*, was also based on an autobiography, that of a white South African lawyer imprisoned for subversion in the early 1960s, but covered a much shorter period of time. The third was *Nicholas Nickleby*.

What all three plays had in common was that they strove to present, in dramatic terms, the relationship between the original work and my perception of it. I did not view my function as being no more than the oil in which the chips fried. Throughout, I wanted to preserve a visible relationship between me, as a writer writing in the late 1970s and early 1980s, and the works I – or, in the case of *Nickleby*, we – had chosen.

From this perspective, it is surely clear that the act of choice itself is the central decision. When Picasso found a bit of an old gas oven in a junkyard, put it on a plinth, signed it, called it 'Venus de Gas', and declared it a piece of sculpture by Picasso, he was making the point that one of the artist's functions is to look out for and reveal those everyday things in the world – whether objects or forms of behaviour – that are usually unnoticed, or taken for granted. The act of choice is in itself an artistic process, and, in Picasso's case, he noticed that a certain bit of rusty metal did indeed look like a kind of classical Venus. In the same way, the adaptor *chooses* to transform a book because he or she feels that that transformation, in itself, will make the statement that a work, which has perhaps grown dusty on forgotten shelves, none the less has something important to say to our times.

Two of the works I've adapted were out of print when I began to work on them, and the third, *Nicholas Nickleby*, had fallen from literary favour. The act of theatrical presentation in the theatre (an event quite specific in time) sought to 'frame' the original work, or, put another way, to perform the function of Picasso's plinth and signature. I decided to adapt *Mary Barnes* because it was a book about people at the centre of the late 1960s counter-culture, and I felt, ten years later, that the time was ripe to look again at the fierce, unique and challenging ideology of that movement. Albie Sachs's *Jail Diary* is a story of the heroism of a left-wing individual, and I adapted it at a time when the left, collectively, was in a mood of pessimism, doubt and, above all, cynicism. And when the RSC asked me to work on its adaptation of *Nicholas Nickleby*, I was happy to do so, because the book presents, in a wonderfully rich and vivid way, the social conflicts of a time, the 1830s, that are in many ways comparable with our own.

This is not to say that most theatrical adaptations are as direct and simple as Picasso's creation of his Venus. All the ones I've done have involved great changes in the original work. In a lot of ways, I find the process of adaptation is very like the normal process of play-making. Most plays – particularly but not exclusively plays on social or public themes – do involve writers in extensive research into the subject in which they're interested. It might be too pat to say that a stage adaptation is an ordinary play researched from a single source, because, obviously, the playwright is considerably more circumscribed, not least by respect for the original author, than he or she would be in choosing a play's incidents and characters from a wide variety of sources. But I think it is true to say that the only difference is that the adaptor is intervening much later than the writer of an original play in the same process of transforming daily life into theatrical art.

The changes one does make in adapting books should, if the adaptation is an honest one, relate all the time to the reason one chose to do it (apart, of course, from the many changes that result from the technical business of telling a story on the stage rather than the page). My adaptations have all been of books written and set in the recent or distant past. When I wrote *Mary Barnes*, I became fascinated by the way, in the late 1960s, that the conventional divisions of human experience were broken down, and, in particular, in the way in which the personal, the political and the spiritual sides of life were made to relate to each other in a way they hadn't related before. Writing ten years on, I needed a metaphor to demonstrate this truth which was, of course, an assumed fact of life at the time when the book was written. So I decided to give each of the three acts – in all of which the schizophrenic Mary Barnes goes through a process of psychic disintegration and reassembly – a specific theme and character. The first act was set within a psychological mode of reality: I was concerned to show the challenge of the so-called 'anti-psychiatry' movement to the conventional relationship of patient and doctor. The second act was constructed round a religious metaphor: Mary Barnes's vision of her suffering as an imitation of Christ's death and resurrection. And the third act, in which Mary began to relate to other people again, was much more social in its flavour: the world outside, in the shape of hippies, Vietnam war protests and so on, intervened in the action for the first time. Of course in reality, and in the book, these three forms of perception mingled together throughout; to isolate them was in part a matter of theatrical clarity, and in part a response to the fact that I had to explain an ideological and historical context as well as describe events.

Similarly, in *The Jail Diary of Albie Sachs*, I was concerned to show that Albie Sachs's imprisonment by the South African authorities took place in 1963, when the present police state in South Africa was in its infancy. Albie Sachs himself, writing shortly afterwards, merely mentioned from time to time the uncertainty of ordinary policemen faced for the first time with their new political role, and the resentment of the uniformed branches of the security forces against the newly prestigious Special Branch. I wanted, writing many years afterwards, to give this much more prominence, and so selected, emphasised and occasionally invented incidents to demonstrate these ironies. Also, I wanted to explore Sachs's internal ambivalence about his own heroism in resisting the authorities in a way that he, obviously, couldn't do in a book about himself. So, again, my selection was made with that in mind, and, again, I found new material, partly from external sources, and partly from my own imagination. The result, I think, was quite clearly a play by a person who was not concerned in the events of his play, about a book by a person who was.

The same problem of writing an adaptation which is in part about the author of the original work came up, again and again, while we were working on *Nicholas Nickleby*.

And as it might have been noticed that throughout I have been saying 'I' about *Mary Barnes* and *Jail Diary* and 'we' about *Nickleby*, I think it is time to give some idea of how the adaptation came to be made. This procedure will also give me the chance to come clean.

During, roughly, the academic year 1978-79, I was in the United States on a fellowship, and I had been in correspondence with Trevor Nunn, artistic director of the RSC, about the possibility of writing a film adaptation of George Eliot's *Felix Holt*. In late October 1979 – I was due to return in November – I received a dramatic transatlantic phone call, from Trevor Nunn, telling me that the RSC had decided to make a version of a Dickens novel, and the choice was already down to two: *Our Mutual Friend* and *Nickleby*. I was asked to think about being the writer, and immediately I phoned my wife, who was in England (it was proving an expensive afternoon), to ask what I should do. The extent of my Dickensian scholarship can be judged from the fact that my first question was 'Is *Nicholas Nickleby* the one with Mrs Gamp in it?', and when we'd established that no, it was the one with Dotheboys Hall, her advice was to say yes if it was *Mutual Friend* and no if it was *Nickleby*. Happily, as things fell out, I departed from the habits of a lifetime and did not follow my wife's advice. I read the novel on the plane on the way home on the Friday, and started work with the company on the Monday, more unprepared for a project than I had ever been before, or ever intend to be again.

The process of work was one with which the company was familiar from its work on the classics and I was familiar from my work with small-scale touring companies. Basically, the company as a whole would research, discuss, experiment, undertake exercises and consider the results. Some kind of collective view of the work and its subject-matter would then emerge, at which point more conventional theatre processes would take over: the writer, in the case of a new play, would write; and the director or directors would direct the actors. But the collective voice would not be silenced even now; the rewriting and rehearsal processes would be influenced by the fact that the company as a whole was pursuing a collective purpose. This, as I say, was a familiar process to most of us; but none of us had ever attempted it on anything like this scale. We began by sitting round in a large, 45-person circle, to talk about the novel, our reaction to it, our memory of other Dickens adaptations – we saw one or two of the movies – and so on. Then we began the exercise work, which was to last four or five weeks before a single part was cast or a single word written.

While preparing this, I was very struck by how many of the ideas that came up in those first weeks ended up as key elements of the adaptation. Indeed, the story of the adaptation *as a text* (as a theatrical production, things are rather different) can be largely told through the exploratory period, and three exercises in particular.

The first was the research project. Pairs of actors were assigned a subject to research and prepare a short submission on; the subjects covered Dickens himself, his life and his times, and various aspects, in particular, of the world of the 1830s. They were all good, but the most useful to me were the projects on social etiquette and manners, which significantly affected the eventual creation of Fanny Squeers, Mrs Nickleby, the Wititterlies and the Kenwigs, of whom more later; an extraordinarily comprehensive report on sports and pastimes – which was immensely helpful for Hawk and his entourage; and a *son et lumière* presentation on the early Victorian theatre, which had not a little influence on the way we portrayed the engagement of a certain young actor with a provincial company of no mean repute. But I think most important of all were the projects on science, technology, the Empire and medicine, because they gave flesh and substance to our growing view that the 1830s were in many ways a mirror of our own times; they were the decade when the great technological revolution that had been brewing for fifty years suddenly flapped its great iron wings and flew. Two years before *Nickleby* was begun, Samuel Morse had built his first telegraph: four years before that, Michael

Faraday discovered electro-magnetism, in the same year as Charles Darwin set off on his voyage of exploration with the *Beagle*. And *Nickleby* was finished only ten years after the first steam locomotive line opened in the United States, between, if this matter is of interest, Baltimore and Ohio. Industrialism, it must have seemed, had taken nature by the throat and commanded it to bend to its will; as, meanwhile, imperialism was opening up the great uncharted continents to exploration and discovery.

But behind the unparalleled sense of excitement and opportunity lay a sense, too, of great if undefined loss. The old certainties – particularly those of the rural English village – were dissolving. Hundreds of thousands were crowding into the cities, where the old rules appeared no longer to apply. True, the outmoded hierarchies and snobberies were swept away by the winds of change; but something else had gone too: the idea of a social hierarchy which not only granted immeasurable rights to the powerful, but imposed obligations on them too. Less than ten years after *Nickleby* was written, two other great nineteenth-century literary figures were to describe what was happening in the following terms:

> The bourgeoisie, wherever it has got the upper hand, has put an end to all feudal, patriarchal, idyllic relations. It has pitilessly torn asunder the motley feudal ties that bound man to his 'natural superiors' and has left remaining no other nexus between man and man than naked self-interest, than callous 'cash payment' ... The bourgeoisie has torn away from the family its sentimental veil, and has reduced the family relation to a mere money relation ... All fixed, fast-frozen relations, with their train of ancient and venerable prejudices and opinions are swept away, all new formed ones become antiquated before they can ossify. All that is solid melts into air, all that is holy is profaned, and man is at last compelled to face, with sober senses, his real conditions of life and his relations with his kind.

When we began, we had only one rule: we were going to adapt the whole of *Nicholas Nickleby*, or, at the very least, we were going to tell the whole story. Anyone who knows the novel will understand that this principle forms itself quickly into a society for the protection of the Kenwigs plot, virtually the only section of the story that could be snipped out in its entirety. But we realized quickly that this plot encapsulated, in comic form, the obsessions of the whole. Mrs Kenwigs, who has married beneath her, is desperately concerned to keep on the right side of her tax-collector uncle, whose promised covenant to her large and growing family is her only guarantee that her children will be kept in the manner – and manners – to which she is determined they will grow accustomed. The point, of course, is that 50 years earlier Mrs Kenwigs would not have married beneath her, and the rules and regulations of family life would see to it that her inheritance would either be on the way or conversely not; but *there would be no doubt in the matter*. As there would be no doubt that Ralph Nickleby would look after his brother's widow and her children, or that Madeline Bray's predicament would be solved, one way or another, in a manner befitting her station. What the research we did on the 1830s demonstrated was that the technological revolution, and the social upheavals that followed from it, had created a world of unfathomable economic opportunity but also one assailed by bottomless social doubt.

The projects revealed something else too. Human beings were making the most incredible discoveries about how to adapt and control their external environment; but their knowledge of their own bodies had hardly progressed beyond the middle ages. Death – nasty, brutish and sudden – lurked behind the spinning jenny and waited in the next carriage of the railway locomotive, mocking humankind's Promethean pretensions. And that reality brings me to the second major exercise we undertook, and to the whole question of Smike.

The second exercise was a simple one. Each actor was sent away to prepare a two-minute presentation, from the book, of an aspect of a character in the novel. Performers were not restricted to age or sex or the part they wanted to play; some viewed it as an unofficial audition, but many others did not (Roger Rees, who ended up playing Nicholas, did his two minutes on Mr Brooker; the actors who were to end up as Ralph and indeed Smike himself presented variations on the Gentleman in Small Clothes). There were eight Smikes, including two actresses, and all of them were full of perception. One actor, for example, spotted the tiny passage in which Smike, who has borrowed a book from Nicholas, attempts to do with it what he has seen Nicholas doing. His failure to make the thing work – Smike was not only illiterate but, one assumed, ignorant even of the principle of what reading was – took the whole of the actor's two minutes, and was breathtaking. Even more significant was another performer who brought his own experience to bear on the almost equally tiny incident in the novel when Smike, having been extensively tutored by Nicholas, performs the part of the apothecary in *Romeo and Juliet*, to Nicholas's Romeo. The actor's two minutes showed Smike in the wings, waiting for his cue, and desperately going through the lines that Nicholas has drummed into him. So obsessed was he, indeed, that he missed the actual cue. It was moving and very funny, and it turned out to be the tip of an inverted pyramid in terms of the construction of the play.

A little later, when we had decided on a two-evening structure for the final work (how we ever thought we could do it in one go is a mystery), Trevor Nunn said that he thought the first part should end with a huge triumphant Crummlesian moment: Nicholas and Smike at a high point, surrounded by their strange new friends, with only the knowledge of Kate's persecution by Sir Mulberry Hawk to undermine the sense of happiness and achievement. I had read that, in the eighteenth century, *Romeo and Juliet* was frequently performed with a happy ending, and I thought that ending a well-known tragedy in uncontrolled mirth would be a cheerful metaphor for Nicholas and Smike's unawareness of the storm clouds that were lowering. Then, when writing the scene in which Nicholas rehearses Smike as the apothecary, I realised that many lines applied to other characters and other situations (Newman Noggs, 'so poor and full of wretchedness', Ralph's gold, 'worst poison to men's souls', and Kate's poverty, but not her will, consenting), and I constructed a double scene in which the London and Portsmouth events weaved in and out of each other. It was then pointed out – I think by Trevor Nunn – that the second half of *Romeo* had other resonances too: particularly, the Capulets' project of marrying Juliet to Paris had distinct echoes in Ralph's use of Kate as a bait for Lord Frederick Verisopht. And so that scene was inter-cut with Ralph's dinner party as well.

But matters did not stop there. I had already decided that one way to make Smike – a character who could easily slide into easy sentiment – work as a part was to develop those aspects of his dialogue which were at least equivalent to the medically observable behaviour of retarded or schizophrenic people. (At the same time, and marvellously, the actor David Threlfall developed the physical characteristics of a twenty-year-old who had suffered profound environmental and nutritional deprivation.) One frequent habit of schizophrenics is to invest particular words and phrases with an immense metaphorical and often punning significance; there is a wonderful passage in R.D. Laing's *The Divided Self* where he makes intelligible a young schizophenic's obsession with the idea that she is called Miss Taylor on the basis of a series of interlocking puns which culminate in her self-definition as a 'tailored maid'. I initially took Smike's obsession with the words 'home' and 'away' (for him, reversed: 'home' was dangerous and nasty, and 'away' was potentially cosy and comfortable), invested them with meaning, reversed them and turned them back again; and the same things happened with Squeers's imposed definition of Smike as an 'outcast, noun substantive'. But then I realised that if echoes of Smike's misery would be of immense significance to him, then memories of his period of greatest contentment would be so too. So the words of the apothecary scene – Smike's greatest triumph – kept reappearing on his lips in part two of the play, and formed the basis of his dying speech, which concluded with the apothecary's opening words 'Who calls? Who calls so loud?'

Genuinely, then, a whole track of the play was based on one actor's perception in a two-minute improvisation. Similarly, the third initial project, which dealt with narrative techniques, was an open sesame for the solution of a number of pressing dramatic problems. The exercises on how the company could collectively represent key passages of the book were most obviously useful in two great descriptive passages in Part Two of the play, which were assembled largely by the directors, with very little textual interference by me. But the revelation that it was possible to use Dickens's narrative in a vast number of ways, and, particularly, that characters could step out from themselves and narrate their own feelings about themselves or other people, in the third person, was a mighty discovery. Specifically, it opened the door to the solution of a problem that was obsessing me, which was how to make the young women in the novel active participants, rather than insipid victims, in the story. At a simple level, we found that by transferring certain key passages about Kate Nickleby from reported speech ('Kate thought', 'Kate felt') to direct speech, we were creating a much gutsier character, and one, furthermore, who was clearly capable of surviving the privations and sufferings to which she is subjected in the story. (Incidentally, this trick of looking at what the women actually do, rather than what they say, helped with Madeline Bray as well. In the novel, she spends the scene of her greatest crisis, when she is about to be married off to the ghastly Arthur Gride, in a dead faint; we woke her up, and she is an active, indeed the most active, participant in the scene where Nicholas and Kate interrupt Arthur Gride's gruesome wedding morning.)

The use of narrative was also important, in a more complex way, in our treatment of Fanny Squeers. All Dickens's petty snobbery, London contempt for the provinces, and, dare I say it, sexism, come out in his own comments on Fanny; but his portrayal of her is imbued with much greater understanding of the desperately limited options open to a plain and not very bright little girl, stuck in the middle of an appalling family on the edge of a bleak Northern moor, and blessed, if that is the word, with an extremely pretty and only friend. No surprise, then, that she resorts to a pathetic and grandiose gentility; and it is evidence of Nicholas Nickleby's lack of sensitivity in the early part of the novel that he treats her with such undisguised contempt. Theatrically we represented this reality by using Dickens's own words about Nicholas's feelings, initially, and then by using Dickens's own long paragraph of attack on Fanny, but put into Nicholas's own mouth, to turn the audience's own attitude from one of contemptuous mirth against Fanny to a kind of sympathy with, or at the very least understanding of, her situation. And by establishing the principle that Nicholas's attitudes to the women who fall for him are revealed by his own third person narrative, we were able to make clear the progression from his boorish dismissal of Fanny, through his ironically detached flirting with Miss Snevellicci, to his passionate declaration that he would know his beloved Madeline Bray 'in ten thousand'.

Much of the ultimate shape of the plays, therefore, was defined during these first three exercises. I should add a fourth, which was a series of long discussions between me, the two directors, and the assistant director, in which we hammered out, in thematic form, the story we wanted to tell, which revolved, in a way we did not quite expect, around the figure of Nicholas Nickleby himself. It is possible to view the character, in the original novel, as a kind of courier, the chap at the front of the bus, who, though of little interest himself, introduces you to the wonderful sights you are passing. Increasingly, we discovered that the novel's title is no accident. Nicholas comes to London an innocent and is rudely thrown up against cynicism, brutality and sham. He discovers that goodness is not a function of status, indeed that more often than not human decency is to be found among the low-castes or outcasts, rather than in the halls of the great; and he and we discover this truth in the most theatrical manner, through the relationships that Nicholas forges, of antagonism or friendship, with moneylenders, rakes, schoolmasters, members of parliament and misers (on the one hand), and bluff and simple corn-dealers, alcoholic clerks, and mentally-retarded simpletons (on the other). For Nicholas, all that is solid has indeed melted into air, all that he thought of as holy has been profaned, and, as Marx and Engels predicted, he is at last compelled to face, with sober senses, his real conditions of life and his relations with his kind.

As I've said, I firmly believe – although somewhat to my retrospective surprise – that the main thematic structure of our *Nickleby* was built in those early sessions, and as someone who is committed to collaborative play-making techniques, it's a pleasant discovery. Even when we moved into the more conventional business of writing the text, designing the set, and rehearsing the shows, however, our initial ideas had to be developed and deepened, and indeed thrust along through the great length of the novel (predictably, much of the exercise work had concentrated on the early part of the book). Most importantly, we had to sort out the great struggle between two radically different types of capitalist – Ralph Nickleby on the one hand, and the benevolent Cheerybles on the other – which forms the arch of the last third of the story.

In a review of the New York production, in the conservative journal *Commentary*, I was berated for deliberately missing the point of *Nicholas Nickleby* by choosing to emphasise the social criticism which I believe lies at the heart of the novel. 'Far from being the result of unjust social arrangements,' the reviewer stated, 'violence in *Nickleby* is a consequence of the original, inborn nature of man, in which aggression forms a constituent instinct.' Indeed, the whole novel 'subverts the notion that nature endows all creatures with innocent and praiseworthy impulses', and, 'For Dickens, the state of nature is not holy but Hobbesian, the war of all against all.' And indeed, citing Burke as well as Hobbes (he might have added Hume), the reviewer goes on to argue that the point of the philanthropic Cheerybles is that, being without a wicked instinct, they are fairy-tale figures, too good to be true; and further that *Nickleby* as a whole was a staging-post en route to the wholesale attack on the original barbarism of man that lies at the centre of *Barnaby Rudge*.

Well, yes, you can see it like that, but I – and we – became much more convinced by the thesis put forward by George Orwell in his incomparable essay on Dickens (a constant script-side companion). As Orwell pointed out, Dickens has been seized upon as a champion by supporters of all ideologies and religions. He has been claimed as a fellow-traveller by Catholics and humanists, by Communists and capitalists, by the most ardent revolutionaries, and – like the *Commentary* reviewer – the most avid supporters of reaction. But, for Orwell, Dickens fits neatly into none of these categories. 'In every page of his work', he writes, 'one can see a consciousness that society is wrong somewhere at the root,' but Dickens provides no specific solutions to the social ills he describes. Indeed, it's possible to extract from his work a message that, at first glance, looks like an enormous platitude: 'If men would behave decently the world would be decent.' Orwell was by no means convinced, however, that this perception is as shallow as it sounds. 'Most revolutionaries,' he goes on,

> are potential Tories, because they imagine that everything can be put right by altering the *shape* of society; once that change is effected, as it sometimes is, they see no need for any other. Dickens has not this kind of mental coarseness. The vagueness of his discontent is a mark of its permanence. What he is out against is not this or that institution, but, as Chesterton put it, 'an expression on the human face'.

For me, what is wrong with the conservative view of Dickens is contained in Orwell's simple sentence, 'If men *would* behave decently the world *would* be decent.' Dickens's vision is *conditional*. Of course he was horrified by the brute instincts of the mob, see *Barnaby Rudge*, see *A Tale of Two Cities*, and see the forces unleashed at the break-up of Dotheboys Hall, which I hope we represented honestly. But Dickens is not just positing his horror at and pessimism about what *is*, he is also expressing not just a hope but a conviction that things *could be* different. Of course the Cheerybles are impossible – they dole out largesse to the needy with a gay abandon which in the real world would drive their business into bankruptcy in an afternoon. But surely Dickens is asking, wouldn't it be good if the Cheerybles could exist, or, to return to the Communist Manifesto, wouldn't it be wonderful if one could retain all the obligations and kindnesses and generosities of rural relationships, and somehow impose them on the exciting, challenging and democratic age that technology was ushering forth? Or, put even more simply, wouldn't it be great if iron capitalism could have a smiling feudal face? The Cheerybles are not there to be scoffed at as fairies, beside the cold reality of Ralph Nickleby. They are – they must be – at least a possibility.

And Dickens provides ample proof that they are. Ralph Nickleby is a classic Hobbesian figure; he knows the world, he knows himself, and at base both of them are about naked self-interest. But, as it turns out, Ralph's judgements about other people and indeed about himself are consistently and grossly wrong. The gull Lord Verisopht, the unctuous Mr Snawley, the besotted Madame Mantalini, the drudge Newman Noggs, and the supposedly self-seeking Nicholas himself, all *in fact* turn out to be considerably nobler, finer and more selfless creatures than Ralph believes them to be. And at the very end, he suffers the frightful realisation that *he himself*, through his love for his niece and his desperate grief at the death of his son, is not the man he thought himself to be, is *better* than he thought himself to be, and the discovery kills him.

I don't think any of us realised fully the importance, for representing the conditional essence of the novel, of a development in the narrative principle which occurred quite early, but didn't reach fullness until we began work on the second play. The directors were strongly of the view that the whole company should be regarded as the story-teller of the whole tale: that they had possession of it, collectively, they all knew how it began, continued and ended, and their joint ownership of it was more important than any individual's part. And the theatrical effect of that, particularly towards the end, was that our 40 actors – who knew how it was to end – were expressing a huge, collective 'wouldn't it be good if' aspiration, as they watched and told the unfolding events. This distancing device, which in Brecht is supposed to clear the mind of emotion, had in our case the effect of directing and deepening the audience's own visceral longing for Ralph's vision of the world to be disproved.

I think it will be clear what I'm saying. I began talking about our *Nicholas Nickleby* as a play about Charles Dickens. Often, in radio adaptations, there is actually a character called Charles Dickens, who reads selected pieces of narrative. We decided really rather early that no one was going to don a frock coat, beard and mustache, and stand at the side of the stage with a big book. Nor was our collective story-teller to be viewed as a 40-strong embodiment of the Great Man. Because what they were was a group of late twentieth-century actors, who sympathised profoundly with what Dickens wrote and his aspirations for society and the human beings within it, but who were telling his story six generations later, and who knew 150 years' worth of things about men and women and their affairs that Charles Dickens did not know.

There was a lot of comment, in the press and elsewhere, about the way we chose to end *Nicholas Nickleby*. What happens is that the concluding chapter – in which we hear how our heroes and heroines enjoyed an absurdly happy ever-after – is represented as a narration by a kind of Christmas family photograph of the central protagonists, surrounded by the rest of the company singing the most Dickensian of carols, 'God rest you merry, gentlemen'. As the carol reaches its climax, however, Nicholas, alone, notices that, outside in the snow, a Dotheboys Hall boy, the boy in fact who took over from Smike as the Squeers's general factotum, is sitting in the bleak darkness. Nicholas leaves the party, goes to the boy, picks him up in his arms, and, watched by his wife and his sister, holds the child out to us, as a reminder that for every Smike you save there are still thousands out there, in the cold. I have on previous occasions justified this departure from the text by pointing to the fact that the novel does indeed end with Nicholas and Kate's children playing round the grave of Smike, and their eyes filling with tears, as 'they spoke low and softly of their poor dead cousin'. But I think that I was probably being dishonest. Orwell points to the unsatisfactory ending of the novels, where all conflicts appear to be resolved by the acquisition of 'a hundred thousand pounds, a quaint old house with plenty of ivy on it, a sweetly womanly wife, a horde of children, and no work', a world where 'everything is safe, soft, peaceful, and, above all, domestic'. Clearly, the conditional operates here *par excellence*: 'Wouldn't it be just marvellous', Dickens is saying, 'if it could be Christmas every day?' But I think we, with our 150 years of experience of things turning into air, are more certain than he was that it can't be Christmas all year round, and more doubtful that decency alone can warm what Marx and Engels call 'the icy water of egotistical calculation'. And, while I believe that Dickens was aware, if only subconsciously, of the impossibility, or at the very least the conditionality, of his ending, of his freezing of his characters' lives into an unending and unchanging state of pure contentment, I think that our ending was not just the conclusion of an adaptation of a Charles Dickens novel, but of a play of which Dickens himself was the subject-matter.

I began by attempting to justify the business of adaptation as a legitimate artistic process. Whatever may be thought of what we did to *Nicholas Nickleby*, I hope I have justified that position at least. I know that the directors of *Nicholas Nickleby* gave real directions, the designers produced real designs, and the actors delivered real performances. I like to think – well, no, actually, I *do* think – that I wrote a real play.

Public Theatre in a Private Age

I want to talk about a generation of British playwrights, indeed my generation of British playwrights, and how I think we view what we're doing now, fifteen or twenty years after we started writing. In doing so I'm aware that any notion of a 'school' of playwrights is deep anathema both to playgoers and to writers themselves. I well remember a discussion among contemporary playwrights in the mid-1970s, set up and tape-recorded by *Gambit* magazine, at the beginning of which the editor, John Calder, attempted to impose one of two forgettable labels on the writers present. All of us, from the most ideologically individualist to the most collectivist, spurned with outrage the suggestion that our work might have developed in concert with anyone else's, or that we might have been influenced by each other, or even that we were aware that each other's work was going on. In fact, however, I think there is a definable movement, even 'school', even if Mr Calder's attempt to impose a definition fell on stony ground.

I spent most of 1979 in the United States, and was struck by the lack of any sense of a community of playwrights in America. There are good new playwrights there, a few sharing our concerns for the social and the political, but they are so isolated from each other, as well as from the processes of theatre making, that they are forced constantly to work within a structure and an aesthetic that has been created by and for others – commercial producers and their stars – a structure and an aesthetic which seems to act not for their work but against it. Practically, this means that American playwrights are not supported, in the main, by directors and actors who have grown up with their work and understand it; still less have they been able to work with companies created to serve their work and new work in general.

Both countries had a baby-boom in the late 1940s, and a university boom in the 1960s, to accommodate the consequent late-teenage boom, but for various reasons – mostly, I think, to do with the lack of mass state subsidy – there did not develop in America either the vast army of actors and designers and directors who started off doing new work in the late 1960s – and in many cases stuck with it – nor were there, or are there, in America many equivalents of those companies set up for, and sometimes by, new writers – there are no Portables or Joint Stocks or Everymans or Warehouses. As a consequence there is no sense of common endeavour, no sense that the problems and challenges raised by one writer's play are answered by another's. And there are certainly very few American playwrights who share those principles and purposes which I think do unite many of my generation of British playwrights, a belief in collaborative production processes, an aspiration to an audience wider than the usual metropolitan coterie, an open attitude to form, a concern with the public world and its relation to the private world, and a commitment to radical social change.

For we – who came into the theatre on or about the date of the abolition of theatre censorship and the beginnings of the great expansion of subsidy of the late 1960s and early 1970s – are playwrights of a particular kind. Unlike, say, Arnold Wesker or Brendan Behan, we've tended to choose subject matter that is at some distance from our own experience; unlike Brecht or John Arden or Edward Bond, we've largely written about our own country in the present day or recent past; and unlike Shaw, we have been dealing with a world which, in our view, is, sadly, not teetering on the edge of a rational order. The barrier between human beings and the just city no longer looks like a diaphanous veil, simply waiting to be rent in twain by the cutting edge of Fabian analysis; but something more akin to an electrified barbed-wire fence or the Berlin Wall.

So, in *Magnificence*, Howard Brenton sought to explain urban terrorism, what was both brave and true, but also desperately wrong with it, and, in *Brassneck*, he and David Hare described how English provincial cities had been carved up by corruption since the war. Hare's own *Plenty* charted Britain's post-war boom and decline through the example of the diplomatic service. And Griffiths's *The Party* tried to make sense of the proto-revolution of 1968, while his *Comedians* did the same job on the relationship between laughter and ideology. And, in Stephen Poliakoff's *Strawberry Fields* and my *Destiny*, two very different writers attempted to analyse the reasons for the rise of neo-fascism in contemporary England.

But what all those plays had in common, apart from their zeal to explain contemporary phenomena – often through plays that started some time ago and eventually arrived at the present day – was that the people who wrote them had come into the theatre at a time when there was a consensus shared between play-makers and their audiences that British society was rotten at the root, and that it was the proper business of the theatre to anatomise its rottenness and point the way to radical change. And, importantly, they came into the theatre also at a time when this view of things appeared to flower in a hundred and one different ways. I lived in the late 1960s and early 1970s in the Yorkshire city of Bradford, which for reasons best known to itself had become a kind of Northern centre for the counter-culture, and which played host to a veritable Kew Gardens of exotic theatrical blooms, both home-grown and imported, during the two immensely successful Bradford Festivals. (So successful were they, by the by, with so many people having such an obviously wonderful time, that the city authorities refused to finance a third, on the grounds that so much unambiguous pleasure had to be bad for you.) Here, performance artists were careering around the city on pink bicycles ridden in Red Arrow formation; there, Howard Brenton's *Scott of the Antarctic* was being performed in the ice-rink, with myself essaying the small but nonetheless significant role of the Almighty; while, somewhere else, Portable Theatre was presenting an early David Hare or Snoo Wilson, Welfare State were enacting a pagan child's naming ceremony –

with real goats – and Albert Hunt's Art College Theatre Group were staging a full-scale mock-up of an American President Election – with live elephant – in the streets of the city. And, somewhere else again, in clubs and pubs, agitprop groups were relating contemporary labour history, and joining, in their own way, the general and universal call for the overthrow of all fixed things.

As the 1970s progressed, however, this fragile unity between street theatre, social realism, agiprop and performance art – or, put another way, between the university and the art college traditions – began to splinter.

I think that the demise of Albert Hunt's art college group – they of the live elephant – was particularly symbolic. Albert's group had always combined the visual, surreal, pop art tradition of performance art with the explanatory energy of agitprop; in one of the group's greatest successes – *John Ford's Cuban Missile Crisis* – a polemic against President Kennedy's brinkmanship was wonderfully contained within the metaphor of a Hollywood Western directed by John Ford. In another, the conservative role of religion was confronted head on by a performance of the Oberammergau passion play in which the leading parts were played by Adolf Hitler, Herman Goering and Josef Goebbels; and in a third, *The Destruction of Dresden*, the climax was a breath-taking, silent sequence in which the performers tore up cardboard boxes for 22 minutes, the precise length of the RAF's raid on the refugee-swollen German city in spring 1945. But, as time went on, the input of this tradition into the work of groups like Portable Theatre drained away, and the art groups themselves (like Welfare State, John Bull's Puncture Repair Kit, the People Show and others) developed their own performance circuits and their own devotees. Further, the agitprop groups – those who saw the proper function of their craft as being, in the words of the early Shaw, 'to induce people to vote on the progressive side at the next county council elections' – became progressively distanced from those who saw the business of play-making in a less measurably utilitarian light; and this split was stretched by the perception that while agitprop continued to be performed in non-theatre environments, on tour and for very little money, a number of radical writers began to see their work done on large, centrally heated stages, in the provinces and in London, and even at the National Theatre itself.

I don't think, however, that these divisions – between those who worked in touring theatre and those who wrote for large conventional states, between those dedicated to agitprop and those committed to realism, between people who refused to sup with the Lucifer of television and those who saw it as purist and elitist to eat anywhere else – had a great deal of effect on the growing *audience* for the new theatre, an audience that was drawn largely from the same, free orange juice generation, and which had all been touched, in some way or another, by the radicalism of the late 1960s, and which was now employed, by and large, in the social or educational sectors of the public service, in political pressure groups or in the media. As I have said elsewhere, the relative – and I must hammer the word 'relative' – failure by socialist theatre to create a new, mass working-class audience tended to mask the fact that a rather different audience *had* been built up, which was large enough to sustain the mushrooming number of touring groups and community theatres, and, to keep shows like *Accidental Death of an Anarchist, Steaming, Trafford Tanzi* and *Woza Albert*, going for long periods in the West End.

What it was not large enough to do – or, more accurately, rich enough to do – was to compose, on its own or with its friends and relations, the audience for new radical work in the great institutional theatres, although it did provide a sufficient foundation of support to justify the risk of presenting the occasional Hare, Brenton, Bond, Gems or Edgar on a main stage at the National or the RSC. But the success of politically radical work on such stages could only be sustained *over time* if there was a general consensus among the mass of the audience that the ideals of egalitarian collectivism were at least *morally* superior to the alternative ideologies on aesthetic offer, that such ideals were if nothing else the *ethical* common sense of the age. And while it was the case in the mid-1970s that the National and RSC audiences saw the witnessing of the expropriation of their class as a smashing way to spend an evening, by the late 1970s and early 1980s this was no longer so. The capture of the commanding heights of the moral economy, first by the individualist right, then by the consensual centre, and finally by the Spirit of Goose Green, changed the attitude of the play-going middle class to the new radical theatre from one of nervous acquiescence to one of impatient rejection.

This did not mean that our great stages were suddenly flooded with right-wing plays: though in *Night and Day*, for the theatre, and *Professional Foul*, for television, Tom Stoppard stacked the cards so grossly against his left-wing villains – a drunken, boorish journalist and an insensitive lecherous sociologist – that, if any of us had tried the same gambit the other way round, we would have been howled off the stage. What happened in general was an altogether more subtle privatisation of concern, which reflected the way in which the political and social obsessions of the 1960s had become personalised and thus rendered harmless in the 1970s, as the 'we' decade turned into the 'me' decade, the Pot Generation matured into the Perrier Generation, and the concern for the future of Planet Earth mutated into an obsession with the state of Planet Body, as the middle classes of Britain and America jogged slowly to the right. So by 1980, the demand was no longer for plays about the masses resisting the disablement of class or racial oppression, but for drama which dealt with individual cripples overcoming literal disabilities. In New York and then in London, the wheelchair, or at the very least the crutch, seemed to become a compulsory theatrical prop; perhaps the paradigm was the unexpected Broadway success of Lanford Wilson's *The Fifth of July*, in which the hero is a homosexual, legless Vietnam War veteran, who achieves personal growth through teaching dumb children to speak. Elsewhere, the maimed protagonist appeared in the *Elephant Man* (the deformed), *Duet for One* (the paralysed), *Children of a Lesser God* (the deaf), and, (I regret to say) in *Nicholas Nickleby* (the retarded).

And, further, for those socialist playwrights who not only wanted, but needed, to contribute to the discourse of the left as a whole – to hold a mirror up to our side as well as the other – there was in these mean times a further painful conundrum. Do we attempt through our work seriously to participate in the debate that is going on on the left after the major reverses it's suffered – a contribution which would inevitably involve a fair amount of dirty political washing, left twisting slowly in the wind? Or do we view our function as socialist artists as being the palm court orchestra on the *Titanic* – providing at least a little cheer and comfort, a bit of confirmation and even celebration of the old ideals – as our comrades call for lifeboats and the waters lap about our heels?

All of what I've said so far is an attempt to define the universe in which my generation of left-wing writers are now trying to write, or, in many cases, not succeeding in doing so. Trevor Griffiths didn't write a stage play between 1976 and 1981. There was a similar gap between David Hare's *Plenty* and *A Map of the World*. Stephen Poliakoff has been concentrating on writing for television, and Barry Keeffe announced that he, too, had ordered his long spoon. While Howard Brenton and Edward Bond continued to write stage-plays, which veered wildly in style from allegory to agitprop and back again, other contemporary playwrights were found fishing in the strange tributary waters of translation and the adaptation of long nineteenth-century novels. In the early 1970s, playwrights viewed the audience as an adversary, and wanted, in Brenton's evocative phrase, 'to piss in their eyeballs', but all that happened was that the public rolled on its back, stuck its legs in the air, and begged for more. Now the audience really was an enemy, and we had to face up to the problem of finding ways of telling them things they almost certainly didn't want to hear.

I want to discuss some of the strategies that political playwrights and playmakers have tried, or are trying, or perhaps ought to try, in the project of explaining public events in a privatised age. Inevitably, such debates begin with the question of whether playwrights should present the surface reality of human behaviour, or what they regard as the essence of the conditions they're describing, whether what the audience is shown is the supposedly objective situation, or the the subjective reaction of the participants to it. Clearly, agitprop or cartoon theatre is on the far edge of the objective end of that spectrum; the subjective factor is more or less eliminated, and the employer is shown as a Victorian archetype oppressing a downtrodden labourer in cloth cap and waistcoat – not because the playmakers are unaware that Arthur Scargill probably dresses better than Ian MacGregor, but because the important message is that essential class relationships have not changed.

In 1977, I gave a long talk at a conference in Cambridge in which I argued that what had happened in the 1970s was a progression from agitprop to a more complex and, I thought, more mature social realism among political playwrights and companies. It was then pointed out that, while that model might be applicable in some cases (notably, cynics remarked, in mine) it certainly didn't apply, for instance, to John McGrath's touring socialist theatre company, 7:84, where the process had been exactly the reverse. And, further, two writers who have never been directly associated with agitprop, Edward Bond and Howard Brenton, appeared to turn to that form in the early 1980s in, respectively, *The Worlds* and *A Short Sharp Shock*.

So it seems that reports of the death of this lively form have been much exaggerated. And it's easy to understand why this is so: agitprop was born in a period when the battle lines seemed clearly drawn, between American imperialism and the movement for national liberation abroad, and between a monolithic corporate capital and a newly vigorous labour movement at home. Now international Reaganism and domestic Thatcherism – and the reverse for that matter – have re-drawn the same thick, black borders across a political map previously muddied by the complexities of a demoralised working-class movement in Britain, and the renewed brutalities of revolutionary regimes overseas. But I must admit that I still share the reservation about agitprop graphically expressed by David Hare at the same Cambridge conference, which was that the form inevitably implied that the author had settled all the major questions of the story before the play had even begun. In that sense, agitprop caricature is a fundamentally elitist device, and its tendency towards a kind of breathless, hectic hyper-energy results, it seems to me, from the awareness that the form denies the writer one of the most potent weapons in the dramatic armoury. It is demonstrable, I think, that the most dynamic moments of most plays occur when the attitudes of the characters, or the audience's attitudes to the characters, undergoes a radical change, what the Greeks called a 'peripeteia'. The first three acts of *King Lear* are all about the growing, ghastly realisation that this appalling old man really is more sinned against than sinning. And it seems to me that that change of attitude cannot and would not work if the dice were so clearly loaded that the truth was really apparent from the word go. Shakespeare is clearly not presenting both sides of the question out of any chimerical sense of balance or objectivity – his own point of view becomes abundantly clear. But it *becomes* clear, rather than being clear from the start, because without the sense that there is some justice in the arguments of Regan, Goneril and Edmund, the awareness of the massive injustice of what they subsequently do would lack not only dramatic power but dramatic credibility. Similarly, those detractors of Brecht who claim that the richness and vitality of Mother Courage are a theatrical error, the artist beating the Marxist by a short head, miss the point that Courage's dreadful mistake of believing that she can live off the war without it living off her would be nothing more than a sad little parable without our visceral sense that the character is strong and alive enough to believe otherwise. In fact, Brecht has written a tragedy rather than a parable, or, to use words he would have preferred, an epic rather than a fable, precisely because he wants us to share his massive emotional investment in a personality whose terrible miscalculations emerge, like alcohol dripping through charcoal, throughout the entire length of his play.

If agitprop reveals the objective at the expense of the subjective, then the form of naturalism does precisely the opposite. Recognisable, surface behaviour is all. As the critic Terry Eagleton put it, naturalism 'merely photographically reproduces the surface phenomena of society'. For John Berger, the form has 'no basis for selection outside the present; its ideal aim would be to produce a replica'. The naturalist writer, as George Steiner remarks, 'looks upon the world as upon a warehouse of whose contents he must make a feverish inventory'. But all three critics would acknowledge that the naturalist project of being no more than a lens is doomed from the start; because the photograph must be cropped somewhere, the stocktaking must begin and end at one point or another, and the object to be replicated must be chosen from the infinity of objects in the world. And what has made the tendentiousness of naturalism much more important than the form's aspiration to neutrality is that naturalism has become the dominant form of the world's dominant dramatic medium, and that thereby the world-view of television soap opera – that life is a continuous, endlessly repeated series of equivalent domestic conflicts and reconciliations, as predictable and unchanging as the cogs and wheels of a clock – mediates and informs the way we observe and judge naturalist endeavours of a much more serious kind.

Let me give one example, which is that of the work of Mike Leigh, who pioneered the technique of devising plays around characters invented by actors. What Leigh does is to discuss with each individual performer a character that he or she would like to create, the actors then go off and develop their character, through research, observation and improvisation, and only when the characters have been fully developed in the minds of the individual performers does Leigh bring them together, and place them in situations of conflict with one another. What this technique produces is work of extraordinary, naturalistic perception; but what it also appears to produce is an attitude to the characters of little more than rank contempt. Leigh has tended to concentrate on the subject-matter of working-class and lower-middle-class life, and it is the Catch 22 of naturalism that, being only interested in what can be seen or heard, it is bound to imply that a poor environment reveals a poverty of spirit, and a limited vocabulary a pettiness of mind. But even the articulate suffer from Leigh's method, because by constructing his characters independently of each other, he denies them the possibility that their personalities might have been shaped through interaction with others. A recent Leigh television film, *Home Sweet Home*, concerned three postmen, the drabness of whose situation was matched by the wretchedness of their response to it. At the end of the film, the most interesting postman is confronted by a social worker who proceeds to spew out a seemingly endless stream of sub-Marxist consciousness, to the postman's evident perplexity, embarrassment and annoyance. Now, I don't know many postmen, in their home environment at least, but I do know more leftist social workers than I care to think about, and I know that the actor's observation of how they talk was remarkably acute in every respect except the one for which he himself was not responsible; which was, of course, the situation Mike Leigh put him in. The model for the social worker probably did talk just like that, in the pub or at home or wherever, but I cannot believe he would have done so in the first, or I suspect any subsequent, meeting with a client, and thus a perceptive piece of observation turned into a contemptuous caricature.

And I don't think it's a coincidence that super-subjective naturalism ends up at the same point as super-objective agitprop. Mike Leigh's technique reflects the world-view of his chosen form, which is that the human personality is as it is wherever it is, that some mothers will always 'ave 'em, that there's one in every family, and that J.R. would be J.R. whether drilling for oil or digging for turnips. And there is an equally iron determinism in the idea that human beings are inevitably locked into the cogs and wheels of historical necessity. And both end up with caricature and contempt, because both are elitist views of human beings, and neither of them are true.

The Italian philosopher Benedetto Croce made a famous distinction between history and chronicle. The historian attempts to penetrate the core of events by entering into history and reliving in his own mind the experiences of the past; the chronicler treats his materials as inert and empty of determinate content. In the world of letters, clearly, the chronicler is a naturalist and the historian a social-realist, one who, again in Terry Eagleton's words, 'penetrates through the accidental phenomena of social life to disclose the essences or essentials of a condition, selecting and combining them into a total form and fleshing them out in concrete experience'. Both parts of that equation are important: the essences must be disclosed, but the form of their disclosure must be concrete and recognisable. Social realism is obviously a synthesis – dare I say it, even a dialectical one – of the surface perception of naturalism and the social analysis that underlies agitprop plays. To explain, it is first necessary to be recognisable, and only then, having won the audience's trust, to place those recognisable phenomena within the context of a perceived political truth. It is indeed in this combination of recognition with perception that the political power of theatre lies.

Let me give an example from my own work. Now, it is possible, indeed I have done so, to write in a scholarly journal a cogent and comprehensive analysis of those social classes and segments of classes that tend to support fascist movements. You can do a punchier version of the same thing in a newspaper. What you *can't* do in a journal or a newspaper or a book is to show what goes on in the minds and souls of individual members of those groups as, in times of crisis and despair, they slip over into barbarism. In my play *Destiny* I had a scene where a group of people met together to form a branch of a neo-fascist party. On the page, the scene probably looked rather mechanical – the characters were selected very carefully to be representative of the various different groups and interests, and at the end of the scene a leader of the party made a speech in which he cleverly brought together all of the disparate and indeed contradictory interests and fears of his audience, weaving them neatly into the classic Nazi conspiracy theory of history. On the page, as I say, I'm sure the scene looked as if it had been written from a chart, which, as it happens, was the case. But on the stage, I think what happened was that the recognisability of the characters in that situation – the draughty hall, the empty seats, the howling microphone, the echoing silences and bowel-shrivelling crossed purposes – gave flesh and substance to my analysis of their actual and subsequent behaviour, and the hopes and fears of the real people portrayed combined with the hopes and fears of the real people watching to create a genuinely mutual understanding of why they came and why they stayed, which it is the unique capacity of the theatre to create.

Similarly, when I was thinking about my more recent play, *Maydays*, I was concerned that a left-wing theatre should address itself to the yawning gap between the world as we'd like it to be, in the heat of the night, and the one we actually confront in the cold light of dawn. In the play, I wanted to look at how the much publicised shift to the right looks from the insides of the skulls of people in mid-flight (or, in the case of Alliance supporters, mid-leap-frog). And, as in *Destiny*, I wanted to show my defectors as recognisable people with recognisable concerns, and, perhaps unlike *Destiny*, concerns that would directly touch the type of audience which attends the Barbican Theatre. But, again, I didn't want the play merely to be a series of psychological case studies – I wanted to set three generations of defectors within an analysis of the 25 years of history covered by the play. So what I hoped would happen was that the audience would recognise the characters from the inside, but be able, simultaneously, like a sudden film-cut from close-up to wide-angle, to look at how these individual journeys were defined by the collective journey of an epoch.

In other words, I suppose I think that, buffeted and battered through the old hulk may be, there is life in a social realism yet. Indeed, perhaps it is the only current form of political theatre that appears to be able to survive a period in which political ideas in the theatre are so deeply resented. Critics are by and large rotten theorists of the art they review, but they do have a kind of primitive, instinctual horse-sense about what audiences are thinking, and the hammering they rained down in the early 1980s on the heads of Howard Brenton, Howard Barker and Edward Bond demonstrates, I think, that powerful metaphor alone cannot give credibility to unpopular ideas. Take, for example, Robert Cushman, reviewing Barker's *The Love of a Good Man* in the *Observer* in January 1980:

> As it happens, I share the growing dislike for the kind of play which *The Love of a Good Man* has generally been taken to be, the kind in which a playwright presents a received view of a Britain which he bothers less and less to check against the facts and which is dressed up in some suspect metaphor, bound to be described by someone as 'a powerful image'.

And listen, too, to John Elsom, discussing the theatrical output of the same year in the *Listener*.

> What I have most missed, with a few notable exceptions, among the new plays this year has been the kind of broadly well-informed outlooks, an urban sophistication, which can come from reading more than one newspaper and from appreciating, if not agreeing with, more than one point of view ... I am not looking for a view which tallies with my own, but for one which makes an effort to understand, or contribute to an understanding, of the world in which we live. Too often, I have sat in the theatre and simply felt that the audience was more sophisticated than the play which they were watching, and, for simple technical reasons, when a dramatist fails to add to the general stock of knowledge about his theme, he loses control of his audience and hence the play suffers.

The message we should take from both these critics is, obviously, that sensible playwrights would be best advised to lower their heads, avoid overall metaphors like the plague, and hope against hope that the rigour and detail of their observation will justify the construct they put on the phenomena they describe. Let us, in short, anatomise Reagan, see what breeds about his heart, but do so only on the basis of sound factual research. And as I personally do a lot of research, and I don't use overall metaphors very much, and indeed am about as unreconstructed a social realist as you are likely to find outside Paris in the nineteenth century, with any luck I'll continue doing quite nicely.

And yet. And yet. If I think back over my last ten or so years of playgoing, the things I remember are the moments when, suddenly, the iron discipline of social realism cracked apart, the muscles relaxed, and some great blooming metaphor twisted up like a flower out of the shell. I think of Howard Brenton's playpen of screwed-up newspaper in *Christie in Love*, the moment when David Hare's tatty Blackpool motel room split apart at the end of *Plenty* to reveal the vasty fields of France at the moment of liberation, and, pre-eminently, the extraordinary performance of Gethin Price at the end of the second act of Trevor Griffiths' *Comedians*. But behind the pleasure I feel at those memories is a rather different feeling, which can only be described as a gnawing sense of loss.

I think it will be clear where I'm heading. Somewhere between the streets of Bradford and the stages of the National Theatre on the one hand, and the working men's clubs of Liverpool on the other, a connection was broken, and that connection was with the kind of imagery which is an assumed fact of theatrical life in most of the other countries in Europe, but which in this country has seemed to be confined to those visual artists who have chosen to make their statements through the theatre. All the images I described a moment ago are, of course, pure performance art. They are the type of things you could have seen regularly in the work of the Welfare State, the People Show and the Pip Simmonds Theatre Group. They were once regularly seen in the work of Portable playwrights too, and I think they should be again.

And indeed there are signs that this has been

happening. We know that performance art is undergoing a major revival – Rational Theatre, Hesitate and Demonstrate, and so on. But what seems to me most important is the way that, hand in hand with alternative cabaret, performance art has influenced the new feminist theatre (and indeed vice versa) to create a style of presentation of radical ideas which owes little to the increasingly arid forms of cartoon agitprop, but is by contrast wacky and individual and lively and provides at least the basis, perhaps, at last, for a synthesis between the literary, cerebral, intellectually rigorous but visually dry work of the university-educated political playwrights of the 1960s and 1970s, and the visually stunning but intellectually thin experiments of the performance artists in and from the arts schools.

In listing – maudlinly no doubt – the many manifold problems that beset us, I mentioned the two seemingly contradictory roles that theatre might play within the drive to revitalise those egalitarian and collectivist ideals to which many of us remain committed. In *Maydays*, I chose – it could be said, and then some – to emphasise the contradictions within and challenges to, rather than the celebration of, the socialist ideal. However, as the play neared the end of what was universally agreed to be its enormous, if not inordinate, length, I kept being pulled towards some kind of confirmation, I kept feeling that surely this time I had won my spurs sufficiently to make the unambiguous, untrammelled confirmation of what I believe which has always seemed arch and forced in the past. And that is the reason for the last scene of the play, and indeed the reason, too, why it doesn't beat about the bush, but sits itself firmly down on our side of the Greenham Common wire.

I'm not sure, in the end, if I or we pulled it off. What I do know is that, faced with the empty, meretricious and indeed literally inhuman spectacles now occupying so many of our stages, those of us who have spent so long creating and defending an alternative content have at last to set about forging an alternative form.

By the Left

Having had a considerable sense of making our own history, those of us who were young, active and red in the late 1960s are more than usually aware that we would not subsequently make it as we pleased; that the traditions of that time would continue to weigh upon us. For some, like the small terrorist groups who constructed a deathly cocktail of old left means and New Left ends, the residue of the late 1960s did become a kind of nightmare, as I pointed out in a piece on Patty Hearst's book *Every Secret Thing* (*Marxism Today*, May 1982). That there were better lessons to be learnt from the 1960s was argued (in the specific) in 'Why Live Aid Came Alive' (*Marxism Today*, September 1985, later extracted in the *Guardian*) and more generally in 'Never Too Old' (*New Socialist*, May 1986), which features what I believe to be the longest single sentence ever printed in a British democratic socialist periodical.

The industrial rebellion of the early 1970s is not generally related to the cultural politics of the late 1960s. By contrast, almost everyone would agree that the 1984-85 miners' strike was characterised by a vital if unofficial alliance between the miners and the new cultural movements of the cities, a matter touched upon in my review of a selection from the strike's voluminous literature ('Strike While the Iron is Hot', *New Statesman*, 16 January 1987). And in addition to everything else it raised, the strike by its very nature forced both participants and supporters to define and challenge the relationship between political and personal morality. In the aftermath of the 1987 election, it became clear that moral issues were going to dominate much of the rhetoric of the Third Term. Since (though not I suspect because of) the publication of 'The Morals Dilemma' (*Marxism Today*, October 1987) this debate has become even more vital and acute on both the left and the right.

New Left Mutations

Shortly after the kidnap of Patty Hearst, on 4 February 1974, her captors issued a tape-recorded communiqué, partly spoken by Patty herself, and partly by one 'General Field Marshal Cinque', who declared that 'The Western Region Adult Unit' of the 'United Federated Forces of the Symbionese Liberation Army' had arrested the nineteen-year-old heiress as a prisoner of war.

For those who followed such things, the existence of the SLA was not news: already there had been communiqués issued, describing the SLA as 'a United and Federated grouping of members of different races and peoples and socialist political parties of the oppressed people of the Fascist and United States of America', or as 'A United Front and Federated coalition of members from the Asian, Black, Brown, Indian, White, Woman, Grey and Gay Liberation Movements'. Shortly after the SLA's first 'combat operation', the assassination of a black schools superintendant in Oakland, the SLA's 'Western Region Youth Unit' (as opposed presumably, to the 'adult' one) claimed responsibility, and when Patty Hearst herself announced that she had voluntarily joined the SLA's forces, it was to the 'information-intelligence unit' that she was attached. And, a few weeks later, when six SLA members perished in a bloody shoot-out with the Los Angeles police, it was announced tht 'the Malcolm X Combat Unit of the Symbionese Liberation Army proudly takes up the banner of the New World Liberation Front'.

It was, of course, all nonsense. The Malcolm X Combat Unit by that stage consisted of two people, plus Patty Hearst herself. The SLA, *in toto*, at its highest point of active membership, comprised one black man, two white men, and five white women. This *was* the Federated Front and all its units; the Youth Unit matured into the Adult Unit in less than two months. Patricia Hearst's book about her experiences (written 'with Alvin Moscow') is not very illuminating on the key question of whether her participation in the SLA's activities (including two armed robberies) was genuinely voluntary; she states that, having been kept blindfold and physically abused in a darkened closet for 57 days, she was offered the choice of walking out free or joining the 'army', and, not believing the first offer to be genuine, took up the second for her own preservation. What is highly interesting is the picture which she and her ghost writer paint of the SLA itself: the personal and moral squalor of its relationships, the unbelievable grandiosity of its aspirations (and the poverty of its real ideas), the obsession with weaponry, and the 'symbiotic' dependence of both the men and the women on a rigidly patriarchal hierarchy of 'command'.

It would be possible, of course, to shrug off the activities of the Symbionese Liberation Army, particularly as seen through the eyes of the heiress to a vast newspaper fortune. The revolutionary left has always picked up its fair share of fantasists and psychopaths, and to see the SLA as bearing relevance to the American New Left in general would be as unfair as judging all black African states by the regime of Idi Amin.

But in fact the SLA was not alone, and if its activities were farcical, then it echoed (in the manner of the old saw) the tragedy of the American New Left as a whole. In early 1968, Students for a Democratic Society, the organisational focus of much of the anti-imperialist movement, had been strong and united enough to force the effective resignation of President Lyndon Johnson. Eighteen months later, SDS lay in pieces, splintered and shattered by a factional in-fight that led to the emergence, on the one hand, of a workerist, Maoist sect; and, on the other, of a small, underground urban guerrilla force called Weatherman.

And the point about Weatherman (or the 'Weather Underground' as it later renamed itself, in response to charges of sexism) was that its members had not been peripheral or marginal to the mass movement: they were among the best and the brightest of those who had led the Civil Rights movement and the campaign against the Vietnam War. And although their political writings were, in terms of the sophistication of their language, obviously way above the grandiose meanderings of the SLA, the two groups shared the belief that the racial minorities of the United States could, if necessary by themselves, undertake a successful revolution against four-fifths of the American population (including a stupified and bought-off white working class) and that the way to herald this revolution was to indulge in individual acts of terror, the nastier the better. Leading Weatherperson Bernadine Dohrn, for example, responded to the Charles Manson murders by commenting: 'Dig it, first they killed those pigs, then they ate dinner in the same room as them, then they even shoved a fork into a victim's stomach. Wild!' And, as Nigel Young pointed out in his book *An Infantile Disorder?*, the Weather Underground, like the SLA four years later,

> created an irrational caricature of the relationships in the larger society; insensitive to the needs of individuals, riven by aggressive rivalry, dominated by hierarchies that used threats and coercion to maintain themselves.

How could it have gone so desperately wrong? SDS had emerged to national attention, in the early 1960s, with a manifesto (the Port Huron Statement) which anticipated many of the concerns of the early 1980s; rejecting the rigidity of the centralised, vanguard party, and the determinism of the economic base, it posited a politics which started from the personal, and which emphasised the vital importance of culture (particularly, the sterility of the mass consumption society) in stunting the real potentialities of the mass of the people. Further, the New Left did not share the old left's hostility towards the individual, moral impulse in politics: it believed firmly that the outcome of the revolution was present in the means of its making. Perhaps such an open, innocent statement could only have been made in America, where the McCarthy witch-hunts have effectively wiped the left slate clean, and left a generation for whom everything was fresh and yet-to-be-discovered. Certainly, the generosity and libertarianism of Port Huron allowed SDS to play an active and leading role in both the Civil Rights and anti-war movements; it allowed radicals and revolutionaries sufficient space to take on board the concerns and life-style of the growing youth counter-culture.

But, ultimately, the New Left was not new enough. Its opponents joked that what was left about it wasn't new, and what was new about it wasn't left, and while the latter statement was fallacious, the former was at least half true. Woven into the fabric, invisible within the brightness of its coat of many colours, older strands remained. And when the full force of the state was hammered down on to the heads of the anti-war and black liberation movements – particularly after Richard Nixon's election – the old organisational imperatives of Leninism combined with the New Left's own hidden determinism and elitism to create a network of tiny, conspiratorial vanguards, of a tightness and zeal that might have frightened the Bolsheviks themselves.

For, if the concept that all human activity flows smoothly from relations at the economic base was determinist, how much more so was the idea that the entire white working class had been bought off, sucked in and swallowed up by corporate control of the means of consumption? If the old left was elitist in believing that it alone could penetrate the con-trick of capitalism, and lead the masses to self-consciousness, how much more elitist had a revolutionary to be, when that con-trick had not only militarised the labour process and corrupted the polity, but had also polluted the most intimate areas of social and personal life? And when, moreover, the particular masses to be mobilised were either economically and geographically disparate, or, even more crucially, *in the minority?*

In other words, the appliction of materialist models of ideology and organisation to a politics based in personal life led the New Left in the late 1960s into a maze of political contradictions, and some philosophical ones as well. If R.D. Laing and other existentialist psychiatrists had trouble in defining the nature of the 'true', individual personality (before it had been corrupted and twisted by the family), then the New Left had even greater problems in locating the 'real' collective personality, underneath all the grime and dirt of the consumer spectacle. 'False consciousness' was an altogether too feeble description of the condition of the masses in the age of the electric toothbrush and the vaginal deodorant; only the most rigorous shock-tactics, the most extreme psychic destruction and reassembly, could unlock the 'true' but hidden revolutionary impulse underneath.

Again, directly to relate the transformation of Patty Hearst – locked in a closet, bombarded with noise, denied all outside contact, sexually abused – with the political re-creation of the Weather Underground would be a gross and unfair analogy. But her description (confirmed by others) of the daily life of the *rest* of the SLA – the constant harangues from the 'leader', the refusal of any modicum of privacy, the perpetual 'military training', the corrosive fury of all personal relations – does compare with what went on in the closed Weather communities in the summer of 1969, as the ex-student radicals attempted to purge the white pig within themselves, in order to emerge as pure and gleaming tools of the revolution; a honing down that was – and could only be – effected by the constant, collective use of the very moral strength, and sense of individual anger at injustice, that had brought them into a new kind of politics all those years before.

The way that the spirit of the early New Left mutated into a crazy world of fantasy and terror – with, it should be said, all possible help from the repressive forces of the state itself – is a cautionary tale. It is not an argument against libertarianism, as such, but it does undermine the idea that the laws which apply to traditional revolutionary organisations somehow cease to operate when the agency of change is no longer confined to the industrial working class. Before her ordeal, Patty Hearst was a mild radical, typical of her generation. Now she describes herself as a conservative (and an anti-feminist conservative to boot). Both her class origins and her terrible experiences make her totally exceptional. But how many of the millions of Vietnam-generation Americans who voted for Ronald Reagan had, after an initial enthusiasm for radical or even revolutionary politics, been excluded and finally repelled by what the New Left eventually became?

When the SLA – or, strictly speaking, its information-intelligence unit – first removed its captive's blindfold, a strange little conversation took place. Seeing only eight people, Patty Hearst asked, not unreasonably, where all the other units were. The General Field-Marshal burst out laughing. 'What other units?' he asked her. 'This is all there is, baby. We're the whole army. You're looking at it.' The sad truth is that, in all probability, that's just the way they wanted it to be.

Why Live Aid Came Alive

The Live Aid concert gave a number of fabulously rich people the opportunity (at the cost of a few hours of their time) to parade their compassion in front of one of the largest television audiences in history. Among them were a number of performers known for their highly dubious opinions – including both the stars whose reactionary remarks led to the formation of Rock against Racism. Top of the American bill was a former protester now turned born-again Christian, and the British line-up was headed by a former Beatle last in the news for tearing up a striking teacher's leaflet. The organiser of the event – whose stage act used to include the projection of pornographic films – owns properties in Chelsea and Kent, and has been nominated for a prize founded by an arms manufacturer and given in the past to Henry Kissinger and Menacham Begin. Not surprisingly, the event was almost totally lacking in any political content, and indeed began with the showing of a specially recorded video in which two multimillionaires announced that 'the time is right for dancing in the streets' (try telling *that* to the starving of Ethiopia!) And the jamboree ended (in Britain) with the communal singing of the ethnocentric 'Do They Know it's Christmas' and (in America) with the presumptuous 'We are the World'.

Much of the above is true. So why didn't it feel like that? Why did it feel that despite the tarnished reputations of Bowie, Clapton, McCartney, Dylan *et al.*, for once they were on the right side? Why indeed, amid all the undoubtedly blatant commercialism, and undubitably mawkish sentimentality, was it impossible to prevent the odd tear creeping into the corner of at least one eye?

Clear Rules and Bad Examples

Before answering that question it's useful, I think, to pose another, which is why the reaction *of the right* to Live Aid was so embarrassed and half-hearted. And the answer to *that*, I think, is that by its very existence, let alone its triumphant success, Live Aid gashed a great gaping hole in the contemporary Conservative portrait of the modern malaise.

Since the riots of 1981, the Conservative leadership has regarded the state of the nation's youth as a matter of particular concern. Initially, this took the form of Cabinet committees solemnly considering how children could be taught to manage their pocket money; then Mrs Thatcher and her Ministers began to complain (in the context of the riots and with increasing frequency) that children were no longer given the clear rules they need and indeed want, and without which they cannot learn the ancient and necessary virtues of discipline and self-restraint. Increasingly, such notions were associated with the baleful effects of the welfare state – which was supposed to foster in the young (along with the insidious propaganda of left-wing teachers and social workers) the idea that their every appetite was an entitlement, and that they bore no personal responsibility for the amelioration of their condition.

Further, the argument ran, the decline of religious, social and familial sanctions – and the promotion of 'morally relative' and 'permissive' ideas in the educational and communications media – led to a situation in which any denial of gratification was viewed as a legitimate excuse for violence. And finally, this condition was blamed on (and also, by a subtle sleight of hand, extended to) those adult groupings who were held at one and the same time to be setting children a bad example (Sir Keith Joseph's constant refrain to the teachers) and to be themselves in the position of greedy children, unable to restrain their clamorous demands on the paternal state. As Mrs Thatcher remarked in April, of humanity in general and the British populace in particular, 'You don't get the best out of them, unless you are really rather firm.'[1]

Heysel Stadium

This model was reiterated with considerable force – if not
positive glee – in the immediate aftermath of the tragedy
of the Heysel stadium in Brussels. In the *Spectator*, Richard
West wrote that

> the collapse of teaching and discipline in our schools, thanks
> largely to Shirley Williams, is nowhere more evident than in
> Liverpool ... [where] a whole generation of pampered,
> undisciplined children has grown up with the habit of
> petulance, envy, greed and wanton cruelty – as seen last week
> on the television screens of the world.[2]

In the same publication, Auberon Waugh identified the
hooligans as 'our wonderful, overpaid "workers" on a
spree'[3], and in the *Sunday Telegraph* demanded that from
now on the 'Calibans' be kept 'locked up in their caves'.[4] In
the *Guardian*, Mary Whitehouse pointed the finger of
blame at 'the soft-centred, self-interested, liberal-humanist
sentiment which has beguiled our universities, schools and
indeed churches' and which now 'has demanded a terrible
price in human delusion and consequent suffering'.[5] In
the *Daily Mail*, Anthony Burgess asked 'What has gone
wrong with the lower orders?',[6] a question answered by
Lynda Lee Potter, who defined the message of the
'gratification society' as follows:

> If you're lazy, go on social security; if you lust after children,
> rent an obscene video; if you're depressed swallow valium ...
> if a fellow worker dares to defy you, chuck a load of concrete
> at him; if you don't like the look of a rival football supporter,
> kill him.[7]

For Brian Walden (in the *Evening Standard*), Heysel
showed that 'if the working classes in our cities ... are not
restrained by Christian morality, then they are not
restrained at all',[8] while for George Gale (in the *Express*),

'we have positively and enthusiastically endorsed indiscipline' in a period when 'permissiveness has been the motto of the age'.[9]

But it was the *Daily Telegraph* that presented the model in its starkest form. Attesting that 'in matters of public behaviour great improvement occurred between the middle of the last century and the middle of this one', the paper's leader-writers went on to argue that 'the post-1945 settlement embodied a reversal' of this trend: 'It became fashionable among the middle classes to sneer at family, respectability and middle-class values, premarital chastity, social disciplines, neatness and thrift.' As a consequence,

> they should not have been surprised when what the Victorian middle classes called 'the lower orders', but to whom they had a sense of responsibility, took those who set intellectual and political fashions in this country at their word ... They failed to understand that ordinary people need simple rules to live by, and that without a framework of social discipline they can very easily become brutalised.[10]

Less than two months after that was written, there was another international event, also involving large numbers of young people, assembled in (on this occasion) two sports stadia. Despite Anthony Burgess's dire warnings about the inevitably atavistic nature of mobs, this gathering was completely, one might almost say eponymously peaceful. Indeed, it was engaged in what is (for the right) the most laudable of purposes – voluntary charitable endeavour. As was pointed out by a left-wing critic of Live Aid (Mark Lewis, in the *Guardian*), the event could well be compared with those Victorian philanthropic activities 'so vigorously encouraged by both Thatcher and Reagan', even if the nineteenth-century do-gooder donated his own wealth, and often chose to do so anonymously.[11] And although Mrs Thatcher's sterner economic gurus might in fact have a bit of trouble with the general concept of overseas aid, even if donated from private sources, surely it was better for 70,000 young persons to be throwing teddy bears at each other rather than beer cans, singing and swaying rather than slinging and slaying?

The New Right and Rock 'n' Roll

So why in the event was the response so incredibly muted? Why did the columnists and leader-writers not queue up behind the *Times*'s Richard Williams to proclaim that 'the Wembley leg of Saturday's extraordinary Live Aid concert felt like the healing of our own nation', proving that, despite Heysel, 'young people could gather peacefully in large numbers, drawn as much by a "good cause" as by the chance to worship the gods of popular entertainment'?[12] Indeed, apart from Williams and (initially) two put-downs in the *Guardian*, there was hardly a murmur in the feature pages at all, and while every serious daily ran a leader on Heysel, only one (the *Daily Telegraph*, commented on Live Aid, which was described as 'wholly admirable in its intent', but only in contrast with the pop industry's more usual 'venality, greed and corruption'.[13]

The reason for both the reticence and the carping appears at first to be a matter of taste. As the anti-libertarian writer Mary Kenny wrote in the *Sunday Telegraph*, 'it seems churlish indeed to utter objections to the very charitable accomplishment of Bob Geldof', but, churlish or no, it was none the less 'a pity that so much of the rock music sound is so horrible'.[14] Similarly, though in reverse, Auberon Waugh was forced to acknowledge that

> This is not the occasion to sneer at the horrible, boring noises these people made or shudder at their dreadful appearance. If a single African life is saved by all this caterwauling, it is obviously a good thing.[15]

But this objection to Live Aid goes way beyond the formal. Anyone reading the social authoritarian right in the post-riot era will have been struck by the importance of rock music in its demonology.

It's not just that Mary Kenny doesn't *like* rock music; she is clearly highly *concerned* that 'this noisy, tuneless, rather barbaric performance is the culture that enfolds our children'.[16] And in his post-Heysel *Express* piece, George Gale made it pellucidly clear why the new right is inherently and implacably hostile to sex, drugs *and* rock and roll: adjuring those who think that 'violence is confined to political extremists' to

> listen to the pop 'music' that is thrust into the eager ears of our children and grandchildren ... Minds indeed become mindless when stuffed with the trash poured out by the pop industry every day, without restraint, without control, without decency, without discipline'.[17]

The Spectre of the 1960s

Such lacunae have been listed in such a context by other commentators too. In 1983, Colin Welch wrote in the *Spectator* of a world from which certain virtues are completely missing, those virtues including 'all fidelity, restraint, thrift, sobriety, taste and discipline',[18] a world evoked, as he saw it, by the work of the Beatles. And like Gale, Welch is sure that it was not just the Beatles, but the era in which they flowered, which was at desperate fault:

> To define the world of the 1960s is to adumbrate the damage it did and is still doing. It was a world in which hallowed connections were severed or weakened: between crime or naughtiness and punishment; between effort, skill, accomplishment and reward. It was a world in which all the laws which make civilisation possible were damned as oppressive ... From this world were banished as hostile the aged, the past and all the mentors who spoke therefrom.[19]

The fact is that, for the contemporary British right, while the whole of the post-war era might have been polluted and enervated by the sickly syrup of welfarism, the 1960s served up the poison in a peculiarly concentrated and virulent form. In the years since 1981, in speech after speech and article after article, Mrs Thatcher and her supporters have specifically blamed the 'permissive society' of the 1960s for the undermining of authority and tradition, and the consequent collapse of social and individual disipline, in the years that followed.[20] Within the last months, indeed, the chorus has been joined by voices as various as Victoria Gillick ('the Gillick parents see themselves specifically in rebellion against the 1960s and the changes in society it spawned'[21]) and Norman Tebbit (who blamed 'the end of National Service and the emergence of flower power and the permissive society of the 1960s' for promoting social violence[22]).

Geldof's Project

And it is this analysis of the root of the national malaise which gives the right problems with Live Aid's content as well as its form. Not only have commentators like Welch and Gale condemned the music as the transmission belt of anarchy, nothing less than the very virus of the plague; in political terms, too, they confront a potent expression of the 1960s in defiant and indeed triumphant flower. For, despite its generational breadth, it was surely obvious that the day belonged to the Jaggers, Bowies and Baezes, not because they're better people than the Spandau Ballets and the Whams, but because for them such unalloyed idealism was a familiar accompaniment of the music. Who can doubt indeed that in its commitment to the power of will and the politics of conscience, Live Aid was consciously attempting to evoke Woodstock and conjure the Concert for Bangladesh?

And who can doubt either that even as an act of philanthropy Live Aid departed in significant respects from the accepted Victorian model. Non-governmental it may well have been, individual and private it certainly wasn't. And despite Mrs Thatcher's last-minute message of congratulation – rushed by motorcycle from Number Ten, and praising Geldof for, guess what, setting a good example to the young – it was clear from their broadcast confrontation over EEC food surpluses that Geldof's project is to shame *governments* into higher aid spending. In that sense, Geldof and his lieutenants were far from being long-haired Nuffields or Barnardos in blue jeans. As Hugo Young pointed out in his perceptive *Guardian* piece (a welcome if belated antidote to Terry Coleman and Mark

Lewis), Live Aid has given the lie to the notion that overseas aid is at the bottom of the public's priority pile. It has challenged the government's own aid programme (more accurately, *de*-programme) by demonstrating that 'the crisis which governments take least seriously is the one which, in certain circumstances, the people take most seriously'. In that sense, Live Aid was, for Mrs Thatcher and her supporters, truly 'a message from the prince of darkness'.[23]

Learning the Lessons

So what should the left learn from Live Aid? Should it indeed (for there is no more double-edged slogan than 'my enemy's enemy is my friend') learn anything at all?

It seems to me that if there are lessons to be learnt, they are lessons that have been on offer, in one form or another, for the best part of twenty years; ever since, indeed, that period whose continued influence so disturbs our leaders. In other words, despite some tart words on *World in Action*, Live Aid is an event with its roots in the 1960s in more ways even than the right is aware of, and that was one of its particular virtues.

First of all, Live Aid was a mass *cultural* mobilisation, but one a million miles removed from the clammy, deadening form of that idea traditional on the left, notably because the culture through which people were being mass-mobilised has genuine mass appeal. Indeed, it reminds us of the immense resource of rock and roll music – the only popular form with the faintest radical credentials that has ever gained significant purchase in the working class. And of course, one of the reasons why a fabulously rich rock musician is *not* the same as an even moderately wealthy property speculator is precisely because throughout its history rock music has consistently returned to its origins as working-class protest music, and whenever it has temporarily slipped into being anything else, it's a sure sign that a new burst of oppositional energy – punk in the late 1970s, the Beatles in 1963 – is going to come along to drag it, twisting and shouting, back to its roots.

Second, the event was by definition *international*, though once again, not in any traditional sense. Part of its internationalism rested precisely on its shared culture, of course, and, in that, it was directly comparable with the youth uprising in support of the Vietnamese revolution, surely the most significant international left mobilisation since the Spanish Civil War. And like that campaign – and *unlike* Spain – its international context can only be understood through the technology and vocabulary of electronics – the global village not only of the jet aeroplane but also of the communications satellite. Live Aid began with Bob Geldof watching a television programme, and ended up with him making one.

North and South

And third, of course, and most importantly, Live Aid sought culturally to mobilise billions of people, all across the northern hemisphere, on behalf of the tens of billions of the south. By definition, the event was about the relatively rich extending their hands to the absolutely poor, and it demonstrated dramatically the energies that can be unleashed on behalf of others, energies which, Hugo Young argued, could be mobilised to such an extent for no other imaginable cause. This is not to say that Live Aid's cause was soft or bland – indeed, for socialists, it must be welcome to see an idealistic campaign that seeks to confront the arbitrary cruelties of nature with the exercise of collective human organisation and will. Rather, it provided a potent challenge to the strenuous efforts of contemporary Conservatism to create a commonsense rationale for selfishness and individual greed on all fronts.

In this sense, perhaps, Hugo Young is being unduly pessimistic about the power of the spirit of Live Aid to infect the domestic as well as the international arena. Clearly, it would have been impossible to mobilise anything like as extensively for the miners. However, if Live Aid has triumphantly demonstrated that (*pace* the traditional right-wing argument) charity need not begin at home, it surely doesn't imply that it can't be reimported. If

– contrary to Thatcherite superstition – people can care for strangers, cannot the same well-springs sustain the poor within our gates?

I am aware that much of points one and two, and almost all of point three, are arguments viewed with the deepest suspicion. However, the conventional wisdom that people are best mobilised around their own oppression – or at least on behalf of their own collective self-interest – is by no means fully confirmed by recent history. From getting the Americans out of Vietnam to stopping the South African cricket tour of Britain, from the Anti-Nazi League to Greenham Common, campaigns for others (or on behalf of the species as a whole) have proved remarkably successful, and indeed resilient. And it's perhaps not completely coincidental that it's been those movements – rather than more conventional industrial mobilisations – which have shown the greatest imagination in their use of form, from the poster and badge art of the anti-war movement and the Anti-Nazi League, to the powerful theatrical symbolism of the practice of the new peace campaigners.

If there has been one theme running through all the debates that have occupied the left since 1983, it has been that the socialist vision of the 1945 government, once so potent, has now run its course. The true message of Live Aid for the left, it seems to me, is that there is another period of rather more recent history, which undertook experiments in democratic, egalitarian and collective political forms even more radical than those of the 1940s, and whose principles and ideas still inform the best of what is happening today, from municipal decentralisation and green politics to the continued creativity of feminism. Shortly after the Woodstock Rock Festival of 1969 – the apogee of 1960s idealism, the moment when the politics and the culture finally embraced – a similar event was held in Altamont, California, during which at least four people were brutally killed by Hells Angels, providing by comparison a potent symbol of the flower generation going murderously sour. In the wake of the 13th of July, however, perhaps it is less fanciful than it was to believe that the 1960s found their enduring form at Woodstock rather than Altamont, and even the 1980s not so much in the Heysel Stadium, as in those of Wembley and Philadelphia.

Notes

1. *Evening Standard*, 11 April 1985.
2. *Spectator*, 8 June 1985.
3. Ibid.
4. *Sunday Telegraph*, 2 June 1985.
5. *Guardian*, 10 June 1985.
6. *Daily Mail*, 31 May 1985.
7. Ibid., 5 June 1985.
8. *Evening Standard*, 4 June 1985.
9. *Daily Express*, 31 May 1985.
10. *Daily Telegraph*, 3 June 1985.
11. *Guardian*, 15 July 1985.
12. *Times*, 15 July 1985.
13. *Daily Telegraph*, 15 July 1985.
14. *Sunday Telegraph*, 21 July 1985.
15. *Spectator*, 20 July 1985.
16. *Sunday Telegraph*, 21 July 1985.
17. *Daily Express*, 31 May 1985.
18. *Spectator*, 17 December 1983.
19. *Spectator*, 20 October 1984.
20. See my 'Bitter Harvest', *New Socialist*, September 1983.
21. *Sunday Telegraph*, 7 July 1985.
22. *Daily Mail*, 25 July 1985.
23. *Guardian*, 18 July 1985.

Never Too Old

The question of values – and indeed of the 'socialist vision' – has played a prominent part in the debate on how to rebuild Labour as a party of government. There appears now to be an emerging consensus that the Labour Party can rely neither on the instinctive loyalties of the white working class, nor on the arithmetical assembly of minority interests, to secure it a majority. But the leadership is well aware that part of its task must be to mobilise significant sectors of the 'haves' (including large numbers of white workers) on behalf of the 'have-nots'; as well as convincing the majority that Labour's policies are in the short- and long-term interests of the people as a whole.

In fact, of course, the Labour Party faces a complex of distinct, if sometimes overlapping, tasks. It must, of course, persuade a majority that the political economy would benefit from socialism. But it must surely also convince large numbers of people to vote in the interests of groups to which they do not presently belong (though they may in the future), for classes or sections of classes which they are highly unlikely ever to join (or certainly, to imagine that they will), for categories into which they fall, but to which they might not yet feel exclusive loyalty, and for policies whose fears for the future of the planet as a whole they may not yet share.

But even having done so, no one believes that it is enough to win people over to the cause of the poor, the sick or the old, to convince women of the virtues of feminism, nor the population as a whole of the iniquities of Trident and Cruise. The 1985 *Social Attitudes* report confirms that on many key issues the British think further to the left than they vote. (28 per cent of the population voted Labour in 1983: two years later, 39 per cent thought that the government should increase services *and* taxes; a miserly 6 per cent supports government policy of reducing both). We do not have to believe that human beings are naturally selfish to be aware of the need for their natural altruism and social idealism to be buttressed against the subtle blandishments of their individual self-interest (particularly when those temptations are presented in such seductively alluring terms as 'individual liberty' and 'getting the state off our backs'). And it is of course the business of radical politicians to erect a network of such defences, to repoint and where necessary demolish and rebuild them when, in time, they crumble and decay.

If the term 'socialist vision' has any meaning beyond the merely sentimental, then it must imply a coherent and credible set of assumptions about the collective capacities of human beings. It is not enough to proclaim a list of values, however admirable (as Anthony Barnett tartly puts it, 'socialists for sunshine'). Nor however can serious socialists resort to the old Trotskyite tactic of defining a vision of the future in quite specific contrast to any actually-existing socialist society (all of them too incurably reformist or hopelessly degenerate to merit a moment's consideration). But most socialists would now also agree that the hitherto dominant image of post-war welfare socialism – though both coherent and credible – is no longer seen as a desirable model on which a new society can be built.

There is, however, a rather more recent epoch of social experiment, from which lessons can perhaps still be drawn, an epoch in which many if not all of the movements and campaigns whose achievements are redefining the left agenda were founded. Yet while many left-wing commentators acknowledge their importance, they appear to remain nervous about dating their birth, and even more circumspect about admitting the extra-ordinary preponderance in radical politics generally (from the single issue groups to borough and constituency Labour Parties) of actual people who were also formed in that same period, the era bounded roughly by the assassinations of John F. Kennedy and Sharon Tate or, put another way, between the flowering and break-up of the Beatles.

The decline and fall of the political image of the 1960s has been a remarkable phenomenon. In the previous decade, Cold Warriors frightened their children with Krushchev's attributed threat to the Western democracies: 'We will bury you.' Who then could fail to be attracted to the New Left's 1960s promise: 'We won't need to bury you: we will just outlive you.' And yet, by the mid-1970s, the putative outlivers were reduced to the status of the superannuated greaser of Jethro Tull's mordant imagination, 'too old to rock and roll, but too young to die'.

On the surface, it is easy to see why the 1960s have proved so easy to dismiss. The political forms of the period *were* vulnerable to charges of lack of seriousness, the dominant issues of the decade *were* social and cultural rather than economic and traditionally 'political', its direct achievements did dramatically undershoot its aspirations, and its emphasis on the importance (indeed, the apparently magical qualities) of physical youth was peculiarly irksome, particularly for those not privileged to have been born in the period immediately following the Second World War.

There are, however, several things to be said about even the most irritating characteristics of the 1960s. The first is that, *even of itself*, the generation that reached majority in the 1960s comprises a disproportionately large group of people, as Senator Gary Hart discovered during the 1984 Democratic primary campaign. And while some of the feted yumpies and yuppies doubtless voted against Mondale because they disagreed with his welfarist economics, it is equally certain that many of the 53 million Americans who passed the age of twenty while American ground troops fought in Vietnam were unable to stomach the nomination of a Democratic presidential candidate whose political mentors had started and led the war, and whose main financial backers – the labour unions – had promoted its continuation so militantly (and indeed physically). And in this country – where the numerical bulge is if anything more striking – it's worth any serious political party noting that there were 4.3 million people aged between fifteen and nineteen in the United Kingdom in 1966, nearly half a million *more* than those aged between twenty and twenty-four. On the other side of the bulge, there were to be over half a million *less* young people leaving their teens between 1972 and 1976.

The striking preponderance of radical activists now edging their way towards the age of 40 thus reflects demographic reality. Another fact worth noting is that they share with all those who followed them a political experience sharply distinct from what went before. You would need now to be over 55 to have been grown-up during the construction of the welfare state, and, indeed, to be nudging 50 to have had adult experience of a political universe in which the far left was dominated by a single, monolithic party. It is thus nearly 40 years since the zenith of Fabian centralism, and thirty since the revolutionary wing of the movement ceased to be dominated by Stalinism. For the majority of people now alive, therefore, the left has always presented a pluralistic face, and has indeed (with some significant exceptions, like the Liverpool District Labour Party) been more associated with attacking authority – if not promoting downright anarchy – that with the dead hand of centralised control.

This reality is of great significance as the first post-Stalinist generation passes its experience on to its successor. We are now living through another major boom in the new adult population which, like its predecessor in the 1960s, is using its size and consequent cultural clout to redefine fashion and taste in its own image, an image once again characterised by the eccentricity of its hairstyles, the height of its hemlines, and the oppositional energy of its politics. Thus, we are once again in an era in which the political agenda is being rewritten by the young, and for which the experience of the 1960s can and is proving of invaluable benefit. Not only have the campaigns of the 1980s developed the concerns and drawn on the tactics of the 1960s (from anti-nukes to animal rights); the new activists have inevitably called upon the services of that network of alternative institutions, periodicals, and resource centres created in the 1960s. Perhaps the most dramatic example of this collaboration between the generations was the anti-fascist and anti-racist movement of the late 1970s, which owed much of its considerable success to its use of techniques first developed during the anti-war movement of a decade before, from the use of badges and T-shirts as emblems of belonging and solidarity, via the cheerful and (for a campaign initiated by the Socialist Workers Party) uncharacteristic pluralism of its offshoots (Vets and Grannies Against the War inspiring Schoolkids and Skateboards Against the Nazis), to that highly effective compound of rally and rockfest which we dubbed a carnival, the Americans called Woodstock, and Bob Geldof re-invented as Live Aid.

This view is certainly shared by the Conservatives, which accounts for the recent and dramatic change in their angle of attack on the left. Despite the occasional ritual obsequies in the direction of economic libertarianism, the party has now almost completely reverted to its more familiar role as the defender of tradition and authority against the forces of infantile disorder, forces most extensively unleashed, they would argue, between 1965 and 1974. Indeed, Norman Tebbit's famous Disraeli lecture of November 1985, in which he blamed the 'permissives' of the 1960s for 'today's violent society', was merely the culmination of a whole series of speeches by government ministers and their supporters on the same theme. Even his keynote phrase ('thus was sown the wind; and we are now reaping the whirlwind') was cribbed from a piece on the Toxteth riots, written by George Gale in July 1981, and echoed by Margaret Thatcher herself in a speech the following spring.

The analysis has been as consistent as the phraseology. The Conservative ideologues have observed – and indeed in their paranoia if anything exaggerated – the extent to which the permissively educated, radical young of the 1960s – now ensconced in the schools, polytechnics, social services departments and television studios – are busily engaged in transmitting their values to the generations they teach, counsel, inform and entertain. This model of the 1960s as a kind of abscess, in which all the debilitating poisons of the post-war era congregate, has been taken up in countless thinkpieces, on subjects as various as education, architecture and contraception, in which 'moaning 60s has-beens', relive the era of 'matted hair and mind-numbing mantras', 'the revolting students of the 1960s' mutate into 'the revolting teachers of today', and 'unashamedly ageing rockists' fail to get their mind round the fact that 'Woodstock took place 16 years ago'.

The success of this campaign can be deduced from the number of people *on the left* who have capitulated to it (the above quotations are from the *Daily Mail*, the *Observer*, the *Spectator* and *Marxism Today* respectively). Even sadder is the way in which the class of 68 itself has become crippled with generational guilt, and surrendered to the increasingly fashionable view that the 1960s was the decade that gave us tower blocks, Charles Manson, herpes simplex and *nothing else*.

So it's worth reminding both boomers and non-boomers alike, that for all its undoubted silliness and grandiosity, and despite the sourness of many aspects of its many ends, that confluence of movements and experiments and campaigns and indeed trends that have been collectively dubbed 'the 1960s' added up to the most concentrated upsurge of political inventiveness within the progressive and socialist movements, certainly since the 1940s and arguably since the immediate aftermath of the Russian Revolution; that in terms of theory it saw an inchoate New Left (on both sides of the Atlantic) develop its instinctive anti-Stalinism into new and thrilling spheres of political inquiry and action, enabling radical politics for the first time to operate not only in the traditional, socio-economic dimensions of the industrialised world, but also (and simultaneously) in the as yet largely ignored reaches of the Third World, the previously uncharted territories of the family, sexuality and 'lifestyle', and via those matters into the hitherto forbidden reaches of the human personality, in its most public but also in its most intimate and private manifestations; that, culturally, it was one of only two periods this century (the other being the early 1920s), in

which the political and artistic avant-garde walked hand in
hand, and in which (and partly thereby) radical art was
able to gain a significant purchase on a mass audience
(from Ken Loach's television films to progressive rock);
that it saw as a consequence the cultural enfranchisement
of vast layers of the working class, particularly but not
exclusively the young, as they bought (or made) clothes,
books, artefacts and, of course, music, in their own accents
and on their own terms; that in addition to all the
unquantifiable changes in social, sexual, familial, economic, political and racial relationships that resulted from
the incalculable changes in lifestyle, behaviour, social
forms, modes of living and political perception, it is
possible to point to a list of solid, specific and irreversible
victories, from the desegregation of the southern
American states to the up-ending of French society
post-May 1968, and pre-eminently to the most significant
international left-wing mobilisation since the Spanish Civil
War, the world-wide movement in support of the
Vietnamese Revolution, which *en route* to forcing
American withdrawal brought down one President, and
provoked another into the actions that would bring him
down too; and that even in Britain, even in this remote
little backwater, the decade saw not only the reproduction
(albeit on a smaller scale) of the student and youth
uprisings of America, Europe and Japan, and parallel
experiments in new social forms and new methods of
cultural intervention (from communes to collectives, from
political theatre to the underground press), but also the
development of a culture of insubordination and a
vocabulary of protest, which was to be incorporated, with
dramatic effect, into the great industrial struggles of the
1970s, as the rediscovery of the sit-in and the squat were
transformed – pumpkin like – into the industrial work-in
and the factory occupation; and which would continue to
set a tactical agenda, as the industrial upsurge waned, for
the most ultimately original developments of the
counter-culture and the New Left, which were of course
those complementary movements which sought to address
and challenge the oppression of women by men, and the

exploitation by both of the planet on whose finite and threatened resources we all ultimately depend. And it is worth underlining the point that in addition to being provoked by the worst of the 1960s, the women's liberation movement was enabled by the best of it; that it took over and extended a vocabulary of authenticity and autonomy, adumbrated by movements as various as Black Power and anti-psychiatry, in the same way as the greens of the 1970s developed the challenge to monolithic, inhuman capitalism that had been first articulated by 1960s radicals of quite another shade.

To list the decade's achievements is to chart both the breadth and the limits of its concerns. With significant but small exceptions, almost all the great issues were social. Indeed, the principal accusation of the far left against the 1960s was that, in its obsession with the 'soft' issues of social, sexual and racial oppression, (and, worst of all, 'lifestyle'), it ignored the 'hard' issues of economic exploitation, that the battle of the bedroom (and even more, the fight for the planet) represented an unnecessary deviation from the 'real' (or 'primary') arena of the factory picket line. And, of course, there is still a significant faction of people on the left who, when they hear the word 'superstructure', reach at once for their base.

But the fact is that, on the basis of solid achievement, the 'soft' social gains of the last twenty years have proved considerably more resilient than the left's 'hard' economic victories. In early 1974, the miners brought down the Heath government, with a strike mounted to resist wage controls; within eighteen months, the trade union movement (including the NUM) had capitulated to Harold Wilson's incomes policy. In the same period, however, the women's liberation movement was leading an eventually victorious mass campaign in defence of the 1968 Abortion Act (an achievement which was repeated when the Corrie Bill attempted to succeed where the James White amendment had failed). Since 1979, Margaret Thatcher has implemented considerable tracts of the economic agenda proposed by the radical right in the 1970s, from the dismantling of Labour's employment protection legislation to the undermining of the closed shop and privatisation of key public enterprises. On the social front, however, virtually the entire pre-1979 edifice remains stubbornly intact. Despite the most sustained attacks – by the very same free market gurus – on the iniquities of the Equal Opportunities Commission and the wickedness of the Commission for Racial Equality, despite the growing volume of moralistic attacks on single parents, gays, young blacks and other 'minorities' (and the deafening crescendo of law and order agitation), the institutions and the legislation of the permissive 1960s and the anti-discriminatory 1970s remain resolutely in place, the Abortion Act remains unmolested, the Race Relations Act unrepealed, Gillick defeated and (against all predictions) the rope unrestored. And who can dispute that the most successful element of the miners' campaign against pit closures was the activities of the miners' wives' groups, and the alliances forged by the support groups with a wide variety of social forces, while the least successful, equally obviously, was the mobilisation of industrial trade unionists (which didn't happen) and mass picketing (which didn't work).

And even in terms of public attitudes, the old saw that the left does well on economic issues but badly on the social ones doesn't hold water. There remain, of course, substantial majorities who think there should be more hanging and less blacks. But on other social questions there are some surprises. For example, a surprisingly high proportion of people (compared, that is, to the number who vote Labour) feel nuclear weapons of any colour make us less secure, and there is on both sides of the Atlantic a quantified shift in the female vote, to the left, on the grounds of hostility to militarism. (The much publicised 'gender gap' in American voting patterns has tended to obscure a similar shift here. In 1983, Gallup reported that for the first time more men had voted Tory than women.) Despite hostility to 'immigrants', and somewhat blinkered views of sex-roles, the 1985 Social

Attitudes Report shows massive support for anti-discrimination legislation (partly because over 80 per cent think that women are discriminated against to some extent at work). When Audience Selection surveyed Londoners in October 1984, they found an unsurprisingly comfortable 69 per cent against abolition of the GLC, but also a dramatically high proportion of people who support not only the GLC's right to exist, but also its more controversial (and satirised) social policies: 62 per cent approved of the GLC's support for ethnic minorities, and 63 per cent of its support for women (gays, as is usual, did less well). And while the trade unions remain massively unpopular in general, the fight of the GCHQ workers to retain their right to organise is supported by 69 per cent (at the same time, as Anthony King pointed out in the *Guardian* of 8 November 1985, as the number who think Britain is less free under Thatcher has increased from 21 to 35 per cent).

And it is worth remarking, in support of the argument that socially progressive and libertarian causes are by no means inevitably unpopular, that the most significant party political event of the last five years has been the emergence of a new formation – of undoubted if regrettable popularity among millions of former Labour voters – whose activists, members and supporters, in poll after poll and survey after survey, are either in the centre or (on trade union matters) to the right-of-centre on economic issues, but stand to the left on social questions. As Anthony Heath, Roger Jowell and John Curtice pointed out in a perceptive piece in a recent *Marxism Today*, higher-educated people in the public sector salariat tend towards liberal views, and large numbers of such people appear to support the Alliance. As the 1960s saw an unprecedented expansion in higher education, and the 1970s the emergence of that very salariat as a social force, the location of at least one of Labour's Lost Millions is no longer a mystery.

So it is by no means as certain as some might suppose that a left-wing political party, vigorously campaigning on the issues raised by feminism, environmentalism, anti-racism, libertarianism and the peace movement, would necessarily crash to defeat. And it's worth remarking also that even in the economic sphere, the 1960s saw a number of more than tentative steps towards alternative forms of social ownership. As a few left commentators have argued (notably Stuart Hall, David Coates and Ken Worpole), the roots of, say, the GLC's industrial strategy lie not so much in the 1940s models of nationalisation, but in the publishing collective, the wholefood co-operative, the communal theatre group, the community resource centre, workshop or school. If, as Ken Worpole hopes, there does indeed exist a 'third way between a bureaucratised state apparatus which stifles or regulates all forms of popular creativity and the global ambitions of multinational production',[1] then it is, as Stuart Hall asserts, somewhere in the alternative currents of the 1960s that its roots will be found.[2] Certainly, that perspicacious Conservative Ferdinand Mount is of that view. Writing in *Marxism Today* (June 1985) Mount went to elaborate lengths to define socialism in a way that excluded non-statist, voluntary associations from its remit. He of all people knows that the successful socialist initiatives of the last twenty years have often been as small as they have (on occasions) been beautiful.

There is however one further project of the 1960s – which began in 1956 but flowered ten years on – which also helps to explain the considerable hostility that sections of the left hold towards its politics. For the first time since 1917, an effective challenge to traditional, i.e. Leninist, modes of organisation was posed on the revolutionary wing of the left, a challenge which – like the big bang – still resounds through all its circles, just as the old left's prescriptions (and *pro*scriptions) continue to reverberate, their directives echoing in the oddest places and the least expected tones. What the New Left and the counter-culturalists did was to develop a politics of ideological witness and collective prefigurement that could operate in pluralistic association with fronts of autonomous

movements and campaigns – *and to make it work*. Neither
the Committee of 100 nor the Vietnam Solidarity
Campaign can be said to have 'succeeded' – though the
Stop the 70 Tour and National Abortion Campaign can.
What is certain is that their success is monumental in
comparison, say, with that of the Workers' Revolutionary
Party, or even (apart from its role as progenitor of the
Anti-Nazi League) the SWP. Equally, the victories of the
movements for women's and black liberation in the 1970s
and 1980s were achieved despite rather than because of
the activities of the separatist tendencies in both (with their
strangely reified re-enactments of the tactics and tone of
the Bolshevik sects).

There are of course reasons for the resilience of the old
ways. There is no doubt that the forms of collective
organisation created in or prefigured by the 1960s can be
exhausting and frustrating to be part of, and, for this
reason, the end of the decade saw a reversion by some
activists to the tried-and-tested, if grim, certainties of
democratic centralism (or even, in the case of the Red
Army Faction and the Red Brigades, to Narodnik-style
terrorism). Indeed, one of the reasons for devoting some
scrutiny to the 1960s – unblinkered by scorn but also
untinted by nostalgia – is to learn from the political
experiments of the period, and to develop strategies by
which pluralistic and democratic organisations can
maintain themselves through dull and difficult as well as
exciting times, without collapsing into impotence or
oligarchy.

But a just assessment of the achievements of the 1960s is
not just a matter of political anthropology. In an article
calling for the creation of yet another left party, that wily
Old Left apologist Ralph Miliband listed its ideal
characteristics:

What is needed is a socialist party that would bring together a
lot of different people, with many different concerns and
passions, men and women, young and old, black and white,
blue-collar workers, white-collar workers, and many others,

who would be working in an organisation that was open, democratic and no doubt disputatious, totally committed to the struggle against capitalism, sexism, and racism, and to the struggle against the global counter-revolutionary crusade conducted by the US and its allies.

Such a party, he continued,

would have respect for the demands of women, blacks, peace activists, ecologists, and others in progressive movements; and it would work with them and forge alliances, without trying ever to colonise or use them. Further, it would be acutely sensitive to the immense technological, economic and social changes which occur in the world, and to the bearing which they have on the socialist project, without surrendering any of its fundamental principles, and it would state those principles and its applications in a language that was fresh and accessible.[3]

What many on the left still refuse to acknowledge (including, perhaps, Ralph Miliband) is that neither the form nor the programme of such a party could have been conceived of without the cultural revolution of the late 1960s, and, if it ever did come to pass, it would inevitably need to admit and indeed celebrate its parentage. As it happens, however, there is no need for yet another formation, yet another founding conference, one more constitution. Acknowledged or not, the ideas of the 1960s are already refashioning the Labour Party, at local, municipal and regional level, and are beginning to seep (however slowly and through however many barriers) into the consciousness of the national leadership. The thousands upon thousands of political activists whose politics were formed somewhere en route from 'Love Me Do' to 'Let It Be' should stop apologising, and take heart. As the old song cheerfully (but quite properly) concludes: 'You're never too old/To rock and roll/If you're too young to die.'

The Second Time as Farce

Notes

1. *New Statesman*, 23 November 1984.
2. *Marxism Today*, January 1984.
3. *Guardian*, 5 August 1985.

Strike While the Iron Is Hot

There are remarkably few books about the momentous industrial struggles of the past two decades. The dramatic conflicts of the Heath premiership have been particularly effectively hidden from history. True, there was one (not terribly memorable) account of the Upper Clyde Shipbuilders' work-in, and Penguin published the miners' evidence to the 1972 Wilberforce Inquiry in *A Special Case* but, in book form at least, there was nothing on the 1972 strike as a whole (not even on Saltley); nothing on the 1974 re-run; nothing even on the docks dispute which culminated in the imprisonment and release of the Pentonville Five.

To remark that the 1984-85 miners' strike has been different is something of an understatement. Clearly, if you want your strike to earn Public Lending Right, keep it going for a year. The first wave of strike books emerged in the summer and autumn of 1985 and ranged from the thoughtful and discursive (Huw Beynon's essay compilation *Digging Deeper*) via the punchily polemical (Geoffrey Goodman's pro-miner but anti-Scargill *Miners' Strike*). Now we are reaching the end of the second, largely hardback phase of the publishing offensive, which has included another overall history (Martin Adeney and John Lloyd's *The Miners' Strike: Loss without Limit*) and Sir Ian MacGregor's grisly apologia *The Enemies Within*.

The three books considered here also owe their existence to the cassette recorder and, like Sir Ian's ghost, Rodney Tyler, their editors are suitably diffident about their role (in one case, almost ludicrously so). But in fact all three demonstrate clearly that orature is as refractable as literature; that the most popular of histories can preserve a distinctive authorial vox.

In the case of Tony Parker's pseudonymous, Northumbrian *Red Hill: A Mining Community*, the tone is one of almost unbearable bleakness: despite a couple of statutory women-who-were-utterly-changed-by-it-all, the overriding (indeed overwhelming) impression is of a community visited and subsequently vitiated by the inscrutable workings of an alien destiny – a confrontation which has left many if not most mystified, dazed and numb.

The fact that Peter Gibbon and David Steyne's actual *Thurcroft: A Village and the Miners' Strike* (lodge banner inscription: 'From Obscurity to Respect') feels so dramatically different is partly that South Yorkshire is a different kind of place and played a very different role in the strike. But it's also a function of the perspective the compilers have chosen: despite their insistence that the 'selection of material or comments is not based on giving prominence to the beliefs we find most sympathetic ourselves', they acknowledge that their sources are almost entirely drawn from 'rank-and-file activists'. And, as nearly half of Thurcroft's miners returned before the end of the strike, the decision not to interview scabs makes the book inevitably partial; though its chronological form and wealth of detail make it also an illuminating and often exciting read (even if individuals – characterised by letters rather than invented names – are hard to follow through).

Like MacGregor, Raphael Samuel, Barbara Bloomfield and Guy Boanas were attracted to Margaret Thatcher's most notorious statement for their title. *The Enemy Within: Pit Villages and the Miner's Strike of 1984-5* does report on both sides, particularly in an acute and painful set of interviews from Nottinghamshire. But, apart from Barbara Bloomfield's brave and illuminating essay on the Mardy Women's Support Group, the body of the book is too much of a *bricolage* to match the impact of *Thurcroft* or *Red Hill*.

Its point, however, is that it contains a preface and introduction by Raphael Samuel, bits of both of which have appeared elsewhere in other guises but which, together, form the most cogent and sustained rehearsal of his argument that the strike was a deeply conservative defence 'of the known against the unknown, the local and familiar against the remote and the gigantesque'. Certainly, the establishment may have seen in the strike the unleashing of the brute forces of anarchy and chaos (a view amply confirmed by MacGregor/Tyler, whose thesauri clearly fail them in their quest for suitable epithets for the 'blind hatred' and 'raging madness' of the 'rampaging mobs', nay 'stormtroopers' of South Yorkshire). But, for Samuel, the dispute was a manifestation of something very different; it was a fight not for economic or political gain but 'against losing something', a struggle for no more than 'the right to stay put'. Notions of tradition, of loyalty, of an almost Burkean debt to the past (and obligation to the future): all of these characteristics flow from the strike's essentially conservative character.

There is of course much truth in this, confirmed on many pages of *Thurcroft* and *Red Hill*. But Samuel himself hints at its major limitation when he describes the strike as 'not so much an expression of community as a discovery of it'. Almost every book on the miners' strike has made mention of the network of support groups that mushroomed throughout the country; almost all, too, go on to disparage them. Lloyd and Adeney are particularly dismissive of the Labour left idea that the strike forged new bonds between urban activists and the miners; Samuel himself mourns the failure of this alliance to live up to its promise. Both perspectives seem, however, to be predicated on the assumption that the influence of the relationship was all one-way; ignoring the perception of those like Bea Campbell who have pointed out that the strike saw a considerable cultural revolution *in the coalfields*, a revolution which included the very rediscovery (aided and abetted by left academics like Samuel), of a past which had in many cases suffered the same fate as the South Wales Lodge libraries, dismantled to make way for bar extensions or banks of electronic games.

Far from being restricted to the ranks of the hard left, many of the support groups were heavily peopled by representatives of that 'ex-New Left class of '68' whose supposed growing 'hostility to the strike', is, for Samuel, such a baleful characteristic of the contemporary left scene. Anyone tempted to embrace Samuel's gloomy vision (or Adeney and Lloyd's gleeful celebration of the collapse of the 'vanguardist' delusion of the city-coalfield alliance) might reflect that the 1984-85 miners' strike saw *for the first time* a real political welding of the industrial aspirations of the working class with the social concerns of the socialist intelligentsia, a welding which obviously included the education of that intelligentsia in the realities of privation and struggle; but also involved immeasurable changes in the attitudes of a goodly proportion of miners themselves to issues of law and order, race, sexuality and gender. Naturally, Raphael Samuel emphasises the conservative dimension of the women's support groups, their defence of kinship, hearth and home, and it's true that the women of *Thurcroft* and *Red Hill* pepper their histories with caveats of the 'I'm no women's libber but ...' variety. But men of village and city will ignore that 'but' at their peril; often, the dazed incomprehension communicated so graphically in Tony Parker's book results from the realisation that a sacked miner may never work again; sometimes it results also from the loss of a wife.

In assessing the achievements of the strike, one Thurcroft activist said, 'Well, we gave them a good run for their money. In years to come there might be something to come out of that.' Almost every one of the now voluminous number of oral histories of the 1984-85 miners' strike represents, in microcosm, a fragment of the alliance out of which some of that something might come.

The Morals Dilemma

From child abuse to 'race commissars', from street crime to video violence, the silly season was dominated by tales of individual iniquity and talk of its political redress. And while August may be, as the saying goes, a uniquely wicked month, it is clear that causes and cures of anti-social behaviour will continue to influence policy debate.

This is, of course, a territory in which the personal has always been political. Moral attitudes have always informed social policy, as Bernard Shaw trenchantly noted in *Pygmalion*, when he has Arthur Doolittle define the essential distinction between the deserving and the undeserving poor. Four years ago, when the then still crusading *Sunday Times* exposed the full misery of single-parenthood in Hackney, correspondents were quick to point out that the mother in question didn't *have* to have her baby, that wrecked cars and old mattresses are dumped by *somebody*, and graffiti doesn't scrawl itself.

Moral judgements of personal behaviour are thus – and have always been – a crucial component of the *political* debate over social policy. It is not a debate that the left has been doing that well in recently. True, the election campaign demonstrated that Labour still led the other parties in the arena of provision of the universal caring and welfare services – the health service, school education, the retirement pension. But as soon as care becomes selective and discretionary, as soon as its notional recipient gains a face and a history, the public's capacity for social compassion became significantly limited. Even the plight of the unemployed appeared to excite less universal concern than hitherto.

The reason for this is simple. Throughout the second

term, the Conservatives devoted much energy to the ancient sport of victim-blaming, developing and honing a variety of interlocking ideological mechanisms which relocated the causes of unemployment, poverty and even racism within the behaviour of the victimised groups themselves, increasingly defined in terms of personal morality. One obvious example is the way in which the single-parent family has been transferred from the deserving to the undeserving column of the social ledger.

Another was the not always unspoken assumption that the social pathologies popularly associated with the inner city underclass – from domestic violence and drug abuse to soccer hooligans and vandals – demonstrated not only economic but ethical weakness; as Conservative ideologue Ferdinand Mount put it, the right's use of the word 'demoralised' usefully elides loss of morale with lack of morality, thus allowing the moral *responsibility* for the condition of the wretched to flip effortlessly from us to them.[1] Allied with this was the idea that those sections of the underclass who might notice that they had bootstraps to pull themselves up by, were being encouraged by left-liberal teachers, social workers and others to the view that society owed them a living, and if it refused to honour the debt, they were entitled to appropriate it.

This individualising of guilt not only allowed the Conservatives to evade blame for the evils of unemployment; it also let their own people off the hook. A key element of the hysterical assault on anti-racism that marked the concluding months of Thatcherism Mark Two was the idea that racism was not a structural fault but a moral failing, and that for a local or national government to pursue a collective strategy against it was as absurd a notion as a collective campaign against sin; that an anti-racism campaign or even a Race Relations bureaucracy was as ludicrous a concept as a conscious strategy of Anti-Slothism, an Envy Monitoring Unit or Gluttony Awareness Training.

Race is a particularly dramatic example of an issue where the arenas of social policy, politics and personal morality overlap: soft (if not downright subversive) teachers are seen to be miseducating young blacks into exaggerated expectations, and the idea that if denied them, they have the right (on the grounds of 'centuries of oppression') to take what they cannot earn, if not by crime then by riot. The idea that the left gives the poor permission to commit crime (a notion most fully developed by conservative sociologists and criminologists in America) is one of the most potent components of the Conservative moral package.

All of the above I believe to be dangerously true. And yet I don't think I was alone in sensing, during the election, that the Conservative claim to inherent superiority in even the personal moral arenas was beginning to crumble. Wasn't there a growing suspicion (lurking in the darker corners of the opinion polls) that the Tory moral line was contradictory and indeed hypocritical; that its rejection of any environmental explanation for deviant behaviour was just a bit damn convenient; and that too often it appeared to promote one moral law for the rich (and/or respectable) and quite another for the poor?

Perhaps the most dramatic evidence for the contradictions of Conservative moralism has been provided by the indecisiveness of its chief ideologues on the question of child sexual abuse. On the surface, what could be a juicier issue for Tory moralists than mass outbreaks of child-molesting in high unemployment areas (even better, in the very heart of the wingeing North); what more suitable a St George than Dr Marietta Higgs, as she takes on the dragons of paedophilia on behalf of the vulnerable and the innocent? But of course the difference between the Cleveland case and (say) the notorious cases of unchecked (if non-sexual) abuse of children in Brent and elsewhere, is that the abuser is not a boyfriend but a husband, and the colluder not a single parent but a wife. So instead of bleeding-heart social workers failing to protect the innocent against the immoral, we are faced with meddling doctors, boldly going where they've no business to, attempting to tear apart what the marriage service quite clearly states no man (or even less, a woman) should put asunder.

If the Tory moral critique of the underclass – on which its

evasion of responsibility for unemployment rests – is, indeed contradictory and hypocritical, then the left has a huge opportunity to seize the initiative, to set the agenda for the development of codes of personal behaviour appropriate to the post-religious (not to mention the post-industrial) age. What might prevent it taking full advantage of that opportunity is its own considerable confusion and consequent vulnerability on questions concerned with personal morality, a confusion obvious enough in the ideology of the 'old left' but equally present in sectors of the new.

The traditional left position on personal morality is of course well known, and much caricatured. It is most often articulated in those endless quotations from V.I. Lenin (who in this respect, though of course few others, has much to answer for) to the effect that there is no morality above the interests of the proletarian revolution, a principle which arises itself not out of any moral nihilism but the belief that human behaviour is entirely a function of its environment, that the superstructure is a mere glove puppet, manipulated by the iron fingers of the implacable base. In this respect, for the left to develop a doctrine of personal morality *under capitalism* is as pointless a project as the development of a subaquine lawnmower or the proverbial chocolate teapot: once socialism arrives, the programme of the human machine will be rewritten, and its behaviourial outlook accordingly changed, changed utterly.

It is this delusion which has left such a vacuum in the actual moral arena of socialism in practice, and allowed the familiar forms of normative and collective controls on deviance to have their sway in the socialist countries (and indeed in not a few Western Communist parties), with their firm, lower-middle-class philistinism, their unremitting, humourless positivism, and the tendency of all forms of collective activity to aspire to the condition of a scout camp. By contrast, the leaders of the New Left were from the start aware that the New, unalienated Person would not necessarily emerge unaided from the chrysalis of the revolution, and that the creation of that person had to be considered, and even practised for, in the here-and-now.

As a consequence, New Left documents like the American SDS's 1962 Port Huron Statement are fiercely moralistic (perhaps the most famous passage of the document begins: 'We regard men as infinitely precious and possessed of unfulfilled capacities for reason, freedom and love ...'), and their tone extended into the late 1960s, when the notion of socialist prefigurement, the collective and the commune as a laboratory for the development of new forms of social and personal relationship, as a rehearsal for the revolution, excited the young masses flooding into the European and American protest movements as much as they irritated the Communists and Trotskyists. And this notion became, of course, even more enticing when it became clear that one of the routes towards self-cultivation and creativity was the following of personal instinct into hitherto forbidden areas of sensual and sexual behaviour ('if it feels good, do it').

It was the uninhibited assertion of this principle that led many in the New Left to suspect that the virtues of doing one's own thing had its limits, and the new social movements threw up new analyses of the causes of anti-social behaviour, and indeed new, often biological determinisms (based on gender and race), which were in many cases as metallically constructed and crudely applied as the class determinisms on which they were in a real sense modelled.

Both old and new left, therefore, have difficulties with the idea that the left should address issues of personal behaviour, certainly in the here-and-now. For the libertarians, it's an authoritarian interference in its project of personal and social emancipation; for the class, race and gender determinists, such an undertaking is pointless (for the social symptoms of capitalism, imperialism and patriarchy cannot be cured in advance of the disease).

I am increasingly convinced that the Left *must* develop a politics of personal behaviour that goes beyond crude determinism or easy libertarianism, not least (but also not only) because if it does not do so it leaves the field wide open for the right to impose its own analysis and its own solutions. But in doing so, it is equally important to reassert that there *are* material factors in deviant behaviour which remain, if not a sufficient, then at least a necessary part of any credible analysis of its causes.

For of course it is no more than common sense that the poor are tempted to crime more often (and more understandably) than the rich; that material deprivation is a more obviously effective seed-bed for moral squalor than material abundance; that the denial of human function and identity implied and imposed by unemployment is more liable to lead to inertia, frustration and anger than to a sensitive and mature use of increased leisure time (as Bea Campbell pointed out in *Wagon Pier Revisited*, the poor can't afford *The Pauper's Cookbook*; nor are they actually that likely to get access to the perquisites of an improving hobby) and that – to take on that favoured right-wing canard – although of course poverty is indeed *relative*, and though it is absolutely true that the most miserable of our citizens is markedly better off than the vast majority of Ethiopians (and also, in some respects, than eighteenth-century royalty), a moment's thought about one's *own* attitudes to one's *own* material conditions compared to those around one makes it abundantly clear that someone suffering from relative deprivation is nonetheless really deprived.

So why, with such pressing arguments for the environmental interpretation of anti-social behaviour, does the left need to go any further? It is not only because such factors do not fully explain why some people do and others don't react violently or criminally to the miseries of their lives. Nor is it entirely because, in terms of practical political policy, the redress of the environmental root causes is (to put it mildly) the long-term solution to a problem experienced bitterly and urgently, by people who should but often don't support the left, in the here-and-now.

No, if the left is to confront the issues of personal deviant behaviour in the present tense, and if it doesn't (as it shouldn't) propose to have any truck with populist, punitive solutions, then it will have (first) to admit that individual anti-social behaviour is a real problem, and that vandalism, hooliganism, drug addiction, domestic violence and sexual abuse are phenomena that should and must be addressed by any political tendency seriously aspiring to power. Second, it will have to confront and challenge the model which the Tories have so self-confidently promoted, of a *cultural* breakdown, rooted in the 1960s and embracing factors as diffuse as modern architecture, progressive education, liberation theology and rock and roll.

Happily, on this question, the Tories are by no means invulnerable. True, they can still trumpet the claim that 'sour media mores' have, as it were, given 'social permission' for anti-social behaviour; and in the same way that the left should not flirt with the law and order lobby, it should not collude with the censor.

But there are at least three elements of the culture of our time which can be seen to contribute to such behaviour and which can and should be directly laid at the Thatcher door. The first – as began to be hinted at during the election – is a positive glorification of individual greed and self-aggrandisement which is seen at its most dramatic in the currency exchanges of the City of London, but which has had a palpable knock-on effect in almost all areas of economic exchange; a legitimisation of selfishness and carelessness for the interests and needs of others which has seeped over from the market place into almost all areas of public and indeed private and family life.

Second, there has been from the Falklands onwards a frightening upsurge of a kind of atavistic, tribal chauvinism, which has not only turned multi-racial estates into nightmare zones (a phenomenon the left has consistently – and rightly – attributed in large part to a climate created by this government), but also blighted the football terraces, afflicted public transport and ruined countless holidays and recreational resorts, here and overseas.

The left should not be coy about making such

connections. You do not have to think that *Rambo* should be banned to regard it (and indeed works of the *Death Wish* school) as an outgrowth of a culture of militarism, tribalism and individual aggression that has been deliberately promoted by the very government that is now trying to blame it all on us. Nor should we ignore the fact that both the rampant individualism and the aggressive chauvinism of Thatcherite culture is a function of the reassertion of masculinity and the anti-feminist backlash. Much of the familial and sexual violence we see in the inner cities and on the estates (and, as it ought to, but perhaps shouldn't, go without saying, behind the privet hedge and beyond the raked driveway) is a function of this pressing crisis of masculinity, the importance of which has tended to be underestimated in the search for less threatening explanations of phenomena like child sexual abuse. As Julie Birchill recently argued, if it is indeed true that most abusers were themselves abused, then you would expect two-thirds of the former to be women (the proportions of the latter), whereas in fact, of course, 90 per cent are men.[2] As she put it: 'Men are at bay: they are getting nastier and nastier as women get stronger, and they have not finished yet'; an assertion that Michael Ryan, with his privately made, privately hired videos, and his privately bought and legally sold armoury, was about to prove.

A realistic, mountable campaign against sexism and racism, a consistent effort to demonstrate the connection between economic greed and personal selfishness, militant nationalism and racial abuse, triumphalist masculinity and male violence, could and should be presented by Labour as a major component of its social and its *law and order* programmes. The answer to such a campaign no doubt would be the re-playing of an argument consistently wheeled out by Norman Tebbit, Rhodes Boyson and the like (and which featured prominently in the Tory's final election broadcast). It is that the only ultimate non-punitive sanction against anti-social behaviour is provided by shared and accepted values (usually religious) passed on to each new generation by institutions which command universal respect (notably the family).

And although it is vital that the left asserts the still dramatic and pressing material causes of social deviance, and the connection between such deviance and a *Zeitgeist* which this government has eagerly promoted, its most important task is to challenge the argument that the only conceivable moral code for the late twentieth century is a religious one, and the only feasible medium for its transmission is familial. Indeed, it must remind a large number of people (including much of the present leadership of the Labour Party) that active Christian belief is a minority conviction, and membership of a traditional nuclear family a minority location. And having done so, it must go on to look at the way in which its own institutions might develop acceptable and feasible codes of personal behaviour, and means to transmit those codes through society.

The idea that the institutions of British democratic socialism might contain within themselves the potential to reform social behaviour has its critics. One of the most credible is Jeremy Seabrook, who has argued passionately and consistently that the working-class family formed and forms the only realistic bastion against the assaults of capitalism, but that this bastion has been neutralised by the promotion of consumerism, which effectively destroyed the bonds of affection, commitment and solidarity which kept working-class families and their communities together; and, most importantly of all, that those new groupings that have sought to substitute themselves for the family have proved – by virtue of their very ersatz nature – entirely inadequate to perform the traditional familial functions of protection, confirmation and care.

Thus, in *Working Class Childhood*, Seabrook analyses his own community – an informal but conscious grouping of those who, like him, 'escaped' from working-class backgrounds in provincial cities and came to the big one in search of enlightenment and liberation. For Seabrook, however, the attempt by this 'elective kinship' to 'reconstitute the roles' of actual kinship, the group's 'fumbling after structures', its 'need for institutions and permanence', was doomed to failure. As he put it, the group *does* manage to rally round if one is, say, terminally ill – but every member knows that

> We can in all conscience withdraw, so that the surviving members of the blood-family or the statutory services can take over. We have the best of both worlds; although, somehow, it doesn't seem to amount to very much.

The argument is a powerful one, but perhaps it is unnecessarily pessimistic. For whether or not the old, traditional ties, bonds and roles were as consistently warm and sustaining as Seabrook describes them, it is clear that in many cases they were and are going to continue to be unbearably restrictive and limiting as well, and that durable models of effective 'elective kinship', based around codes of interpersonal and social behaviour appropriate to our times, are going to have to be found.

And there are perhaps at least the prototypes of such models around us. The haunting tragedy of AIDS has brought into stark relief what many in the gay constituency knew already (particularly those who lived in gay communities), that a kinship based on a shared oppression can be as mutually sustaining as that of the family, and in many ways more binding and less conditional. For while the AIDS crisis has thrown up genuinely heart-warming cases of supermums embracing both fact and person, it is clear that the real, sustained and reliable support for victims and their companions has been provided from within the community itself. The work of the Terrence Higgins Trust, and particularly the buddy system, is evidence of the existence of a genuine moral community which mocks the malice and spite of the false moralists whose response to suffering is to persecute, isolate and criminalise the sufferers.

The considerable achievements of the gay community in confronting the crisis that (at present) afflicts it particularly is perhaps the most dramatic contemporary example of the creation of new moral communities, in response to the changing nature and structure of the contemporary world. It is by no means the only one. Many of the institutions of the labour movement have begun to assimilate (if not before time) the elements of new codes of interpersonal behaviour that grew out of feminism and anti-racism, and have developed institutional forms (of which the appointment of equal opportunity officers in trade unions is only one obvious example) to promote these values. And such initiatives have of course been the very lifeblood of the newer institutions of the progressive movement which have been such a feature of the last twenty years.

It is true of course that many a commune, co-operative and collective has fallen by the wayside – often because of hack-handed attempts by those of a scout-masterly mentality to impose systems of normative control if not actual coercion inappropriate to small-scale, voluntary associations. But many have survived too, and been refashioned in forms (particularly in the housing field) appropriate to the contemporary inner-city landscape, providing imaginative alternative models for the collective implementation of social objectives at the personal level.

And finally, of course, there is the way in which the two great political movements of the 1960s and 1970s – indeed in a real way political *inventions* of the 1960s and 1970s – challenged the personal behaviour of individuals. I have already made the point that no socialist code of personal behaviour could avoid drawing much of its general and specific content from feminism. It should also be remembered that feminism's challenge to coercive and violent personal behaviour has been most acute in what one could call enemy territory: it is in the home itself that feminism has fought hardest and it could be argued had its most intense if not its most extensive purchase on the personal behaviour of women and men.

But also important is the way in which the various branches of the ecological movement, collectively and individually, have influenced and informed our treatment of both our external and internal environment. Individualistic and even narcissistic may the health movement have been; but it would be ahistorical to deny its roots in the political movement against pollution and for social ecology, and blinkered to ignore its potential as a political paradigm. It is perhaps not entirely a coincidence that a major manifestation of a recent upsurge in collective moral consciousness – Live Aid and outgrowths – should take the form of a worldwide act of environmental self-help, a global physical jerk. Certainly the *moral content* of the health movement – its assertion of social responsibility for the personal as well as the global environment – contains further clues for the content and form of a new social code.

Socialism is at base about challenging and eliminating unequal power relations by and on behalf of the powerless. It is completely appropriate that it should extend that project from the macrocosm to the microcosm, from the unequal relations of classes to the unequal relations of individuals.

No one can deny the problems associated with any consistent attempt by the left to challenge the abuses of personal power. The ghosts of the 1930s haunt the concept, and (in certain town halls and elsewhere) poison the practice. In the most enlightened circles, the spectres of censorship, priggishness and just plain bullying lurk beneath the surface of the rhetoric. There is much to guard against, much to be ever mindful of. But if the left is seriously to address society's present and indeed its own recent past, then personal behaviour cannot remain off political limits. After all, the connection between the two was *our* slogan, *our* insight, *our* perception. The right has tried to take it over. It's time it got took back.

Notes

1. *Spectator*, 11 July 1987.
2. *New Society*, 24 July 1987.

Future Stages

At the end of my talk 'Public Theatre in a Private Age', I expressed the hope that a new synthesis of the visual and the verbal in the theatre might lead to a resurgence of the radical innovation of the late 1960s and early 70s. When Bernard Crick asked me to give the 1986 George Orwell Memorial Lecture (an offer I was to put it mildly eager to accept), I decided to return to that theme in more detail. 'Festivals of the Oppressed' was first delivered on 6 November 1986; it has been published in *New Formations* (Number 3, Winter 1987) and *Race & Class* (Vol. XXIX No. 4, Spring 1988).

Festivals of the Oppressed

It's always risky for writers to theorise about their work, and it's especially dangerous to do so without benefit of hindsight. The reason why I am embarking on this dangerous project is because I think we in the arts are in the middle of a war which, whether we know it or like it or not, is being fought in the language if not always on the actual terrain of theory, and we've got to get in there and engage. The war is of course that between the last few brave defenders of modernism, of the avant-garde project, of the arts this century, and the ever expanding hordes of not so much post- as unambiguously *anti*-modernists, responding with unalloyed glee to every new aesthetic demystified, each new theory debunked, each new building demolished. Reading the despatches from the battlefront, however, I am struck by a strange delusion, in the minds of the most fervent of the shock troops of reactionary chic. That delusion is the idea that the artistic and the political avant-garde, the modernist and the Marxist traditions, have been if not in bed together then at least always fellow-travellers, walking in more or less the same direction down roughly the same side of the street.

In fact it seems that there have been only two periods this century when that was even remotely true: the first being the early 1920s, the era of expressionism, futurism, constructivism and dada; and the second being the late 1960s, the period in which I reached adulthood. And it's perhaps because of the fact that I am a militantly unrepentant child of that time that I am particularly concerned to see the development of my art-form within the context of the social and political changes taking place around it.

For a playwright this isn't hard to do, because I think it's undeniable that the main mouthpiece of political radicalism in the arts in post-war Britain has been the play, and except for a few brief shining televisual moments, the stage play in particular. Further I think that plays have not only expanded the vocabulary of social protest but contributed to its agenda. In 1956, it was a stage play – John Osborne's *Look Back in Anger* – which invented the angry young man, the socially uprooted, existentially precarious child of the 1944 Education Act, appalled by Suez but paralysed by Hungary; in the mid-1960s it was a television film – Jeremy Sandford's *Cathy Come Home* – which exposed the public squalor which private affluence had allowed to accumulate and fester in the cities, and articulated the passionate but essentially social-democratic demand that urban homelessness be planned away.

And in the late 1960s, it was the theatre – albeit not always in theatre buildings – which expressed in the starkest terms the politics of the then burgeoning new revolutionary left. In particular, theatre voiced the conviction that the working class had been seduced from its true revolutionary purpose by the lush blandishments of consumerism, that the future of the revolutionary project lay primarily with the peasants of the Third World, and that the only function for white radicals in the metropolitan countries was to act as a kind of fifth column, to operate, as it were, behind enemy lines, to undermine the enemy's morale and to disrupt the numbing razzmatazz of the capitalist spectacle. For political militants like the German Red Army Fraction – and, on a comparatively miniscule scale, the British Angry Brigade – the ripping away of capitalism's dainty consumerist screen was a literal matter of bombing boutiques. For the new playwrights and playmakers of the late 1960s, the site of struggle was metaphorical, using cultural forms to subvert and disarm the *Zeitgeist*. You could say, indeed, that the artistic project was if anything closer to the heart of the late 1960s than the political or paramilitary one, and if you did, you could well be right.

My own intervention in this discourse began at a

particularly significant juncture. My first professionally produced play was finished in June 1970, the month of Edward Heath's election victory; within months it was clear that reports of the death of the working class had been much exaggerated. Indeed, ironically, it appeared that the working class had learnt lessons from its own memorialists, as new (or perhaps more accurately, rediscovered) political forms like the sit-in, the work-in and the occupation joined the more conventional mass strike in the armoury of industrial protest. It is no surprise that young, radical theatre-makers threw themselves eagerly into the struggle, producing plays which trumpeted their solidarity with the insurgent dockers, shipyard workers, railmen and miners, rising to a crescendo in early 1974, when the second of two great miners' strikes brought the Heath Government to its knees.

But, of course, this seeming unity of purpose masked deepening divisions on the left, divisions mirrored among socialist playmakers. In the late 1960s, there had been a sort of fragile accord among the various manifestations and fractions of the New Left, as differences were sunk in the interests of the struggle against the Vietnam war. And while hippies and yippies, funkies and tankies demonstrated and even worked together (with only the Socialist Labour League permanently rehearsing the impeccably principled reasons Why They Were Not Marching), the equally disparate branches of the theatrical left felt themselves to be operating within a shared artistic and political consensus that could encompass a spectrum from the steeliest social realist or agitpropagator to the wackiest exponent of the wildest reaches of the avant-garde.

Beneath the superficial certainties of the early 1970s, however, this alliance was beginning to splinter and fragment. Like the burgeoning Trotskyite groups, some political playmakers saw the working-class militancy of the early 1970s as a spectacular confirmation of traditional Marxism-Leninism. Others, like the libertarian and anarchist groupings, were attracted to increasingly radical forms of social experimentation, posing a dramatic challenge to traditional forms and hierarchies in the here and now. And as the libertarians in the squats became progressively distanced from the Leninists outside the factory gates, so the performance artists (in particular) grew increasingly remote from the more didactically political groups with whom they had previously collaborated.

Obscured by the struggle, these contradictions appeared in stark relief in the wake of the Tory defeat of February 1974, and the dramatic evaporation of proletarian militancy which followed. Every generation of socialists confronts a moment of truth, when the glad confidences of morning must give way to more considered and durable forms of commitment (the moment when the fainthearts start packing their bags, rehearsing their excuses and looking for the exit). For the British class of 68, I think that moment was the spring and summer of 1975, as inflation nudged 30 per cent, the unions surrendered to the Wilson pay policy, the left slid to abject defeat over Europe, and the long looked-for victory of the peoples of Indo-China gave birth, among other things, to Pol Pot's Kampuchea. Increasingly, the limits of economic militancy were becoming clearer, with even the most zealous Trotskyite beginning to suspect that, far from having struck to bring down the government, the miners might well have brought down the government in order to win their strike. At the same time, the political inadequacies, and terrible human consequences, of the totalist revolutionary model were bitterly reaffirmed.

Even the positive developments were riven with painful contradictions. One of the effects of the industrial upsurge of 1972-74 was to delay, or at least to mask, the growth of feminism in Britain – but by 1975 the women's movement was able to mount and sustain a highly successful mass campaign against the threatened amendments to the Abortion Act. Similarly, while the white aristocrats of labour had withdrawn from the commanding heights of the struggle, black and Asian workers were demonstrating, in the sweatshops of the East Midlands and elsewhere, that they were not prepared to submit to exploitation just because Labour was in power. But of course both these movements posed a challenge not just to the class enemy without but to the comrades and brothers within. In 1972 feminist demands were ignored, if not derided, in the interests of the industrial struggle against the Tory government; as the dockers marched against Heath it was conveniently forgotten that four years before significant numbers of the same dockers had marched for the racist ideas of Enoch Powell. But by the end of 1975 the 68 generation had lost its innocence, and the section of that generation that had gone into the theatre began to appreciate that anybody seriously attempting to represent the times that followed was inevitably going to be dealing with complexity, contradiction and even just plain doubt.

The political theatre of the late 1970s reflected the new mood in a number of ways. Overall, political plays became more analytical, more discursive, more about worrying contradictions than amplifying great blasts of anguish or triumph. In the mainstream theatre, the so-called 'state of England' play sought to analyse the social malaise in historical and cultural rather than crudely economic terms; in the alternative theatre, plays were as likely to address the debilitating effects of working-class alcoholism as the dastardly machinations of late capitalism or the craven reformism of the labour bureaucracies. And the emerging feminist theatre took considerable pleasure – and gave it, too – in using theatre not so much as a platform for the proclamation of eternal truths, but rather as a laboratory for the testing, under various conditions, of new ways of relating to each other and the world, often through forms that stood at perversely oblique angles to the content they sought to embrace. Thus male aggression was armlocked in the wrestling ring, and glamour demystified amid the sequined glitter of the late night cabaret.

The fact that neither socialist nor feminist theatre – nor any combination of the foregoing – was prepared for the Thatcherite blitzkrieg did not of course distinguish it markedly from the rest of the left-wing population. Similarly, many radical playmakers initially saw the Thatcher government as no more than a re-run of the early 1970s, and the early 1980s consequently saw something of a revival of the kind of cartoon agitprop that had been in such vogue ten years before. But it didn't take long for people inside the theatre to realise what was painfully being realised outside it too – that Thatcherism was not Heathism in skirts, that it was a new and much more dangerous phenomenon because its combination of energetic and bracing economic liberalism with the no-nonsense, home truth certainties of social tradition and authority succeeded in appealing to at least something in a sufficiently large majority of people to threaten almost permanent electoral success. And against that the traditional forms of agitprop theatre, all those funny voices and jokeshop police hats and gameshow metaphors, seemed, to put it mildly, an inadequate response.

Before considering what an adequate response might look like, I think it's useful to consider how the theatre as a whole has responded to the challenge of the New Order. In some ways, the new realism has not been entirely negative. There was something rather cosy and self-regarding about the middle-class, proto-yuppie audience in the Warehouse or the Royal Court (or on occasions at the National), thrilling to calls for their own expropriation, and applauding the collapse of civilisation as they relied on it. Similarly in the arena of production, I'm sure I wasn't alone in feeling that the ascetic minimalism of the late 1970s had outlived its usefulness – in welcoming the end of the epoch in which all theatrical art aspired to the condition of Jonathan Miller's famously stark, one bench *Measure for Measure* (with some stern, uncompromising spirits asserting that even that bench was a bit lush). But it's now clear that the revival of theatrical spectacle – the move that gave us the National's remarkable *Oresteia* and *Mysteries*, and I suppose the RSC's *Nicholas Nickleby* also – has mutated into the much regarded phenomenon of the New British Musical, ever more dazzling in form, ever more empty of content. And I'm sure I'm not alone in noticing that in addition to people speaking *less* – the very condition of the medium – *people* are speaking less in British musicals; that a common factor in the recent West End smasheroos is the absence of human beings in the cast of characters. *The Little Shop of Horrors* stars a man-eating plant. *Cats* is about small furry domestic animals. *Chess* concerns a game in which two silent men – backed in this case by banks of television monitors – move small pieces of turned wood across a checkered board. One of the stars of *Time* is a hologram and the other is Cliff Richard. And, if *A Chorus Line* was the paradigmatic Me Decade musical, the profession solemnly and narcissistically contemplating its own navel, then surely *Starlight Express* is the quintessential musical of the 1980s, with a cast consisting entirely of inanimate objects, computer programmed not to roller-skate into each other, the first genuine artefact of the post-human age. But even when the New Musical does address itself to dreary old people and their boring old doings in the world, it seems to do so in a way designed to maximise a kind of collective, emotional wash of togetherness, while and by way of eliminating any element or notion that might strike a note of discord and disturb the major chord harmony of the whole.

It is this which leads a playwright like Howard Barker specifically to reject the possibility of a genuine communality in the theatre, insisting that 'we must overcome the urge to do things in unison', on the grounds that 'the baying of the audience in pursuit of unity is a sound of despair'.[1] But against Barker's call for the reassertion of the tragic principle in theatre – a form which he acknowledges is and will remain a minority, indeed elitist interest – a popular playmaker like John McGrath – of the socialist touring group 7:84 – would reassert the old late 1960s principles of a popular theatre based round the real and palpable solidarities of class.[2] McGrath is a highly committed playmaker, who has made considerable personal sacrifices in career terms in order to pursue the creation of a mass, popular audience for socialist theatre. The fact that he hasn't succeeded in urban England is not for want of trying. Nor is it due in large part – though I suspect it makes a contribution – to the delusion that complexity and ambiguity in the theatre are part of a wicked capitalist plot, masterminded by the running dogs of the Royal Court Theatre, to deviate the proletariat from its true class interests, as opposed to being the ways in which most people experience most of their lives most of the time. (I do think, however, that it's highly dangerous to argue that left-wing playmakers shouldn't honestly confront the undoubted crisis that socialism is presently facing, in case some non-socialist might overhear and snitch on them.)

But I think the real problem with McGrath's project – and we've crossed pens on this before – is the notion that there is a genuine, rooted popular culture out there, and that if you take variety shows, club entertainment and pantomime and inject them with socialist content, then you've somehow set up a bridgehead in popular cultural space, you're part of a lived tradition that stretches back, and via which you can place workers' contemporary experience within the context of their history. Well, I'm sorry, but I still don't buy it. I think that the forms that have survived the televisual onslaught – including poor old panto – have been so extensively corrupted with that very televisual culture that they no longer have any usable relationship with autochthonous folk forms at all. How indeed could it be otherwise. The dramatic Making of the English Working Class in the eighteenth and early nineteenth centuries depended, of course, on the equally conclusive Unmaking of the English Peasantry. The massiveness of the depopulation of the countryside, the extraordinary privations of early industrial life, the conscious and considerable efforts of the manufacturers to suppress ancient festivities in the interests of labour discipline, effectively wiped out the living memory of ancient forms. Everywhere there is rupture, and even in the countryside the folk song, the morris dance and the mummers' play are not remembered but reclaimed, an act of social archaeologoy. And let us not delude ourselves either that even in the most militant pit villages – where if there was a living industrial tradition you'd expect to find it – the ballad, the brass band or even the lodge library or billiard room are central elements in people's lives today.

It's in this perhaps dispiriting context that we have to ask what contribution our medium can make to the struggles against our mean, greedy and increasingly frightening times; times inhabited and, indeed, in many ways defined by the most painful and often genuinely horrifying contradictions between human behaviour as we would will it – and sometimes glimpse it – and the actuality of much human action as it actually is. In the spring of 1985, as the fire that was to kill 54 people in Bradford City's football stadium took hold, supporters of the opposing team stood in front of the stand chanting 'burn, burn, burn'. After the tragedy of Heysel stadium, in which 38 Juventus fans, most of them Italians, were crushed to death following an attack by British hooligans, supporters of the Florence team ran through the streets of their city shouting 'Viva Liverpool'. But still, and at the same time, in Bradford, acts of extraordinary heroism were being performed, as ordinary civilians ran into the burning stand to rescue the trapped, came out with their hair burning, and went back in again to rescue more. And although there were undoubtedly acts of gratuitous viciousness during the 1984-85 miners' strike, on all sides against all others, nobody involved in any way with that struggle could avoid being heartened and moved by the constant acts of bravery, by the consideration and kindness shown by people suffering the most extreme privation to their comrades and to the strangers who supported them.

While similarly, but on the level of day-to-day experience, anyone who lives and/or works in a city has felt not just the contradiction between but the cohabitation of the cruel and the creative, the squalid and the stylish, a vital culture of resistance breeding on the very grey fungus of despair. This can be sensed in the hinterland around many city centres, where the gay bar or club is next door to the surviving workshop or wholesaler; where the community resource centre has set up shop beside the left-wing bookshop in the middle of the main Bengali area or Chinatown.

And I've spent much time thinking about what kind of play might best treat of these contradictions, or even more, might seek to *inhabit* them, and the strange places where they grow. And I was sure it wouldn't be agitprop, which can only present models of the world, and even then (frankly) not very sophisticated ones; nor naturalism, which can only treat of the personal; nor even social realism, with its precise choice of acceptably 'typical' characters, carefully positioned in 'total' contexts, a form which for me had grown too dry, too rational, in some ways too abstract, to grapple with the stories of our times. I knew in short entirely what sort of play *wouldn't* do; but I remained unsure about what kind of play *would* do until I realised that quite unintentionally I was already writing one.

The director and writer Ann Jellicoe is best known for her play *The Knack*, and for her tenure as Literary Manager of the Royal Court Theatre in one of its more heroic periods. In the 1970s she moved to Lyme Regis in Dorset, and about nine years ago began to develop in her region a method of playmaking by which local stories were told by local people, but written, directed and designed by professionals. In 1984, I was asked to do Community Play No. 10, in the county town of Dorchester. The tale we hit upon was that of a titanic if historically doubtful contest of wills between a crusading local vicar (the original of Revd Clare in Thomas Hardy's *Tess of the d'Urbevilles*) and the (female) founder of the local brewery. The piece had a cast of 180, and featured a race meeting, a Grand Equestrian Parade (in support of our brave lads at Balaclava) and a major cholera epidemic. Considering how to make these sequences, I raised with Ann the possibility of setting up defined groups of people to work on the individual episodes, in the manner of the medieval guilds making the mystery plays. Ann was hostile to the idea, which initially surprised me, but I soon understood why. We were, she explained, making not a pageant but a play, a thing of breadth, bulk and shape, to which all participants should have an equal relationship. But while the distinction between a play and a pageant seemed to be apposite, it struck me that if *Entertaining Strangers* is a play, then it's an odd one. It's written to be performed, for a start, in the promenade manner, on platforms surrounding and in the midst of the audience; further, its action is often multi-focused, with several incidents occurring at once, albeit usually in the context of one event. Certainly, I thought, there should at least be a metaphorical definition that could embrace these peculiarities. And it didn't take me too much time – though I suspect it would have taken a more assiduous reader of the works of Mikhail Bakhtin even less – to realise that my play is a kind of theatrical carnival. And in rewriting the play for production at the National Theatre – a project minutely informed by a belated but painstaking reading of *Rabelais and His World* – I have increased and I hope deepened its carnivalesque character.[3]

Earlier I argued that – to a greater extent than most European countries – our dynastic links to the folk-festive past have been ruptured. And of course we should feel highly impoverished, if not a little ashamed, as we contemplate the continued richness of the ancient folk traditions of Japan or Burma, or even Hungary or Spain. But we can at least comfort ourselves with the thought that our deracinated, cosmopolitan rootlessness affords us an opportunity denied more settled nations. For, if there are indeed few living links with our own ancient folk-forms, then the world is our oyster. We can draw on the forms of medieval Italy, or indeed Renaissance France; we can plunder Eastern Europe and ravage the Orient. And of course we can look as well to those forms which we have ourselves imported to our shores. For you can question whether the folk ballad still lives, or argue about panto or debate 'Whither Mumming?'. But there's surely no doubt that the biggest single working-class cultural event in Britain, now, and perhaps for two hundred years, is of West Indian origin, and is of course the carnival held every August in the streets of Notting Hill. And the fact that it has formed the paradigm for similar events up and down the country demonstrates that here at least is a tradition which doesn't need a preservation order slapped on it to survive.

For the maker of *theatrical* carnivals, the real carnival to be witnessed yearly along and about Ladbroke Grove provides a number of important clues. The first, of course, is the way that unlike more conventional forms of even outdoor entertainment and festivity, carnival collapses the division between participant and spectator. Even Goethe, in his teutonically dour and disapproving description of the Roman carnival he witnessed in 1787, notes that the carnival reveller is both spectator and actor, and he finds it hard to stop himself being caught up, if only for an instant, with the intoxication of the experience.[4] The reason for this is partly, of course, a matter of location: as Kwesi Owusu points out in his study of *The Struggle for Black Arts in Britain*, Western art has traditionally sought to create illusory spaces – from the museum to the concert hall to the playhouse – where the division between the spectator and the work are the very essence of the architecture.[5] The site of carnival is in real space, in the actual social landscape, where the act of stepping off the pavement into the street transforms a spectator on the sidelines into a part of the action. And this flexibility is bound up with the second important characteristic of carnival, which is that despite its overall coherence, its structure can accommodate and embrace all variety of manifestations at every level of development and sophistication: the most elaborate costumes are cheek-by-jowl with makeshift cardboard masks; the most elegant steel orchestra (or the most effectively amplified reggae band) competes with the solo fiddler on the toy violin or the child on the kazoo.

In this respect, the participatory, unfinished, multi-dimensional carnival is at absolute odds with the prepared, completed, uni-dimensional pageant, a distinction easily demonstrated by comparing two of the popular, mass-festive forms of our time. At a Royal Wedding, although the pavements are thronged, and much is going on, the division between coached participant and pedestrian spectator is clear and unambiguous. Even when observation takes autonomous form, it is one that fits effortlessly into preconceived formations: the jolly cockneys at their street party, the Hooray Henries and Fionas at their Fortnum picnics, the funny foreigners with their backpacks and their instamatics, all click neatly into their pre-ordained position in the jigsaw. How different, however, is that more recent invention, the mass-participation sports event, the London marathon, or Sport Aid. Here the distinction between participant and spectator is often highly blurred, the motivations of the former are highly contradictory and sometimes antagonistic, and – as hapless television interviewers so frequently discover – it's often hard to tell the fun-runner from the record-challenger, as the perfectly equipped athlete in his tasteful Adidas strip is exposed as a dilettante, while the obviously frivolous young lady in charity T-shirt, whiteface make-up and huge plastic ears plods doggedly towards her personal best. At the wedding, everything is exactly what it seems, and if it isn't, the cameras turn briskly away. At the marathon, by contrast, who knows what secret dreams, what challenges and what ambitions lurk beneath the cheery waves, the gritted smiles, the elaborate disguises?

Almost every commentator on carnival has commented on forms of this ambivalence and mystery. In Rome, Goethe noted the constant, and sometimes threatening, confusion of the actual and the fantastical, as attorneys proceed up and down the Corso accusing people of the most extensive criminal activities, or young men set up brawls which go quickly and wildly out of control. Almost everybody, too, has noted how the event challenges and up-ends the social hierarchy. As Henry Porter pointed out in a commentary on the 1975 Venice Carnival, it's no coincidence that socialist administrations have been keen to revive this manifestation of levelling in action.[6] Indeed, an incident which Porter describes – in which two revellers, dressed respectively as Napoleon and Marie Antoinette, march into a bar, jump the queue and demand brandy and cake – could have occurred, in some form or another, at any carnival at any time anywhere in the world. But just as common, and much more significant, is a ritual witnessed by Goethe, in which a dozen *pulcinelle* elect a king, crown him, put a sceptre in his hand, seat him in a decorated carriage and accompany him along the street with music and loud cheers. For, of course, the carnival is a feast of fools, a period of limited duration when hierarchy is not challenged but up-ended, a reversal with which Mikhail Bakhtin was obsesssed and which is exemplified by the election of the King-for-a-day, the Abbot of Unreason, the Lord of Misrule. When Falstaff plays the King to Hal in *Henry IV* part 1, he represents of course an echo of this tradition, But it is worth noting that Shakespeare's benign view of this indulgence does not last throughout his career; by the time he reaches the last plays his vision has grown crusty. First, it is true, the paternal old eye twinkles at the charming naïvety of the *Winter's Tale* clowns, apeing the quality in their absurdly fine new clothes. But then his gaze turns waspish, as it lights upon the distressing spectacle of Caliban. It has been the custom of the aged and secure throughout the ages to see in carnival revelling the threat of a debased and debasing culture, the march of the mindless, anarchy amok. Recently, the image of Caliban has been wheeled out once again, by British conservative commentators like the dreaded Auberon Waugh of the *Spectator* and the *Sunday Telegraph*, demanding that the latter-day descendants of Sycorax be 'driven back into their caves', or whatever it is Auberon Waugh thinks that people outside rural Somerset live in. And it's true of course that carnivals can turn nasty, from the sixteenth-century carnival in Romans investigated by Professor Le Roy Ladurie, to Notting Hill in 1976.[7] But it's equally true that they tend to do so not of their own accord but when they are attacked, by those who have good reason to view them as a threat.

I am aware that Bakhtin's prescient work on carnival has been exploited primarily as a political paradigm. I want for the moment however to express some tentative thoughts about how the principles of carnival might work artistically; but not in the real world of the street but in the illusory space of the theatre. In his remarkable book *Theatre of the Oppressed*, the Latin American theatre-maker Augusto Boal contrasts three dramaturgies: the Aristotelian model in which the spectators passively delegate power to the dramatic character, so that the latter may act and think for them; the Brechtian theatre of the enlightened vanguard, in which the spectators do not delegate their power to think, but still give up the right to act; and Boal's own 'poetics of the oppressed', in which the spectators no longer delegate either power to the character, but exercise them both.[8] In Boal's case, this is partly a literal matter, as he has developed an extensive repertoire of theatre games in which situations are presented by actors to groups who in turn instruct the actors to try out new ways of solving the social/political problems portrayed, before their very eyes. But he has also developed an abstracted, theatrical version of the same idea, what he calls the Joker technique, whereby a character (or rather a character function) outside the space and time of the play acts as a 'contemporary and neighbour of the spectator', an interpreter of the action, a challenger, on the audience's behalf, of its course and outcome.

The jester is of course, again, the Lord of Misrule, as is Dario Fo in his feted retrieval of the medieval strolling story-teller tradition, *Mistero Buffo*.[9] In Britain, too, there are contemporary giullari plying their trade. In the early 1970s, carnival was a key element in the justly famous Bradford Festivals, in both of which a genuine sense of popular street festivity was created by events as disparate as a full-scale mock-up of an American presidential election parade, the recreation of an Edwardian steam-fair amid the disused arches of the abandoned railway station, and the celebration of a custom-built pagan child's naming ceremony, performed by the Welfare State performance group (accompanied, as I remember, by the Mike Westbrook band, a fire-eater and two live goats) beneath the venerable wood beams of the Wool Exchange. Last year I journeyed to Cumbria to visit the Welfare State at their present headquarters (as they put it, half-way between Wordsworth and Windscale). And it was alarming as well as exciting to realise that the spotty teenager grinning bravely through her chickenpox in the corner of director John Fox's living room was the very child whom I'd participated in naming in the Bradford Wool Exchange some fifteen years before. But it was unambiguously cheering to learn that Welfare State were still at it, in ways that bear much relevance to the above. Indeed, one of their more recent creations was an extraordinary compound of community event, pageant, fun-fair and performance, presented on the wharves and in the waters of old dockland, and titled *The Raising of the Titanic*.

But it's my belief that it's possible to go even further than the Welfare State. As I said at the beginning, the early 1970s saw a split between the anarcho-libertarians and the stern class warriors, or in theatrical terms, between performance groups like Welfare State, based in the art colleges, and the linx-eyed social realists from the universities. And despite sterling lyrical work by such as Adrian Mitchell, it seems to me that the one thing Welfare State haven't cracked about total theatre is the place of the text. Is there in the method of *abstraction* of the principles of carnival a way of incorporating the sophistication and complexity of the fully realised theatrical text with the energy and immediacy of the participatory celebration?

One of the remarkable things about proto-carnival theatre as I experienced it in St Mary's Church Dorchester is its amazing flexibility. Somehow, because in the promenade form the audience is able to choose what to look at, to construct its own spatial relationship with the event, it is able to switch not just the direction but the very *mode* of its attention, if not in the twinkling of an eye, then certainly in the turn of a head. Perhaps in fact I shouldn't have been so surprised. It's the custom of theatrical snobs like myself to complain of the exponentially diminishing concentration span of the TV remote control generation, but to forget the positive side of that phenomenon, which is an extraordinary quickness of uptake, a learned capacity to click into highly contrasted narratives and indeed moods at a moment's notice. Most of us had had the sense, watching even quite modern realist plays (and certainly in Ibsen), that the audience is way ahead of the exposition, that while the plot's still *en route* the punters have already arrived. In *Entertaining Strangers*, the audience evinced a remarkable capacity to switch its attention and its mode of perception from a race-meeting to a church, from a participatory drinking song to the witness of a silent man at prayer.

In this form, then, the theatre does seem to be more capable than we might have thought it to present experience with a variance, a simultaneity, and most of all the *unevenness*, which is metaphorically at least akin to the experience of actual carnival in real streets. And my interest in exploiting such characteristics arises out of one of the central projects of Bakhtin's book, which is to contrast the official, religious world of Gothic Europe, in which everything is vertical, complete and hierarchical, with the horizontal, unfinished world of carnival, of which the paradigm is the human body itself, and particularly the lower half of it, with its tumescent protruberances and welcoming hollows, its permanent condition of ingestion and evacuation, the simultaneous site of birth and death. And Bakhtin goes on to relate this characteristic to another traditional function of the ancient feast of fools, which is to evoke the ritual of the dying and reborn king, the ritual echoed dimly in the English Mummers' Play. For Bakhtin, Rabelais's carnival form is uniquely capable of expressing birth and death, good and evil, the elegaic and the grotesque, the transcendent and the base, not as separate or opposite, but as the simultaneous inhabitants of the same processional space – as the sacred and profane were able, in the flash of an eye, to occupy the same space during our performances in Dorchester. In *Rabelais and His World* Bakhtin writes,

> All that exists dies and is born simultaneously, combines the past and the future, the obsolete and the youthful, the old truth and the new truth. However small the part of the existing world we have chosen we shall find in it the same fusion. And this fusion is deeply dynamic: all that exists, both in the whole and in each of its parts, is in the act of becoming.[10]

I think I've already made clear that it is this capacity to express the opposite in the same plane that is, for me, the most exciting aspect of carnival as Bakhtin defines it.

Certainly, that idea is central to the project of developing a theatre that can explore and inhabit the contradictions of our time without either denying their existence or pouring detached scorn on all sides from a great height. It also contains within it the answer to those critics of carnival – both in the abstract and in the theatre – who point to the frequent historical *incorporation* of carnival, an incorporation acknowledged by Bakhtin himself (who describes how even in the Renaissance 'the state encroached upon festive life and turned it into a parade'). That this containment often takes the form of a safety-valve for otherwise explosive social tensions is argued by the Marxist critic Terry Eagleton, who describes carnival as

> a *licensed* affair in every sense, a permissible rupture of hegemony, a contained popular blow-off as disturbing and relatively ineffectual as a revolutionary work of art.[11]

One hardly dare speculate as to the level of ineffectiveness that Eagleton would ascribe to the carnivalesque *in artistic form* (revolutionary or otherwise), but it is pretty clear that he would agree wholeheartedly with Howard Barker that 'a carnival is not a revolution', because 'after the carnival, after the removal of the masks, you are precisely who you were before'. And perhaps the most compelling reasons for that phenomenon lie in the essentially limited nature of carnival, its characteristic as an up-ending of existing hierarchies (and its consequent dependence on them the right way up), and most of all its formal conservatism, its backwardness, its visible roots in ancient and venerable – if peasant – traditions. No surprise then, that the most successful attempts to apply Bakhtin to the present day have taken place in countries which still have a strong repertoire of carnivalesque practices, such as those of Latin America, or upon literatures produced in colonial or ex-colonial societies where social divisions are peculiarly stark and particularly charged.[12]

It is, however, there that the clue lies. For while the political difference between, say, Hampstead and Hackney may not yet be comparable with that between riviera Rio and the barrios, there is no question that it has got considerably *more* charged over recent years, that the sense in Britain's inner cities of living beneath the base of a dominant and irremovable authoritarian hierarchy has increased dramatically and will go on doing so. And, indeed, the fact that, like carnival, some inner-city cultural forms are rooted in tradition, that they express a limited sense of security in an otherwise frightening and threatening world, does not necessarily mean that their expression, and most importantly *their defence*, is not a potentially radical act.[13]

For in the inner city, it seems to me, we do find communities peculiarly receptive to the principles of carnival, even in theatrical form. One of the assumptions about community theatre on the Ann Jellicoe model was that it relied on the existence of an essentially culturally homogenous grouping – such as you would be more likely to find surrounding a school in South Dorset than in Walsall or North London. But the fact that there have been highly successful urban community plays in precisely those places, and elsewhere, often involving groups drawn from the widest possible class and ethnic spectra, demonstrates a perhaps unexpected potential for carnivalesque theatre in the urban environment. But it really should be no surprise. The inner city contains within it the building blocks of a rich alliance between the economically and the socially excluded – an alliance which has already born fruit in the obvious realms of music (the influence of black culture on white working-class music) and fashion (the spread not just of sartorial styles but of a whole attitude to clothing and personal presentation first developed in and by the gay communities). It has also found expression in the alliances that developed between the city and the industrial countryside during the year-long miners' strike; a dispute which was itself, as has been frequently argued, in part a conservative movement in defence of communities and their traditions, but also, as things fell out, a conflict which brought the new politics and cultures of the cities into the coalfields, as well as visa versa.

But finally, the receptiveness of the city to the

carnivalesque lies in its *prefigurative* quality. Augusto Boal describes his theatre in São Paulo as a rehearsal for the revolution, and while that word left my active vocabulary some time ago, I relate very strongly to the idea that the theatre is not just about what is but also what could be. And, as Bakhtin reminds us, during medieval carnival,

> For a short time life came out of its usual, legalised and consecrated furrows and entered into the space of utopian freedom. The very brevity of this freedom increased its fantastical nature and utopian radicalism.[14]

What I suppose most of us are striving for, is a way of combining the cerebral, unearthly detachment of Brecht's theory with the all too earthy, sensual, visceral experience of Bakhtin's carnival, so that in alliance these two forces can finally defeat the puppeteers and manipulators of the spectacle. We are doing so in full knowledge of the dangers of incorporation, of becoming no more than a radical sideshow to divert the masses and dampen their ardour. But, although we must take heed of Shakespeare's perception 'that there is no slander in an allowed fool',[15] there remain fools, in the bard's cannon and elsewhere, whose message of energy and anarchy is by no means welcome at the feast, and would be even less so if informed by the passion and intelligence of those whose analysis of social wrongs is informed by a greater breadth of experience and thought. When that old manipulator Prospero came to the island, he seized it from Sycorax, releasing her slave Ariel, but then enchaining him again, to enchant his creatures with his spells and songs. Now that Ariel is free, perhaps the time has come for him to look down from his flight, and for Sycorax's slave-son Caliban to crawl up from the bowels of the earth, for them to take each other's hands, and show us what a future island, without Sycorax *or* Prospero, what such an island might be like.

Notes

1. *Guardian*, 10 February 1986.
2. See John McGrath, *A Good Night Out*, London 1981.
3. Mikhail Bakhtin, *Rabelais and his World*, Bloomington Indiana 1968.
4. J.W. von Goethe, *Italian Journey*, Harmondsworth 1970, pp. 446-60.
5. Kwesi Owusu, *The Struggle for Black Arts in Britain*, London 1986.
6. *Sunday Times*, 24 February 1985.
7. Emmanuel Le Roy Ladurie, *Carnival in Romans*, Harmondsworth 1981.
8. Augusto Boal, *Theatre of the Oppressed*, London 1979.
9. See Tony Mitchell, *Dario Fo: People's Court Jester*, London 1984.
10. Bakhtin, op. cit., p. 416.
11. Terry Eagleton, *Walter Benjamin, or, Towards a Revolutionary Criticism*, London 1981, p. 148.
12. See Peter Stallybrass and Allon White, *The Politics and Poetics of Transgression*, London 1986, p.11.
13. Paul Gilroy, *There Ain't No Black in the Union Jack*, London 1987.
14. Bakhtin, op. cit., p. 89.
15. See Eagleton, op. cit., p. 148.

After Orwell

It is now generally accepted that George Orwell chose the date 1984 by reversing the last two digits of the year in which his novel was written. In celebration of the actual 1984, I wrote a short story – published in the January edition of *Marxism Today* – which tried to pull the same trick on the Year of That Woman. My piece owes much to the insights of Bob Rowthorn and Eve Brook, but I cannot resist claiming personal credit for the hiving off of 'minority' television networks – and the fate of the Alliance.

1997

It was a bright cold day in April, and the clocks were all set to different time-zones. Harold looked nervously around as he waited for the entry phone to be answered. Eventually it was: he gave the codeword (which today was 'primogeniture'), and he passed quickly into the building as an empty Budweiser can crashed into the wall above his head, fell, and clattered down an open manhole.

Inside the concourse all was clean, and plush and quiet: a million miles removed, it seemed, from the degradation of San Carlos Square just beyond the electronic entrances. (The square was in Islington; it had once been called Mandela, or Mugabe, or some such name: but all that had changed when the Commissioners had taken over from the 'borough council' in the later 1980s). Harold was searched, took the lift to the sixteenth floor, and held up his ID in front of the securiscope, before the mistress of the house deactivated the lasalarm and let him in.

It was his first day working for this couple. They had rung the agency at short notice, wanting a man for 'general duties', and as Harold had only worked for seven days in five weeks, it was welcome, whatever 'general duties' were. His speciality was butling (the agency called it 'stewarding'), but he could turn his hand to ushering, or valeting, or even gardening, and at least the job would last for several days. The next five weeks or so were bad ones for the supply servant trade: with all those public holidays (Jubilee Day, Royal Wedding Day, and next week, naturally, Belgrano Day) you were lucky if you did a full week in the months of May or June.

Nice couple, Harold thought. The point, the mistress said, was that nanny, housekeeper and both the maids had taken William and Dorothy to Merionethshire, and Sue and Bryan were needing somebody to keep the place, you know, just ticking over, for a week or two, until they'd all return. And if he could come in daily, do the plants, switch the freezer over to the generator if the national grid went down (*when* the grid goes down, laughed Bryan), and keep the place in shape, then that would be just fine.

At which point Bryan checked his worldwatch, announcing that if he didn't get to work before the markets closed in Delhi they would have his guts for garters. But he'd be back for sure by 18 GMT.

(Harold knew, of course, that Bryan would not leave the building as he, Harold, had entered it: he would take the lift down to the basement car park, past the service concourse, and drive out through the electronic doors, which would close like a jaw behind him, and off he'd go, past the garbage and the pot-marked pavements and the open manholes, as if he and his family didn't really live in Islington at all.)

By 9.00 (by normal British time, thought Harold sniffily), the flat was empty. Everything was clear. All servant agencies now signed an anti-theft agreement with their clients, and although half your pay was docked against temptation, an agency like Harold's still suffered quite substantial losses. Harold, however, was known for his punctilious honesty (too stupid to steal, people at the agency remarked) and so was one of the few people on the books to be trusted with a job which gave him free run of someone else's home. He started in the kitchen.

The flat was large, and well-equipped, with a gym *and* a solarium. The master, clearly, was a banker: Chase Manhattan, probably, or maybe First National of Tokyo, or even Intermid or EuroWest. Madam, she'd said, was in the civil service (which she'd admitted quite apologetically, as if it was something to be vaguely ashamed of, like being a pornographer or a sociologist). She hadn't told him which of the four ministries she worked for, but from her general demeanour he could guess. He chuckled as he took the pulses out of soak. He could remember when the Government was like an octopus, its interfering tentacles were everywhere (the *Government* owned factories and mines, and even built the roads!). But then, as her last gesture before retirement, the Great Aunt (as she was still affectionately known) had rigorously rolled back the ever-expanding agencies, reducing them to a manageable four. The first was the Department of Security, which ran the army, the police, and dealt with foreign governments; the second was the Department of the Budget, which dealt with all financial matters (it had once been called 'The Treasury', but that implied an open crock of gold, whereas the word 'budget' implied frugality and thrift). The third was the Department of the Family, which dealt with education, health and poor relief, and the final ministry, the Department of the Government, had started life as the Prime Minister's private office, but now oversaw all operations, and since 1986 had been responsible for the work of the Commissioners who ran the cities and the towns. The Departments were colloquially referred to as DOS, DOB, DOF and DOG, and Mrs was undoubtedly a Doffer, probably one of those busybodies who oversaw the FPG.

'Busybodies'. Harold smiled, as he cleared away the carrot juice and bran from the breakfast bar. He was beginning to sound like Jane, who was always railing against this or that. In fact, he'd voted for the Union Party solidly for nearly twenty years, back from the days when it was called 'Conservative'. Whereas in her time Jane had at least considered voting for the lot: the Labour Party, naturally, and the Democratic Labour Party, and the Labour Party (Tribunite), and the Labour Party For The Pact (and the Labour Party heartily opposed to same); but also for the Alliance, and the Alliance (Owenite) and the Liberals and the National Liberals, not to mention all the various varieties of Social Democrat (from 'Real' to 'True' to 'Genuine') that had mushroomed in the wake of '88. In fact, the opposition (or, the 'other parties', if the truth be told) had consistently got higher national votes, and indeed collectively won far more seats, than had been mustered by the Union. But as the largest single non-Governmental group was never more than 70, and each felt personally betrayed by all the others, it didn't make much odds.

Jane didn't take this view. She felt the opposition parties should unite again, as they had in 1988, during the brief Labour-led administration that had provoked such violence and hostility, both without and within its ranks. (Jane understood the jargon of the parties, and so knew why 'pactist' had become such an insult, worse even than 'Hobsbawmist', to which 'pactism' was connected in ways disputed by all groups and factions, including the 'Hobsbawmists' themselves.) She felt that nearly twenty years of virtually uninterrupted Union rule had been a disaster for the country, and while Harold didn't agree, he could understand Jane's point of view. She had been born in Liverpool, then a thriving industrial town (even a city). By the late 80s, however, the only real industry left was one unprivatised car manufacturer, left in business as a kind of *memento mori* for the bad old days (like the one state-owned pit in Rotherham, or the one remaining shipyard on the Clyde). The factory was small and its products massively subsidised by the DOB: but at least it allowed the town to stay sufficiently alive to sustain a minimal level of services, of hospitals and shops and cinemas and schools. Most of the inhabitants of Liverpool, indeed (and the same was true of Leeds and Wolverhampton) were engaged in selling increasingly mediocre and threadbare services and things, not to the outside world, but to each other. And so while all the young and ambitious had long since moved down south (to populate the shanty-towns on Hampstead Heath and Clapham Common), there was this kind of ghost economy remaining in the northern counties, to sustain the ageing population as their once-great cities crumbled quietly around them.

So he could understand how Jane must feel. Her place of birth had once been larger than Northampton; and indeed both Manchester and Coventry had once been much, much bigger than Buckingham or even Norwich. But, as the Great Aunt had so often pointed out, cities like Liverpool and Bradford – far from the European ports, their infrastructure in decay, surrounded by bleak countryside – were unviable in the contemporary world, and there came a point when natural sentiment must give way to the harsh realities of modern times.

He heard a discreet buzz, and looked up at the worldclock. It was 6.00 in Washington, and time to take a coffee break.

At least, in casual work, you could take a break (you couldn't smoke a fag, of course, in a job like this: indeed the doorman frisked you for your packet when you first arrived). In the FEZs, you worked a straight six hours, and woe betide you if nature called. The FEZs (the acronym stood for 'Free Enterprise Zone') were set up in the 80s, to encourage business back to the inner cities, by offering tax and rates and customs concessions, and by exempting firms from all those irritating rules and regulations which had made it so prohibitively difficult to make an honest profit in the past. Now, within the older southern cities (the few FEZs in the north had been dismantled following the long hot summers of 1987 and 1991), the Zones provided almost all the industrial employment, and they even still had unions, and closed shops of a sort (despite the Bill of Rights, which had banned closed shops, as well as guaranteeing everybody's right to purchase private medicine and education). So although you had to work much harder than you'd had to in the old days (and there was nothing wrong with *that*) you got high wages, and the jobs were highly prized, and sometimes even fought over, which explained the wire fences and the checkpoints at the entrances. And with things being as they were, the unions were prepared to turn a blind eye to the upsurge in industrial accidents, which had resulted (malcontents would claim), from the repeal (within the Zones) of the more ludicrously restrictive provisions of the Factory Acts.

Harold sipped his decaff. In the old days, he'd have read the paper, but of course now you could only do that on a screen, and although Madam had said he could use the VDU, he wasn't quite sure he could make it work. He didn't have one in his flat (you couldn't get a rent rebate if you could afford to rent a receiver or a quadreo, which, when you thought about it, was quite fair and reasonable), and the channels were proliferating now at such a rate he didn't understand the system any more. He knew that the old channels – ITV 1-16 – could still be received by everybody, but that for 'minority' networks like the ITNs and BBC, you had to pay. But how you got NBC, or British Satellite (1-17), or Home and Garden (1-6), or ITS (1-9) for Sport, particulary on the ICC (the Independent Control Console, which you pointed at the screen, and pressed a button, and things happened), let alone how you could talk directly to the bank, or to the shops, or to your mother (like as not), or call up Mirrorscreen or Sunscope, was a mystery.

Still, he would have a go. It took some time to find the 'on' switch, and what came 'on' was a list of figures about 'future softs', but by dint of much pressing of the ICC, the channels did start flashing by, and he recognised the logos of the sixteen ITVs – which were showing quiz games – and that must be NBC (a film about rich people in America) or ABC (a play about the wealthy in the United States) or CBS (a serial apparently concerned with the moneyed classes of the USA). And then he passed both Mirrorscreen and Sunscope (which were both announcing details of a competition), and Expresserama and The Daily Mailout (which were broadcasting the winning numbers of a lottery), and he'd have liked to stop, but the ICC appeared to be stuck on channel change, and so on he went, through seven snooker channels and some cricket and the racing live from Munich and through all the ITNs (which were showing maps and charts and little blue and yellow arrows and parliamentary figures jumping up and down and shouting and interviews with high-ups from the DOS) and by now he was developing a headache and at last he found the off-switch and with a kind of sigh the screen went dark and Harold was alone with just his thoughts for company once more.

'Communications', Harold thought, as he dusted round the maids' room. The age of information, the age of universal contact, the world a pulsating, electronic spider's web, with Tokyo as near as Tottenham. Yet somehow he felt, himself, that his horizons had grown narrower and narrower. You couldn't even move about as much as you'd been able to before. They'd stopped running third class on the daytime trains entirely (the executive class passengers had protested at the 'louts and hooligans' who used to shout and play loud music in the cocktail bars), and since Spaghetti Junction had been declared unsafe for traffic the motor coach network had become restricted to a limited area of the south-east and south-west. And even telephones were less efficient than they had been: the 'basic service' (reluctantly provided by ITT, as a condition for their exclusive Government communications franchise) provided only local calls, and the long-distance option, once again, was on the DOF list of 'inessential luxuries' that relief recipients were not entitled to possess.

So Harold felt quite isolated from the world around him, and the sense of all that information on the VDU, just beyond his fingertips, provoked a spasm of impatient anger. Yet, really, if he thought about it, why did *he* need to know what was happening in Singapore, or Spain? Why indeed should *he* feel he had the right (on transport systems paid for by the tax-payers) to bomb around the country as and when he pleased? And was there not indeed an argument that the explosion of communications, into every home, had contributed to the moral atrophy that led ill-educated youths to loot and riot? (To see something on the VDU was to feel entitled to it, as the Parent Power Groups so often pointed out). Was it *not* better for the masses not to know about the riches heaped behind the window-meshes and beyond the locked and power-bolted doors?

The quiet, discreet buzz once again broke through his reverie. Good God, he thought. It was already 9 pm in Sydney. Time for lunch.

'Lunch' was a peeling sandwich in a grimy wine bar. (The place had not been decorated since the early 80s: the art deco lampshades were all grey with grime, and sad remains of ferns lay wilted in the jardinieres). The VDU was (oddly) tuned not to the ITS but to the news – those little blue and yellow arrows once again – but the hubbub was too great for him to hear the news-host's words. He sipped the cheap, keg reisling (wine was much cheaper than beer now, after pressure from the European Agricultural Community). In one corner sat three FEZ workers, looking nervously around them (they'd just received their fat pay-packets, and this was a high-crime area). In another was a group of young men in NNP uniform, who'd been celebrating (or drowning sorrows) with a jug of Heineken.

Harold's son was in the NNP. The New Nation Programme was a compulsory scheme for the nation's youth, which ran from the school leaving age (whether fourteen or above) until the age of twenty. In theory, military conscription was a voluntary option, and indeed, if you showed an electronic aptitude, or could prove your 'social skills', it was easy to avoid the army. But most kids from places like round here ended up in uniform, as indeed had Harold's son, who had gained a place at the North East London Polytechnic's bright new Faculty of Imperial Studies (he wished to specialise in the achievements of the British Raj), until the crisis of Harold's marriage had made the payment of the fees impossible.

It had all been most unfortunate, but it was really no one's fault. Harold's wife had been born in the West Indies, and during his long early 90s period of unemploymemt, she had taken on responsibility for the household bills (although fiscal policy was intended to encourage women to fulfill their primary responsibilities as wives and mothers, the repeal of Equal Pay Acts and the abolition of the wages councils had made them peculiarly attractive to employers in the retail trade). Unfortunately, things had got quite out of hand (commitments had been entered into foolishly while Harold was in work) and she was eventually faced – as so many had been – with the choice of prison for default, or applying to the VRP. (The Voluntary Repatriation Programme was intended to assist the passage home of immigrants who found it hard to adapt themselves to British ways.) And so, to use the jargon, Harold's wife was volrepped to Jamaica, and he was faced with a level of backpayments which made his fantasies about his son seem the most grandiose of delusions.

For two years. Harold had lived alone, in considerable privation (to discourage fickle attitudes to having children out of wedlock, the rules relating to relief entitlements for the single unemployed with children were peculiarly stringent). Then, somewhat to his own surprise, he took what he could only call a mistress. His natural instinct was to marry (like the Government, he tok a dim view of adultery), but under the Divorce Law 1989 (which sought to reaffirm the full solemnity of the marriage vows), there were no provisions for annulment unless adultery or cruelty were proved by one party against the other (for blame must lie somewhere) and although Harold did suspect, deep in his bones, that cruelty had been involved, somewhere along the line, he could not see that it applied to him or his wife, and so the marriage was, at least until the five year separation clause came into play, irrevocable.

Harold's mistress was called Jane. She'd been a 'social worker' (a group of state employees whose job had been to encourage the inadequate to consider that they were 'entitled' to be paid for doing nothing) and a 'feminist' (a political persuasion which held that women were 'oppressed' by the people who looked after them). She had been rationalised in 1994, as part of the DOFs 'Stand On Your Own Feet' policy (or the 'Stew In Your Own Juice' scheme, as Jane had put it, but then, after all, she would).

Before that, however, she'd met Harold. He'd got a little drunk one evening, as he was the first to admit, and she'd been called out to the police station after he'd been picked up sprawling in the street. It had been the night his daughter died, but of course that was no excuse for his behaviour.

Harold looked around him. He was not an emotional man, but thoughts of his daughter always brought a tear into his eye, and he was fearful that it would be noticed. It had been his fault of course: the point of the abolition of all that irksome red tape governing small shopkeepers (who found it hard enough to make ends meet) was quite precisely so the forces of the market rather than interfering busybodies from the ministries could weed out those whose services were inadequate in any way.

It had been a can of meat, from the corner grocer. He'd been 'in a hurry', and he wasn't well, so he hadn't eaten any of it himself. There had been scares about tin cans before, but you never thought that this could happen to you or to your family. But somehow, it was not sufficient – really not *sufficient* – that in protest at the killing of his daughter he could henceforth shop elsewhere.

But despite their unpropitious meeting, Jane had liked him (he'd been – she said still was – a handsome man). And one of those strange unexpected likings started, and led on to one of those even more unexpected loves. And although her views were at best eccentric and at worst downright dangerous, their affection grew and deepened.

It was inevitably clandestine. Jane had not found a new position, and she relied on state relief, and the rules against cohabitation were if anything more strict than they had been in the 70s and 80s (and the FPG was everywhere, of course, aided and abetted by those helpful citizens, the Checkers). And even if they did risk a night together, with much sneaking in and out, then there was still the danger of conception, to take the edge of ease and pleasure off their union. (The Government was particularly concerned about the birthrate among those classes of population generally agreed to be least competent to bring up children, and having failed to introduce legislation making it mandatory on doctors to put 'high-risk' young women on the pill, had developed a whole network of proscriptions which at the least made pregnancy a major crisis for anyone who had at any time been wholly or partly dependent on relief, which meant, now, almost two-thirds of the population. Thus, for such people, 'family aid' – once called 'child benefit' – *reduced* with each new child, the parish housing lists were weighted against the 'irresponsibly fertile', and even midwifery insurance rates were set artificially high. But all of these mild irritations could be instantly removed – one might say, at a stroke – if you participated in the DOFs magnanimous STORC programme, which provided generous, low-interest and long-term loans for 'Surgical Termination of the Reproductive Capability'.

So their love life was at best a nervy business. But he enjoyed their time together, he loved listening to her as she lectured him about the world, and even (on occasions) felt there was something in the things she had to say. For Jane, it had all begun with the development of 'the multinational corporations' (how she could use the jargon with a straight face was a mystery!) and their understanding that all the tiresome controls which so bedevilled business in the West could be avoided by the simple project of moving processes and plant elsewhere. At first, this happened *within* countries (the move from Michigan and Indiana to the sun-belt, the flight from Lancashire and Yorkshire to East Anglia). But then, the corporations realised that this scheme could be internationally applied, by moving plant to southern Europe or to Mexico, and then indeed half-way across the world, to wherever labour was cheapest and most plentiful and pliable, which was why the fastest growing economies were no longer the oil states, or even South Korea and Taiwan, but Malaysia, Indonesia and the Philippines.

This was not to say, of course, that no wealth remained within the 'first world', indeed that's where the *wealth* was, but it did mean that the numbers who had access to it had become geographically as well as socially reduced, to the south and western USA (Phoenix was now larger than Chicago), to Japan and South Korea (Seoul was now richer than Toronto), and to a rough quadrangle in the middle of north-west Europe, bounded by Bristol, Bordeaux, Milan and Cologne (the fate of cities like Hamburg and Vienna had been similar to that of Glasgow and New York). And while the new breed of new technologist, his family and friends, required a growing army of retailers, bankers, nannies, real estate developers, doctors, hairdressers, tutors, decorators, governesses, entertainers, lawyers, gardeners and maids, they required them where they were, in bright new garden cities in attractive countryside, not in Belfast, Rotterdam or even Portugal or Spain. And so, for those left out in the cold, there was decay, and a sullen and resigned despair: and even within the golden parallelogram, there was a permanent and aching sense of insecurity, an insecurity which grew out of the awareness that your livelihood depended not on the provision of a human need, but on the servicing of appetites that were defined in large part by the vicissitudes of taste and fashion. And thus it was, Jane said, that a technology that could have liberated humankind, that (for the first time) could have granted men and women the long-prayed-for means to plan their own societies (indeed, to plan how old technologies should give way to the new), had instead turned those very men and women into random particles, forever zipping round a constantly mutating universe, in search of nuclei that having welcomed them could just as simply cannon them away into the outer darkness once again. It flew, and she would say it with a bitter little smile, in the face of human nature.

And that was indeed the problem. It was not so much that the new, thrusting Britain was a frosty place for the young, unskilled and unemployed, who unless rigidly controlled would take out their frustration on the general populace (though that, of course, was what the Kindred Volunteers were for). Nor was it, entirely, that a system based on the pursuit of individual gain raised expectations among the less thrusting and innovative classes that could not be fulfilled (which was why the Checkers had been so keen to pressurise the cable companies to keep advertisements for luxuries like VDUs and quadreos off all but the most exclusive channels). Nor even was it (absolutely) that, denied so much else, the masses had at least the right to feel part of a nation, with traditions and a heritage, which should be protected both from literal invasion by the dregs of the third world and from the constant sniping of self-styled 'progressive intellectuals' (which is why the Parents Unions' campaign to exclude all patrioticist material from school curricula was such a popular initiative). No, it was above all that while individual and collective selfishness were excellent motivations for the strong and powerful (who set up businesses or ran the army), these instincts did appear to have a deleterious psychological effect on those whose temperaments were less mature (who broke shop windows and rioted at football matches), which observation had eventually led the Government to the paradoxical but (if you thought about it) logical conclusion that the freer your economy became, the greater were the limits and controls that must be placed on individual actions in the social sphere.

Which was why (Jane would conclude) a Government that every five years claimed exclusive franchise on the freedom of the individual ...

But there he stopped remembering the things she said, and indeed felt a kind of chill run through him, as he sat there in the bar, because today Jane was expected to report to the local branch headquarters of the DOF for what was described in the official letter as a 'routine assessment' of her relief position. And as he had told her, begged her, pleaded with her: it might well be just that, so why on earth did she refuse to go?

Good heavens, Harold thought, as he saw a timecheck flash up on the VDU. It was 4.15 in Cape Town. Quickly, he drained his reisling, and hurried back towards San Carlos Square. In such a rush was he, indeed, that he hardly noticed (though he would remember it, it would come back to him), the queues outside the meagre food shops, lines of people dressed in cashmere tracksuits or designer dungarees, people with even, milk-white teeth and fitted spectacles and solarified complexions, people (in short) who were as out of place here as he would have been at a Covent Garden juice-bar or in the grains department of a Sainsbury's.

He apologised profusely, but she didn't seem to hear. (She would be back at 16 GMT, she'd said, and here it was, not 5 am in Anchorage.) Surrounded by bags and boxes, hampers and rucksacks, stuffed with food (but not *her* food: there was white bread, tinned fruit, processed

cheese), she drummed her fingers, stood, paced about, sat
down again; until finally she asked him to assist her, she
and Bryan were leaving now, their plans had changed,
they needed to get all this to the lift, down to the garage, to
await his imminent arrival. And of course Harold did as he
was told, and they were standing in the garage, with the
bags and sacks and boxes, when Bryan screeched in
through the jaw-like doors, and the two of them humped
all the food into the boot, and were indeed about to go
when Madam turned to him, with an expression on her
face which seemed to be half-way between embarrassment,
and a kind of inappropriate contrition.

And she explained, that obviously they'd decided to get
out (out? out of where?), and he might wish to get out too
(out of what? whatever for?), and he mustn't feel that if he
didn't want to stay he should (why shouldn't he?), but
perhaps he had the best idea, why should Merionethshire
be any different (different from what?) and anyway ...

And she slipped a banknote – worth more than his
week's salary – into his hand, and they were gone.

And as he stepped into the lift, he realised that, after all,
he knew.

It had been Jane, of course, who had explained it all. She'd
been a 'peace campaigner', naturally (they all were, all that
sort: it was an outrage, as the Great Aunt said, that they'd
appropriated the word 'peace' when what they were really
advocating was surrender). But unlike her friends, she'd
never really thought that all those little proxy wars (she
called them 'poxy wars') would really escalate; for her, it
wasn't really about territory, or the principles of
international law, or even national pride, or any of the
reasons trotted out by the spokesmen of the DOS, but
more a kind of circus, an entertainment to take people's
minds off what was happening at home.

She'd argued it quite forcibly, in fact, and it had
sounded plausible (it always did, of course, at the time).
The liberation of 'Zimbabwe' in the early 90s (in response
to the appeals of persecuted opposition groups within the
country): had not that followed on the disturbances in

Newcastle and Glasgow in August 1991? And the rescue mission in Belize in October 1987 (in collaboration with American and Guatemalan troops loyal to the Government-in-Exile of Air Marshal President Juan Martinez): had that not effectively cleared everybody's mind of the uprisings in Birmingham and Coventry the month before? And indeed, what about the 'Falklands' (now renamed 'New Bedfordshire') and the naval task force that had sailed just nine months after Brixton, Liverpool and Manchester had burned?

But she had admitted, always, that it could get out of hand, that one of these 'adventures' would prove to be unstoppable; and he knew, because he'd heard it talked of, seen it flashing on the VDUs, of the Sino-Soviet rapprochement, and the Russian-Chinese mutual defence pact, and the growing tension as the Chinese government prepared to repossess Hong Kong at the ending of the British lease on June 30, 1997 ...

The lift had reached the sixteenth floor, and Harold hurried down the corridor. He must find out, now, what was going on. He fumbled for the keycard, slipped it in the lock, and the door slid open, just in time for him to hear the tail-end of a sentence, spoken by a voice he knew.

She'd switched their answering machine on, but in the rush, she'd obviously clocked the receiver on to 'monitor' (by this device, you could hear the voice of whoever it was who was calling, and then decide if you were 'in'). The voice was asking if this was the number of place where a steward of the name of Harold was presently engaged. And if this was so, could he please drop everything, at once, and come. The voice was Jane's.

Harold ran through streets that, if he'd stopped to think, would have seemed strange: either empty, or filled with knots of people, arguing and shouting (or other knots standing silent and resigned), or groups of running men and women, their possessions clutched in plastic bags, their children pulled along behind. And finally he arrived at Jane's address, and the FPG was there already, dragging her across the pavement, from the front door to the wagon and he knew it was too late.

What was she saying? He could hardly hear the words. 'Why now?' – yes, that was it, she was screaming out: 'Why now?'

And as she was pushed into the wagon, her face turned, and she saw him, standing on the corner, and she had just time enough to call: 'Harold, you know what's happening? Do you know where they're taking me?' And she was crying, but laughing too, as if at something infinitely ludicrous, inappropriate and absurd: 'And can you believe it, Harold? That the bastards could be bothered to arrest me *now?*'

The streets were empty, for the little knots had melted, and the running families had reached – or not – their destinations. Harold stumbled over an old toy, left lying in the street. He bumped into someone's open door.

(The VDU was still on, in the front room. Three days ago, the British government had undertaken what was called an 'anticipatory defensive thrust' into mainland Chinese territory.)

Why had no one noticed, when it had begun? The process which had brought Jane to the wagon and – no doubt – would now transfer her to a general utility? It had all been for the very best of motives. It was right that the police should demand the assistance of the populace (who after all, knew their own neighbourhoods). It was correct that education should bear its share of the responsibility for the violence and amorality that reached such epidemic proportions among the young. It was surely obvious that among all those millions of people on relief there were scroungers and deceivers (or, put plainly, cheats), and it was the right of the community to insist that the state's generosity (well, after all, the generosity of the taxpayer) was not abused. And it was clearly just that those who *wouldn't* work (as opposed to those who *couldn't*) should at the very least be obliged to undergo some form of training, to instill into them the basic disciplines they would require on their release.

The Neighbourhood Watch Groups came first (they were set up in the early 80s, on the recommendation of the then Chief Constable of London, after whom the DOS domestic complex – Newman House – was named). At about this time, too, the retraining centres (originally intended just for tramps and vagrants) extended their purview to wider groups of work-shy, including those with homes and families. The Parent Power Groups were started in the wake of calls, for a reassertion of traditional British values in the schools (the name was a kind of in-joke, in the way that in the 60s the word 'revolution' had been used to advertise cosmetics, or the slogan 'power to the people' to promote electrical equipment) but soon they were retitled 'Parents Unions' (For a Responsible Curriculum, Against the Tide of Patriotism in Our Schools).

And the 'Checkers' had begun as unpaid auxiliaries to the Family Patrol Group, to assist those overstretched investigators of relief abuse (the slogan: 'Check Up On The Cheaters'); and the Kindred Volunteers, who grew out of the Neighbourhood Watch Groups, ran patrols throughout the cities in defence of our old people and the children against vandals, muggers, rapists, layabouts and anarchists.

(And Harold passed a hardware store, its wire mesh torn, where eight VDUs were ghostily explaining how, as a diversionary tactic to assist their British allies, the USA had undertaken a 'retaliatory pre-emptive action' from bases in North Turkey, and had already taken Odessa and Donetsk.)

And thus it had been that the Checkers, in collaboration with the General Parents Unions (for did these things not start off in the home), had finally combined with the National Kindred Volunteer Detachments (now combatting the distressing rise in pre-teen crime) to form the Kindred Groups of Britain, who had generously taken on the task of administering the growing network of retraining and re-education centres, now re-named the General Utilities for the Location of all Anti-social Groups, in one of which was Jane.

(And he passed the gaping window of a junk shop, in which appeared to be a kind of strange, brown, box-like object, which was obviously some form of visionless receiver, from which a voice emerged, which explained how, in response to the liberation of the South Ukraine, the forces of the Warsaw Pact – in a 'protectively offensive operation' – had taken Braunschweg and Hanover and were half-way to the Rhine.)

But perhaps it had all been inevitable. And perhaps there had been no alternative. And Harold stopped in the middle of the empty square, and looked up to the sky, which was full of the most majestic white and grey and silver clouds, and he heard the rumble of what he supposed was thunder, and he saw the dazzling flashes of what must be lightning, and he told himself (and for the thousandth time) that once all this was over he would really get his life in order, he would start that little business, he would take advantage of his openings and seize his opportunities, and make something of himself at last.

He clicked his tongue. What *was* he thinking of? To stand here, day-dreaming, in the middle of the afternoon!

The sky was black, the skyline laced with fire. Harold set his shoulders, marched across the square and pressed the buzzer on the entry-phone. He had responsibilities: he had a job to do.

All the rest was in the future.